system shock 2

an • **INCAN MONKEY GOD STUDIOS PRODUCTION**

by • **ALEXX KAY**
DAVID LADYMAN
CHRIS McCUBBIN
MELISSA TYLER

CREDITS/LEGAL

AN INCAN MONKEY GOD STUDIOS PRODUCTION

Written by	Alexx Kay, David Ladyman, Chris McCubbin and Melissa Tyler
Graphic Design by	Sharon Freilich
Edited by	David Ladyman and Alexx Kay
Expert Advice	Harvey "Witchboy" Smith

GAME ART

Lead Designer, Story & Content	Ken Levine
Lead Artist, Creatures, Weapons, Objects, FX	Gareth Hinds
Level Designer (Command, Rickenbacker)	Scott Blinn
Level Designer (Ops, Engineering)	Matt Boynton
2-D Artist (Maps, Signs)	Steve Kimura
2-D Artist (Textures, Interface, Meta-Game)	Michael Swiderek
3-D Artist (Objects)	Mauricio Tejerina
Additional Design	Shawn Swift
Additional Art	Eric Dannerhoj, Bill Bobos
3D Artist, Weapons, Objects, FX, Big Droids	Nate Wells
Arachnids, Psi Reaver, Droids	Mark Lizotte, Eric Dannerhoj, Bill Bobos
High-Poly 3-D SHODAN Head Modeling & Animation, Cover Art	Ryan Lesser, Mammoth Studios

Important:
Prima Publishing has made every effort to determine that the information contained in this book is accurate. However, the publisher makes no warranty, either expressed or implied, as to the accuracy, effectiveness, or completeness of the material in this book; nor does the publisher assume liability for damages, either incidental or consequential, that may result from using the information in this book. The publisher cannot provide information regarding game play, hints and strategies, or problems with hardware or software. Questions should be directed to the support numbers provided by the game and device manufacturers in their documentation. Some game tricks require precise timing and may require repeated attempts before the desired result is achieved.

ISBN: 7615-2493-2

Library of Congress Catalog Card Number: 99-65714

Printed in the United States of America

99 00 01 02 BB 10 9 8 7 6 5 4 3 2 1

TABLE OF CONTENTS

Walkthrough

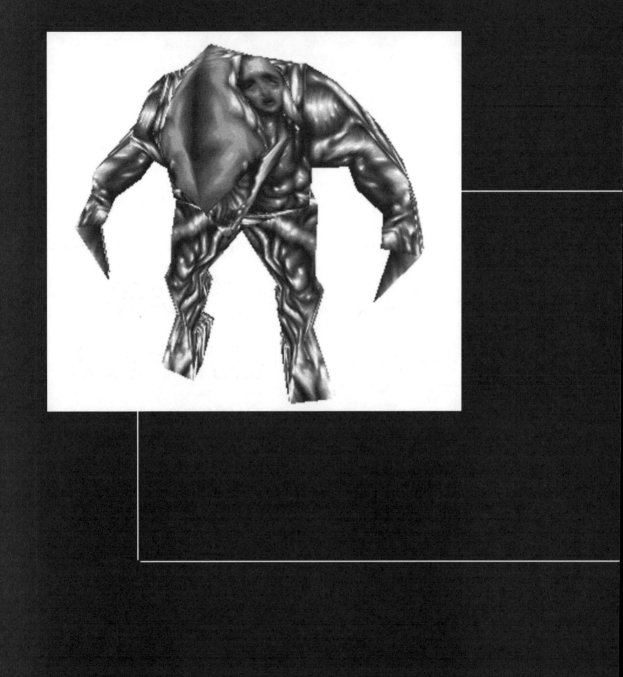

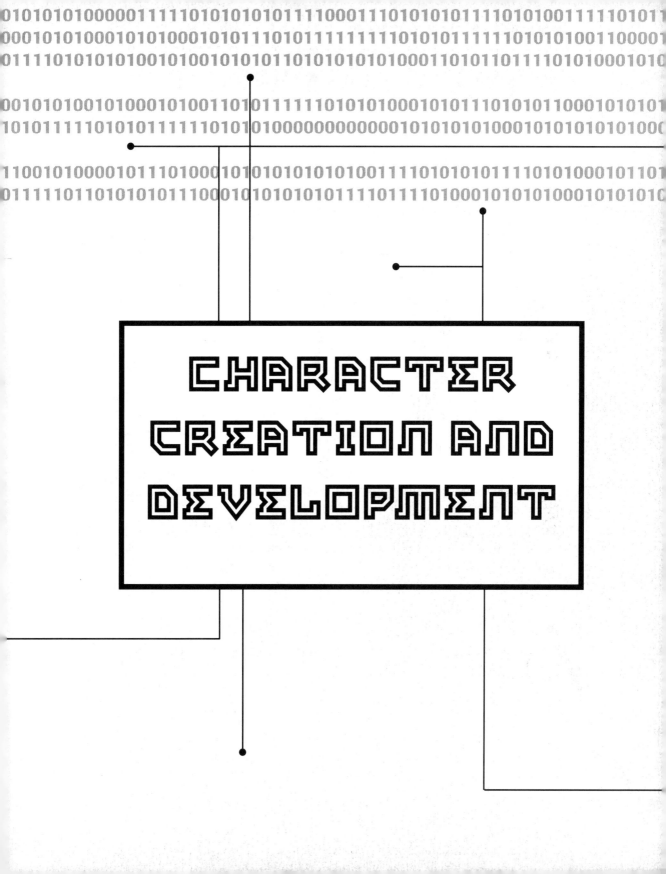

CHARACTER CREATION AND DEVELOPMENT

BRANCH OF SERVICE

Your first and most basic choice is which of the three services you'll enlist in. Each service grants you one unique ability before you begin your first assignment. These default abilities are:

Marines	Standard Weapons +1
Navy	Standard Weapons +1
OSA	Level One Psi disciplines (and a Psi Amp)

After that, you begin the first of three one-year assignments. Each year, you are offered a choice of three available assignments. The assignment choices *completely* change each year … once you pass up an assignment, it's gone for good.

Bargain Hunting

The main thing guiding your choice of assignment should be how you view your character, and how you plan to play the rest of the game. You need to ask yourself how much value each choice will bring you (the relative merits of the various attributes are discussed under **Stats and Skills**, on p. 18).

But a secondary concern that shouldn't be completely ignored is, "am I getting my money's worth?" The improvements you're getting for free during character creation will cost hard-earned cyber modules once you get on board the *Von Braun*. Knowing the relative values of the various assignments can be useful information.

Many of the assignment choices are equal in cyber-module value, while most of those that do have some differentiation are still close. Here are the places to watch out for relative value between your training choices. Note that these values are at the Normal difficulty level; if you're playing at a higher difficulty level, the disparity in value will be higher.

Marines, Year 2. The +2 Standard Weapons choice is worth 14 cyber modules; the other two choices are worth 15.

Navy, Year 2. +1 Maintenance is worth 10 modules, +2 Cybernetic Affinity is worth 11, and +2 Standard Weapons is worth 14.

Navy, Year 3. +1 Research is worth 10 modules; the other choices are worth 11.

OSA, Year 2. +1 Research is worth 10 modules; the other choices are worth 11.

Goodies

Some of the training choices give your character starting equipment when the game proper begins.

If you study +1 Maintenance in the third year of the Marines or the second year of Navy service, you get one maintenance tool.

In the second year of Marine service, if you study Energy Weapons you get a poor-condition laser. If you study Heavy Weapons you get a poor-condition grenade launcher and one clip of fragmentation grenades.

All OSA recruits get a psi amp.

MARINE TOURS OF DUTY

YEAR 1

Supply Ship Gallo

If you're partial to spending time with a lot of high explosives, this posting is for you. There's a lot of heavy lifting, but Ordinance also gets the first pick of the booze and other goodies coming aboard the supply ship Gallo. *Lock and load!*

Feb. 12, 2112. Your stint aboard the UNN *Gallo* is finished. Well, you've spent more exciting years, haven't you, marine? If you ever look at another UNN packing crate, you'll put in a bullet in your head. But you used the time well and bulked up considerably.

You've gained +2 Strength.

Io Survival School

The Navy maintains a survival training school on the surface of Io, the third moon of Jupiter. Pros: There's no better way to improve stamina and survival skills. Cons: The 21.2% mortality rate. Plus you've got to spend the year with a bunch of Navy skanks.

Feb. 12, 2112. Your stint at the Io Survival School is finished. You managed to survive your year there … barely. The encounter with a descendent of a Citadel Station tiger mutant put you in the sickbay for a month. But now you're one tough marine.

You've gained +2 Endurance.

Guadalcanal Training Station

Not every boarding party has the luxury of gravity. So the Corps strongly recommends every one of its brethren gets in some zero-g training. A year aboard the training station Guadalcanal should suffice.

Feb. 12, 2112. Your year on Guadalcanal Station is finished. The place served you well, leatherneck, and you're sleeker than ever. Maybe if you spent less time drinking the lighter fluid they serve in the commissary, you might have done even better.

You've gained +2 Agility.

YEAR 2

UNN Antigua

A tour of duty aboard the Antigua *should let you pick up some one-on-one beam weapon training from the Gunnery Sergeant Malloy. But heads up, she's a world-class SOB.*

Feb. 23, 2113. Time to get off the UNN *Antigua* and back to Wake Island Station, and not a month too soon. Five months into your posting, the Gunnery Sergeant snapped during a training exercise, and killed half a troop with live plasma fire before you tackled her. After that, you were in charge of the exercises, and in the months after, got pretty good with low-energy beam weapons.

You've gained +1 Energy Weapons and +1 Cybernetic Affinity.

Asteroid Belt Ore Facility

The automated asteroid ore facility in JM-432 supply the UNN shipyards, so they're crucial to defense. However, they're also prime candidates for hackers. Somebody's gotten their claws into the primary data loop and they need a team to head in there and blast their way past the automated defense systems.

Feb. 23, 2113. Time to get out of the Asteroid Belt and back to Wake Island Station. You'll probably have nightmares about cramped little tunnels for years, but you and the team got the jobs done. A combination of EMP grenades and high explosives will stop most hostile machinery, and in your year in the Belt, you got a lot of practice at knocking the 'borgs and 'bots right back to the assembly line.

You've gained +1 Heavy Weapons and +1 Cybernetic Affinity.

Port MacArthur Training Facility

Dummy ammunition, live ammunition, moving targets, stationary targets, live targets. The Port MacArthur training facility has enough hardware to warm the heart of any leatherneck.

Feb. 23, 2113. Time to get out of Port MacArthur and back to Wake Island Station. You got to pick up and refill more ammo casings than you can count. You even got to occasionally play the live target in an expert exercise. Still, you can't spend a year at the Mac without learning something. You picked up a good amount of standard weapons skill and even impressed some of the Mac's technicians.

You've gained +2 Standard Weapons.

YEAR 3

UNN Home Office

The UNN secretary general's office needs a full staff of armed guards. When things are dull, it requires a lot of standing around looking good in a uniform — when things are bad, it can require fending off a psi-terrorist assault.

Feb. 9, 2114. Get back to Wake Island Station pronto — your tour of duty at the UNN Home Office is finished. After a year of practice in the honor guard, you look sharp in a uniform. And you're a lot better at keeping your rifle in tip-top-shiny condition. If you had been bored much longer, you might have been tempted to take pot-shots at the tourists. Still, the maintenance skill might come in handy someday.

You've gained +1 Maintenance.

Polidies Trading Station

The Polidies trading station has long been a haven for the black market. However, up until now, they have not interfered with the running of station operations. Recent reports indicate that the Polidies command staff has been overthrown and the station is under the control of a self-appointed Magnate. This must be rectified, and a Marine presence maintained on the station.

Feb. 9, 2114. Get back to Wake Island Station pronto — your year on Polidies Station is finished. Taking on the Magnate's forces was a cakewalk — you hardly spent any ammo at all. The second fight, when his lieutenant made a play for the station, wasn't much harder. The only thing you thought was even mildly interesting was taking apart the black market weapons afterwards to see what sort of fancy mods they'd made.

You've gained +1 Modify.

UNN Antigua (Colony Air Service)

The Colony Air Service gets the dregs of the fleet, and the Antigua *is the dregs of the dregs. You'll learn a lot about recalcitrant machinery on a tour of duty aboard the* Antigua, *if it doesn't blow you to hell and back first.*

Feb. 9, 2114. Get back to Wake Island Station pronto — your tour of duty on the UNN *Antigua* is finished. You kept the *Antigua* running for six months, when every system in the book crashed daily. But your real problems came when the convicts the Air Service was shipping through decided to try a revolt. It took you the rest of the trip to get the smell of explosives out of the air scrubbers, but you learned how to repair the damn things.

You've gained +1 Repair.

NAVY TOURS OF DUTY

YEAR 1

UNN Lucille (Ops Training)

The UNN Lucille *is looking for an Ops training officer to learn the ship's navigation and data control systems. You'll get your feet wet with the high-tech systems, but also expect some heavy lifting.*

February 13, 2112. Your tour of duty aboard the UNN *Lucille* has concluded. You've spent a productive year. Captain Mayer was pleased with your work, especially with the initiative you showed in physical training. A friendly ensign showed you some backdoors into the ship's primary data loop and you spent your time off pumping good old fashioned iron.

You've gained +1 Hack and +1 Strength.

UNN Lucille (Engineering Training)

The UNN Lucille *is looking for an engineer's mate to help maintain the ship's core energy systems. There's some heavy lifting involved, sailor, but you'll learn your away around high-tech equipment.*

February 13, 2112. Your tour of duty aboard the UNN *Lucille* has concluded. You've spent a productive year. Captain Mayer was pleased with your work, especially with your willingness to get your hands dirty. You also showed a special aptitude for fixing what got broken and lugging out what couldn't be fixed.

You've gained +1 Repair and +1 Strength.

UNN Lucille (MIlitary Police)

The UNN Lucille *is looking for volunteers for their military police detachment. Those sailors can get pretty rowdy on these year-long cruises, so you better not be afraid of a tussle.*

February 13, 2112. Your tour of duty aboard the UNN *Lucille* has concluded. You've spent a productive year, though you didn't make a lot of friends. Between toughening up by putting drunken middies in the sickbay, you had plenty of down time in the armory to play with the pretty toys.

You've gained +1 Modify and +1 Strength.

YEAR 2

UNN Carfax (Nav Officer)

The UNN Carfax *is undertaking a mission to examine a newly discovered class B comet approaching the outer solar system. You'll likely pick up some useful skills working with the high-tech navigation systems aboard this newly commissioned heavy cruiser.*

February 11, 2113. Your tour of duty aboard the UNN *Carfax* has concluded. It was a good year for you, but not a great one for the *Carfax*. After taking a surprise hit from a small meteorite that separated from the larger mass, the *Carfax* was forced to limp home, with 123 casualties, including the chief navigation officer. You stepped in and filled his shoes and by then end of the year, you became quite skilled with the neuro-nav interface.

You've gained +2 Cybernetic Affinity.

UNN Pierce (Maintenance Officer)

The UNN Pierce *is ferrying liberated political prisoners back home from their detention near Saturn. The* Pierce *has been assigned a detachment of marines and needs sailors to load, administer and maintain the arms on board the ship.*

February 11, 2113. Your tour of duty aboard the UNN *Pierce* has concluded. Your year's tour was carried out without a hitch, except that one of the prisoners turned out to be a dissident spy. Before and after the excitement of his summary execution, you learned a fair bit about weapon's maintenance from one of the lifers onboard.

You've gained +1 Maintenance.

LaVerne Tactical Training School

LaVerne, Florida, hosts the Navy's premier tactical training school. While maybe not as respected as the Marine's facility at Fort Bush, there's a lot to be learned here.

February 11, 2113. Your tour of duty at the LaVerne Tactical Training School has concluded. A year of firing ranges, mock boarding parties and war games has done you good. You spent plenty of time with military grade pistols, assault rifles and even auto-shotguns.

You've gained +2 Standard Weapons.

YEAR 3

Marie Curie Research Facility

The Navy's Marie Curie research facility on Aquinas 4 is currently conducting research on a new strain of spaceborne virus that killed 220,000 citizens of New Atlanta. To lift the quarantine, we must determine how the virus pierced the city's micro-nanite shielding.

February 9, 2114. Your tour of duty at the Marie Curie Research Facility has concluded. Congratulations on surviving the disaster, sailor. When the saboteurs removed the safety seals and released the virus into the atmospheric control regulators, you were one of the few to reach safety in time. However, you were able to pick up a few odds and ends of research techniques before the crap hit the fan.

You've gained +1 Research.

Io Survival Training Facility

The Navy maintains a survival training school on the surface of Io, the third moon of Jupiter. Pros: There's no better way to improve stamina and survival skills. Cons: The 21.2% mortality rate.

February 9, 2114. Your tour of duty at the Io Survival Training Facility has concluded. You managed to survive your year there … barely. The encounter with a descendent of a Citadel Station tiger mutant put you in the sickbay for a month. You've learned to respect the wonders of biogenetics and have trained your body to excellent physical condition.

You've gained +2 Endurance.

Yamamoto Space Station

The Navy strongly encourages every sailor to undertake some amount of zero-G training. A year at the Yamamoto Space Station in Earth's orbit will more than suffice.

February 9, 2114. Your tour of duty at Yamamoto Station has concluded. You certainly weren't prepared for the events of this year. Captain Willits was never popular with his men, but you never expected half the crew to mutiny. The taut days spent regaining control of the ship with the captain lent you a grace and agility you never knew you were capable of.

You've gained +2 Agility.

OSA TOURS OF DUTY

YEAR 1

TOS Shao Ling (Sensory Deprivation)

The sensory deprivation tanks aboard the TOS Shao Ling *await you. There you will spend a solitary year focused in meditation on electrons and circuitry, and how they may serve your will.*

15 February 2112. Your year in the tanks of the Shao Ling is finished. Your will has grown. Your mind can Freeze your foes in their tracks and you can attune your mind to the inner workings of machines. Second Tier disciplines are within your grasp. You may now take your skills into the field, to pit them against our enemies.

You've mastered Cryokinesis, Psychogenic Cyber Affinity and access to Tier Two Psi disciplines.

TOS Ru Nang (Sensory Deprivation)

The sensory deprivation tanks aboard the TOS Ru Nang *await you. A year in meditation on the nature of matter will grant you power over it.*

15 February 2112. Your year in the tanks of the *Ru Nang* is finished. Your will has grown. Your mind can Freeze your foes in their tracks and Pull distant objects to you. These talents will serve you well. Second Tier disciplines are now within your grasp. You may now take your skills into the field, to pit them against our enemies.

You've mastered Cryokinesis, Kinetic Redirection and access to Tier Two Psi disciplines.

TOS Chu Lun (Sensory Deprivation)

The sensory deprivation tanks aboard the TOS Chu Lun *are modulated for your training. You shall spend a year in contemplation of mass, both yours and that of objects, until you can bend it to your intentions.*

15 February 2112. Your year in the tanks of the *Chu Lun* is finished. Your will has grown. Can you feel it gather to strike? You have learned how to Freeze your foes in their tracks and how to Shield yourself from them as well. Second Tier disciplines are now within your grasp. You may now take your skills into the field, to pit them against our enemies.

You've mastered Cryokinesis, Psycho-Reflective Screen and access to Tier Two Psi disciplines.

YEAR 2

OSA Central Core

Sifting the thoughts of treachery and disloyalty from the morass of emotion and internal conflict that fills most mundane can be disquieting. You shall spend a year building the general strength of your mind while learning how to probe the thoughts of the less capable without losing yourself.

23 February 2113. Your time of service at the OSA Central Core has reached its end. Your year was mostly peaceful, with one major exception. The hired assassin tried to disguise her intentions under a layer of quite explicit daydreams, but you were not deceived. Near the end, you felt the presence of her fading thoughts enter your own mind, and then vanish like clearing mist.

You've gained +2 Psionic Ability.

OSS Ki Luan

Dr. Chandrisvilan's research labs have produced many of this decade's advances in psionic technique. You shall spend a year serving his genius, learning to understand his insights and whims.

23 February 2113. Your time of service on the *Ki Luan* has reached its end. Maintaining patience for a year under the emotional Dr. Chandrisvilan's patronage was difficult. However, careful observation of his technique (and a careful, if illicit, examination of his laboratory notebooks) has led you to a better understanding of the process of research.

You've gained +1 Research.

Io Survival Training Facility

Your body has been neglected in your training of your mind. On Io, you will find soldiers who wish to test their endurance. You will surpass their physical prowess without compromising your mental discipline.

23 February 2113. You are directed to return to Station 74/34A. Your year at the Io Facility has reached its conclusion. You know now that the only real opponent is one who is more cunning than you. You used the cadets around you as prey and learned from their failings. You sense the struggle has greatly enhanced your physical prowess.

You've gained +2 Endurance.

YEAR 3

OSA Central Core

Acts of political terrorism and corporate coercion disturb corporate and political stability. You shall spend a year battling these chaotic elements, both psionically and by physical force.

9 February 2114. You are directed to return to Station 74/34A. Your year with the OSA Central Core has reached its conclusion. You learned the ways of lifting secrets from the minds of enemies and disarming their devices. But when it came time to act, speed, both natural and mentally enhanced, was critical.

You've gained +1 Strength, +1 Agility, and +1 Cybernetic Affinity, and mastered Psychogenic Agility.

OSA Field Base

In the grand scheme, individuals are no more important than pieces on a game board. Occasionally, it becomes necessary to remove a piece, without disturbing the flow of the game. These removals will be done in silence, and with complete secrecy. You shall spend a year learning these skills.

9 February 2114. You are directed to return to Station 74/34A. Your year with the OSA Field Base has reached its conclusion. You have enjoyed your power over life and death, and your careful moves served to prevent great chaos and further death. You learned the art of deadly motion, and the art of complete stillness.

You've gained +1 Strength, +1 Agility, and +1 Cybernetic Affinity, and mastered Neuro-Reflex Dampening.

OSA Field Base

Many threats to security can only be defeated from inside. Your mind shall be carefully blanked, and conditioned with the nature and past of a criminal. Join with the criminal and rebellious, endure their squalor and chaos, and then, when it is time, liquidate them from within.

9 February 2114. Your time of service at the OSA Field Base has reached its end. Even now, your mind is somewhat clouded and you do not recall all the details. You played your part well for most of a year, and your enemies called you friend, until you fell upon them with all your talents.

You've gained +1 Strength, +1 Agility, and +1 Cybernetic Affinity, and mastered Remote Electron Tampering.

STATS AND SKILLS

When you first look at your MFD, everything looks very cool, but you have to ask yourself exactly how useful everything will be. In this section we give some candid assessments of the various stats and abilities … how important they are at the beginning of the game, and how far you want to take them by the end of the game.

Unless you're playing on Easy and find all the cyber modules, you can't afford to buy everything. While all skills and stats have their uses, don't feel obliged to try all of them in a single character. Remember: A jack of all trades is a master of none. Just because something is recommended here , that doesn't mean it's necessarily right for your particular character.

The table below is the basic cost information for your MFD abilities. It's the same information found in your manual, but it's reprinted here for your convenience.

ABILITY COSTS

ABILITY LEVEL	PERSONAL STATISTICS	TECHNICAL SKILLS	WEAPONS SKILLS	PSI TIER	PSI POWER
1	–	10	12	10	3
2	3	5	6	20	5
3	8	8	8	30	8
4	15	12	15	50	12
5	30	25	36	75	20
6	50	50	50	–	–

PERSONAL STATS

Because level 1 is free for all personal stats, stats are a notable bargain at levels 2 through 4. As cyber modules become more available, go ahead and pamper your stats a bit. No reason not to get everything up to at least level 2 fairly early on.

Unless you're planning on seriously pursuing psionics as your primary ability, there's really no reason to boost Psi past 2. (If you are a psionicist, of course, you'll want to put pretty much every module that doesn't go into tiers or powers into your Psi stat, to the exclusion of the other stats.)

Everything else is pretty generally useful, so it's worth it to gradually work them up to 4 or so, as the resources become available. While stat levels 5 and 6 are very useful, they're also very expensive, so once you hit level 4, pause until you've got all your weapons and tech skills up as far as you'll ever want them, then invest in some level 5 or 6 stats.

TECH SKILLS

In this section, more than any other, things are not all equal. In general, the discussion below assumes a character with limited or no psionics. A serious psionic can compensate for many of the problems discussed below through careful selection of powers.

One important aspect of Tech that's not discussed below is software. That's because software is easy … when you find it, install it. Now you have it. Yippee. There are no difficult choices to make about software; they're the closest thing to automatic advancement.

Hacking

Hacking opportunities are ubiquitous. Hacking 1 lets you hack keypads and the security system. This is pretty much a basic survival skill. Hacking 2 lets you hack security crates, which are a vital source of precious resources, particularly early in the game. Hacking 3 lets you hack replicators, which is highly recommended for reasons of basic economy, and once you get to Hacking 3, you'll simply have to get Hacking 4, because that lets you hack turrets … which just *rocks!* So let's just say (especially if you're not a dedicated Psionicist) that you'll want to get to Hacking 4 as quickly as realistically possible.

After that, however, the only thing you need Hacking 5 *or* 6 for is high-security crates. Now high-security crates can be *very* useful, but seriously ask yourself if they're worth 75 cyber modules. If you've saved up your ICE picks, you can get a long way through the high-security crates with them (particularly if you're willing to save before ICE-picking the crate, and restore if it doesn't hold anything you really need). High hack skill also helps reduce the ever-increasing difficulty of hacking into security, as you enter more high security areas.

Maintenance

Grab a Maintenance 2 early on, so you can make constructive use of those maintenance tools that you find from time to time. Basically, however, for about the first half of the game you're better off simply discarding a decrepit weapon whenever you happen to find a better one, and repairing your weapons if they break when nothing better is available.

About the middle of the game, however, this changes dramatically. By the time you start finding and learning to use advanced weapons like the rocket launcher and assault rifle, you'll also start finding more maintenance tools (or being able to afford more). At this point you're wise to start seriously building up your Maintenance skill. At least get to level 4, and levels 5 and 6 are a better value for this skill than almost any other. Not only does level 6 Maintenance allow you to maintain your EMP rifle (an absolute necessity if you actually carry one), but it also allows you to restore any weapon to perfect condition from as low as level 4, with only a single maintenance tool.

Each level of Maintenance lets you store extra charge in your powered items (energy weapons, implants, powered armor). If you use these a lot, Maintenance is invaluable.

Modify

As we mentioned above, under **Maintenance**, during the first part of the game you'll probably be trading weapons frequently, as old ones become decrepit and new ones are found in better condition. During this part of the game, you don't need any Modify skill whatsoever … it'll just soak up your nanites. Once you reach the point where you start keeping and maintaining a single set of weapons, that's the time to modify them to the hilt. Build up Modify skill to 3 or 4 in the mid-game, and modify anything you routinely use. However, instead of building up Modify to 5 or 6 just so you can use it once or twice on your most elite weapons, consider hoarding your French-Epstein devices instead … a few of these will get all your weapons up to their full potential.

Note that in addition to the benefits listed on the Modify panel, each modification also increases base weapon damage by 12.5%.

Repair

Unless you get a decent Maintenance skill right away, you're probably going to need Repair 3 fairly early in the game, for when your shotgun breaks (which it will probably do a lot, at least until your Maintenance improves and maintenance tools become more common). Once that point is reached, however, you're probably pretty safe abandoning Repair entirely in favor of Maintenance (an occasional mishap can be compensated for by simply saving up your auto-repair units). Or you can just spend the extra 12 points, and get Repair 4, which allows you to repair any weapon in the game. Either way, Repair 5 or 6 is simply not a wise investment.

Also note that Repair 3 allows you to fix some broken replicators, of which there are many scattered about the *Von Braun*.

Research

Get Research 1 as quickly as possible, so you can start researching organs and getting the valuable combat bonuses they confer. From there, work your way up to 4 as is convenient – this will let you research most of the implants and the Crystal Shard weapon. You need Research levels beyond 4 for exactly two items – the highest-powered exotic weapon (Research 6), and an alien implant that can seriously turn on you (Research 5). If you're going to be an exotic weapons specialist, you probably want to go all the way to 6. Everyone else can stop at 4, or at least 5.

WEAPONS SKILLS

As quickly as possible you'll want to get Standard Weapons 2 and Energy Weapons 1. This will allow you to use pistols, lasers and shotguns when you find them (which almost anyone will need to get through the early levels). As you find grenade launchers, and then find and Research the crystal shard, you'll want to get Heavy Weapons 1 and Exotic Weapons 1. This combination of skills will get you through 75% of the game (of course, you may want to increase your favorite weapon skill just for the damage bonus).

Don't try to master every weapon skill in the game ... after all, you can't *carry* every weapon in the game. On the other hand, you will want to make use of at least one or two level-6 weapons to get through the tough end game. The solution is to pick a specialization and stick with it. Even psionicists may want to work at least one weapon skill up to 6 (psionicists with Energy 6 and an EMP rifle don't have to take no lip from no robots, ever!). Other characters should probably work two different weapons up that high. There's a good case for one of those level-6 skills to be Energy Weapons (since you don't have to carry ammunition for them) with the second being whatever best fits your character concept and style of play.

PSI OVERLOADING

Overloading generally gives you an effective +2 PSI. However, for most purposes, effective PSI is capped at 8. With a psi booster implant and an alien psi booster hypo, you can raise your PSI (temporarily) to 8. If you do that, overloading will not usually increase your PSI further. A few powers, however, can be overloaded to an effective PSI of 10. They are:
- Cerebro-Stimulated Regeneration
- Molecular Transmutation
- Remote Circuitry Manipulation
- Advanced Cerebro-Stimulated Regeneration
- Metacreative Barrier.

TIER 1 PSIONICS

KINETIC REDIRECTION

Pulls an object toward you.

Duration   1 second per PSI

Projectile Speed   60

Even a character with a minor investment in psionics should take this power. Since telekinetic powers are moderately common aboard the *Von Braun*, many crewmembers have hidden caches of useful equipment in places that can't be physically reached. This power lets you draw the loot to you.

Once you have this power, remember to always examine your surroundings carefully to find these hidden caches.

NEURO-REFLEX DAMPENING

Eliminates all weapon kickback.

Duration   1 minute + 20 seconds per PSI

While not useful for the pure psionic character (the psi amp doesn't have kickback), this power can come in very handy for a psionic with a minor in Standard Weapons, or a standard weapons user with a minor in Psionics. The burst firing mode of the pistol (and later, the assault rifle) is extremely inaccurate if your Agility isn't high. This power makes burst fire effective (and deadly!) for the early-game character.

PROJECTED CRYOKINESIS

Launches a heat-draining projectile at a target.

Base Damage   3 + PSI

Type of Damage   Cold

Projectile Speed   50

All OSA characters get this power in training. For the psi-based character, this is the "basic gun." Note that electronic targets are resistant to cold-based attacks, and will thus take less damage from cryo blasts.

Non-OSA characters with a minor concentration in psionics would be well advised to take this power. When your standard weapon(s) run out of ammo or jam, Projected Cryokinesis makes a good backup.

PSYCHOGENIC AGILITY

Increases your Agility by 2.

Duration   2 minutes + 1 minute per PSI

Useful for when you need that extra burst of speed to run through a dangerous situation. Agility also reduces falling damage, so this can be a good power to activate before attempting a dangerous jump.

You can also use this power to meet minimum Agility requirements for some weapons. This is risky, however, as the weapon will automatically unequip when the power wears off!

PSYCHOGENIC CYBER AFFINITY

Increases your CYB by 2.

Duration   2 minutes + 1 minute per PSI

This power is best suited for a character with a mix of psionic and technical skills. Use it before any attempt to Hack, Modify or Repair to get an extra 10% chance of success. Since it does wear off after a while, it's most efficient if you can line up many technical tasks in quick succession.

Note that Remote Circuitry Manipulation (the psionic hack-at-a-distance power) uses your PSI stat, not your CYB, so these two powers do not work together.

PSYCHO-REFLECTIVE SCREEN

Protects you from 15% of all combat damage.

Duration   20 seconds + 30 seconds per PSI

This power is extremely useful because it affects *all* forms of combat damage, whether physical, energy, psi or any other.

Psycho-Reflective Screens and other psionic shields work well in combination with armor. Psionic shield powers can also be combined for increased protection.

REMOTE ELECTRON TAMPERING

Reduces the duration of any active security alarms.

Duration   5 seconds + 5 seconds per PSI

This power is useful for anyone without any Hacking skill. It is most useful at higher difficulty levels, as security computers (which allow you to deactivate alarms entirely) are far less frequent at these higher levels.

Ideally, you never trigger alarms in the first place. However, if you find yourself having trouble managing this, this power can help minimize the consequences.

TIER 2 PSIONICS

ADRENALINE OVERPRODUCTION

Increases hand-to-hand damage by a factor roughly equal to PSI.
(At PSI 8, damage is multiplied by 9.)

Duration	10 seconds per PSI

Useful for the player who likes hand-to-hand combat, obviously. Even if you don't normally do hand-to-hand combat, this can be combined with Cerebro-Energetic Extension (a psionic 'sword') to inflict amazingly potent damage.

ANTI-ENTROPIC FIELD

While this discipline is active, your ranged weapons cannot break, and their condition will not degrade.

Duration	10 seconds + 20 seconds per PSI

An excellent power for the combined psi/weapons user. Consistent use of this power before getting into fights can reduce or eliminate any need for the Maintenance and Repair skills.

CEREBRO-STIMULATED REGENERATION

Regenerates lost hit points.

Amount Healed	2 hit points per PSI

The basic healing power. Can be useful if you're running low on medical hypos.

LOCALIZED PYROKINESIS

Damages all creatures within its radius. Higher PSI increases damage to enemies.

Damage	5 hit points every 2 seconds
Type of Damage	Incendiary
Radius	5 feet
Duration	15 seconds + 8 seconds per PSI

This power is a useful adjunct for the hand-to-hand combatant. A *really* potent combination is to activate this power and then activate Photonic Redirection (a.k.a. Invisibility). You can walk around and damage monsters without them seeing you!

The glow from the pyrokinetic field can help you navigate in dark areas.

NEURAL DECONTAMINATION

This power provides 80% protection from radiation.

Duration   10 second + 5 seconds per PSI

Once you have this power, you don't really need to carry around the bulky hazard suit any more. Note that this protects you from absorbing the radiation in the first place; it doesn't prevent you from the damage of radiation that's already been absorbed into your body (use anti-radiation hypos for that).

PSYCHOGENIC STRENGTH

Increases your Strength by 2.

Duration   2 minutes + 1 minute per PSI

Useful primarily to improve your hand-to-hand combat damage. While not as potent as Adrenaline Overproduction, it does last considerably longer.

Psychogenic Strength *will* let you carry more objects and use heavier weapons and armor, but you can find yourself in serious trouble if the power runs out unexpectedly.

RECURSIVE PSIONIC AMPLIFICATION

Increases your Psionics by 2. Psi point costs are doubled while active.

Duration   10 seconds + 10 seconds per PSI

While the doubled cost for psi powers is severe, this power can give you the edge you need before going into a dangerous combat situation.

TIER 3 PSIONICS

ELECTRON CASCADE

Recharges a single charged item or weapon.

Recharge amount 20% per point of PSI, up to the maximum allowed by your Maintenance skill

This skill makes the laser pistol a very attractive secondary weapon option for the psionics character. It also can be useful for the Energy Weapons specialist to pick up in the mid-to-late game. Take advantage of this power to recharge powered armor, which runs out of charge much faster than powered implants do.

ENERGY REFLECTION

Provides 50% immunity to all energy-based damage sources.

Duration 20 seconds per PSI

Obviously, this is most useful when facing a creature with an energy-based attack (broadly speaking, all robots and cyborgs).

Energy Reflection and other psionic shields work well in combination with armor. Psionic shield powers can also be combined for increased protection.

ENHANCED MOTION SENSITIVITY

Shows the location of all nearby creatures.

Duration 30 seconds per PSI

This is a good power for the tactical gamer, one who likes to know ahead of time when he's going to be going into combat. It can help you detect some ambush situations and turn the tables on the monsters who think that they'll be surprising *you!*

MOLECULAR DUPLICATION

Use nanites to duplicate one ammo clip or hypo.

Chance of Success 30% + 10% per PSI

It's like having a replicator in your pocket! Sadly, psi hypos have been specifically engineered to be unaffected by this power. Partway through the game, however, you may discover alien psi boosters, that *can* (and should!) be duplicated.

Boost your PSI as high as possible before using this power.

NEURAL TOXIN-BLOCKER

Shields you from 100% of toxin absorption.

Duration   10 seconds + 5 seconds per PSI

Useful for getting through highly toxic areas, or before getting into fights with monsters that have a toxic attack. Note that this power prevents the toxins from getting into your body in the first place, but will *not* prevent toxins you've already been exposed to from damaging you (for that, use anti-toxin hypos).

This power makes it easier to harvest organs from Annelid Eggs, as you don't have to worry about their toxic gases anymore.

PROJECTED PYROKINESIS

Launches a fiery projectile at a target.

Damage   5 + 2 per PSI

Type of Damage   Incendiary

Projectile Speed   50

This is the most damaging "gun" in the OSA arsenal. Sadly, purely mechanical monsters are completely immune to it (though it does do quite well against cyborgs). Annelid Arachnids are particularly vulnerable to fire-based attacks, so this power works well against them.

Note that, since this is a Tier Three power, Projected Cryokinesis actually does more damage per Psi point spent. Projected Pyrokinesis, on the other hand, deals its damage much faster, which is often critical in combat.

PSIONIC HYPNOGENESIS

Targeted non-robotic creature will stand still and docile. If the creature takes damage, the effect ends.

Duration   20 seconds per PSI

This power is excellent for avoiding combat entirely in many instances. Alternatively, it can be used to keep a creature still until you can hit it with a really devastating shot of some kind.

TIER 4 PSIONICS

CEREBRO-ENERGETIC EXTENSION

Turns your psi amp into a powerful melee weapon.

Damage	18 hit points
overhand	24 hit points (with Smasher OS upgrade)
Type of Damage	Standard
Duration	10 seconds per PSI

Useful for the player who likes hand-to-hand combat, obviously. Even if you don't normally engage in hand-to-hand combat, this can be combined with Adrenaline Overproduction for amazingly potent damage.

ELECTRON SUPPRESSION

Immobilize any robotic target.

Duration	3 seconds per PSI

Robots are the natural nemesis of the psionic character. Electron Suppression is a powerful tool to aid you in avoiding or fighting them. The duration is quite short, so use the time well.

MOLECULAR TRANSMUTATION

Converts ammunition and hypos into nanites.

This power is best for the pure psionic character, who has no use for ammunition anyway. The amount of nanites gained is proportional to your PSI, so boost it as high as possible before using this power.

The amount of nanites gained is also affected by difficulty level, so at higher difficulty levels, you may find this power to not be cost-effective on some types of items. Compare how many nanites you get with the proportional cost of a psi hypo (1 psi hypo gives you the same results as using this power 5 times) to see how much (if any) 'profit' you make by using this power on different items. Once you find a recycler, you'll also want to compare how many nanites it gives you, since these are effectively free.

PHOTONIC REDIRECTION

Renders you invisible to all creatures. Attacking will end the effect.

Duration 5 seconds + 5 seconds per PSI

Note that activating any psi power counts as "attacking," and will terminate this power. This is the premiere power for combat avoidance tactics. A *really* potent combination is to activate Localized Pyrokinesis and then activate Photonic Redirection. You can walk around and damage monsters without them seeing you!

PSYCHOGENIC ENDURANCE

Increases your Endurance by 2.

Duration 2 minutes + 1 minute per PSI

Extra hit points are always helpful, especially when going against particularly tough opponents. The extra hit points are lost when the power run out, but this will never reduce you below 1 hit point.

On higher difficulty levels, each point of Endurance gives you fewer hit points (than what you get at lower difficulty levels), making this power arguably less valuable at higher difficulty levels. On the other hand, since you have many fewer hit points to begin with, the additional ones, even if fewer in number, may be proportionally more valuable to you.

REMOTE CIRCUITRY MANIPULATION

Allows you to hack psionically. Uses half your PSI stat (rounded up) in place of both Hacking skill and CYB stat, and costs psi points instead of nanites.

This skill allows the pure psi character to hack, although you'll need to boost your PSI *extremely* high to be even moderately good at dealing with late-game hackable objects.

Note that this power uses your PSI stat, not your CYB, so this power is actually not very useful for a psionic/hacker hybrid.

REMOTE PATTERN DETECTION

Shows the location of many useful items, including nanites, ammo, hypos, implants and audio logs.

Duration 1 minute per PSI

With this power, cleverly hidden caches of loot will no longer evade your notice.

TIER 5 PSIONICS

ADVANCED CEREBRO-STIMULATED REGENERATION

Regenerates lost hit points.

Amount Healed   5 hit points + 5 hit points per PSI

While slightly less efficient than basic Cerebro-Stimulated Regeneration in terms of psi points, this power heals you *much* faster.

EXTERNAL PSIONIC DETONATION

Drops a psionic proximity mine. Does no damage to robots, and double damage to psionically sensitive creatures.

Duration   4 minutes

Damage   30

Type of Damage   Psionic

Radius   10 feet

Projectile Speed 50

This power gives you the psionic equivalent of proximity grenades, without having to learn Heavy Weapons skill. It can be useful for setting traps of various sorts.

IMPOSED NEURAL RESTRUCTURING

Causes a non-robotic target to become hostile toward all non-human creatures.

Duration   10 seconds per PSI, or until damaged by a human

Few things are more fun than making your enemies fight each other instead of you. This power works particularly well on Rumblers in the late game. Note that in the *very* late stages of the game, you may run into monsters who have sufficiently strong psionic abilities to resist this power.

INSTANTANEOUS QUANTUM RELOCATION

The first use of this power sets a "teleport marker." The second use teleports you to it (and clears the marker). You can clear an obsolete teleport marker by hitting *a*T.

This power has many creative uses. It can be a quick shortcut back to the main elevator. It can get you out of a bad combat situation in a hurry. It can teleport you to safety if you fail to make a jump over a long fall. Other applications are left as an exercise for the player.

Note that teleport markers only work within a given sub-level. Going through a bulkhead or elevator will automatically clear any teleport marker in the sub-level you're leaving.

METACREATIVE BARRIER

Creates a wall of psionic force directly in front of you.

Wall's Hit Points   150 + 50 per PSI over 5

Duration   4 minutes

Another good combat avoidance power. This power combines well with Soma Transference; trap a monster with psionic barriers, then drain all of its hit points away.

PSYCHO-REFLECTIVE AURA

Protects you from 60% of all combat damage.

Duration   10 seconds + 20 seconds per PSI

This is amazingly good protection, better even than powered armor.

Psycho-Reflective Aura and other psionic shields work well in combination with armor. Psionic shields can also be combined for increased protection. Put up all three psionic shields and wear powered armor, and even the most powerful foe will do little damage to you … until the shields start wearing off.

SOMA TRANSFERENCE

Drains targeted non-robotic creature of hit points, and adds those hit points to your total.

This power combines well with Metacreative Barrier; trap a monster with psionic barriers, then drain all of its hit points away.

OS UPGRADES

Throughout the entire game you get four — and only four — OS upgrades. These are powerful, and frequently subtle, abilities, and it behooves you to pick them wisely. This section gives you the skinny on just how valuable each upgrade really is, and just what sort of character will benefit most from it.

CYBER-ASSIMILATION

You can extract a diagnostic/repair module from any destroyed robot. Using this item will instantly heal 15 hit points of damage.

This upgrade is especially valuable for the Energy Weapons specialist, who is most effective against robots.

Note that Protocol Droids explode so violently that nothing can be salvaged from them. You can get diagnostic/repair modules from Maintenance Bots, Security Bots and Assault Bots.

CYBERNETICALLY ENHANCED

Allows the use of two implants at once.

This OS upgrade will *not* allow you to use two of the same kind of implant at once. It is especially useful for characters with high Maintenance skill, as they can charge implants to last longer. It's also a good upgrade for researchers, as there are a number of useful alien implants which must be researched before being used. This is an excellent choice for your third or fourth OS upgrade.

LETHAL WEAPON

Increases all hand-to-hand damage by 35 percent (not 50%, as the game might note).

This upgrade is for the player who really likes hand-to-hand combat. Don't take this upgrade if you plan to do most of your fighting with ranged weapons.

If you're specializing in hand-to-hand, it's slightly better to take Lethal Weapon before taking Smasher.

NATURALLY ABLE

One-time bonus of 8 cyber modules.

Beware this upgrade! Early in the game (particularly your first time through) this will look unbelievably attractive, but *don't be fooled!* You'll be tripping over cyber mods throughout the game, but if you take this, you've used up one of your four OS upgrades — it's gone forever. It's a sucker's deal. (Of course, it's possible that you'll happen upon this right at the precise moment when a few extra cyber mods mean the difference between survival and certain death … in that case, do what you gotta do, but don't think you're getting a bargain.)

PACK-RAT

Adds three extra inventory slots.

Extra carrying capacity always comes in handy. On the other hand, if you think you're likely to buy your Strength up to 6 anyway (or 5 and use a BrawnBoost implant), then this OS upgrade is ultimately useless.

PHARMO-FRIENDLY

Extra 20 percent benefit from all hypos.

One of the very best all-around upgrades, particularly if taken early. While every character uses medical hypos, and will thus gain some benefit from this OS upgrade, the characters who will benefit the most are OSA members. They rely on psi hypos for almost everything they do, and getting the maximum benefit out of each one is vital to long-term success.

POWER PSI

Psionic burnout no longer damages you.

Obviously, this is useful for the psi character. Less obviously, it is more useful for the character who is not concentrating *entirely* on psi. As the Psi stat goes up, the chance of psionic burnout goes down, so pure psi characters actually get less benefit from this upgrade than hybrid characters.

REPLICATOR EXPERT

All items in replicators cost 20% less.

All characters will find this one useful. Whatever type of "ammo" you use, you'll find yourself running out if you don't buy supplies occasionally. Combined with Hacking skill, prices can be dropped even more. The earlier in the game you can get it, the better. See **Replicator Item Prices** (p. 87) for a list of lowered prices.

SECURITY EXPERT

+2 Hacking skill (if you already have at least 1 point of Hacking skill) applied only when Hacking security computers.

While you might think that this upgrade is primarily for hacker specialists, you would be wrong. Someone who specializes in Hacking doesn't *need* this upgrade. It is most useful for someone who has Hacking skill as a sub-specialty, but isn't spending all available points in it. While non-hackers will eventually start running into special devices that require higher Hacking skill, Security Expert will allow them to remain competent at the most basic Hacking task, that of temporarily disabling security.

SHARPSHOOTER

Each shot with a ranged (non-psionic) weapon does 15% more damage.

Unless you are strongly specialized in hand-to-hand or psionic combat, this is an excellent OS upgrade. It affects all non-psionic ranged weapons, so a wide variety of characters can benefit from it.

SMASHER

You can execute overhand attacks with melee weapons.

Another upgrade for the hand-to-hand specialist. With Smasher, the overhand attack is as fast as the normal hand-to-hand attack, and does considerably more damage. The only drawback is that it is harder to aim (being on a vertical plane rather than a horizontal one). Keep your crosshairs centered on your foe, though, and you should do fine.

If you're specializing in hand-to-hand, it's slightly better to take the Lethal Weapon OS upgrade before taking Smasher.

SPATIALLY AWARE

Automap for each sub-level is always completely filled in.

While never completely necessary, being able to see the map ahead of time can often give you valuable clues as to where you go next. Unlike the other upgrades, this one has little to do with your character's skills or concept, and everything to do with how you (the player) like to play the game. Some players will find this a god-send; others will find it useless, or even annoying. (And of course, you can always reference the maps in this book.) Do *not* take this as your fourth upgrade; the last few levels of the game do not have automaps, so you would get no benefit from it.

SPEEDY

Movement speed increased by 15 percent.

Especially useful for the players who like to use avoidance tactics. Or for those who, nostalgic for the original *System Shock*, try to finish the game in under 7 hours …

STRONG METABOLISM

Damage from radiation and toxins reduced by 25 percent.

With the Strong Metabolism upgrade, you can worry less about damage from environmental hazards. While these are still problematic, a Strong Metabolism can give you the extra time you need to find an anti-radiation or anti-toxin hypo.

TANK

Increases maximum hit points by 5.

How valuable this upgrade is depends largely on difficulty level. On Easy, it's almost worthless, since you'd rather just boost your Endurance. On Impossible, however, base hit points are lower, while Endurance is much more expensive and gives much less benefit, so Tank can give you as many hit points as spending dozens of cyber modules, and can represent a very significant fraction of your total hit points.

TINKER

Nanite cost for making weapon modifications is 50% cheaper.

Obviously, this upgrade is only useful if you're concentrating somewhat on the Modify skill. Modifications are normally quite expensive, so this is valuable if you want to Modify lots of weapons over the course of the game. This is less valuable at the easier difficulty levels, as there are more French-Epstein devices (free one-use Modify) to be found.

Since Modify skill is normally so expensive, in the normal course of affairs you also want to invest a lot in Maintenance skill, to keep your now-modified weapon in usable condition. With cheaper modification costs, you can afford to throw away a modified weapon now and then, and modify a new weapon in better condition.

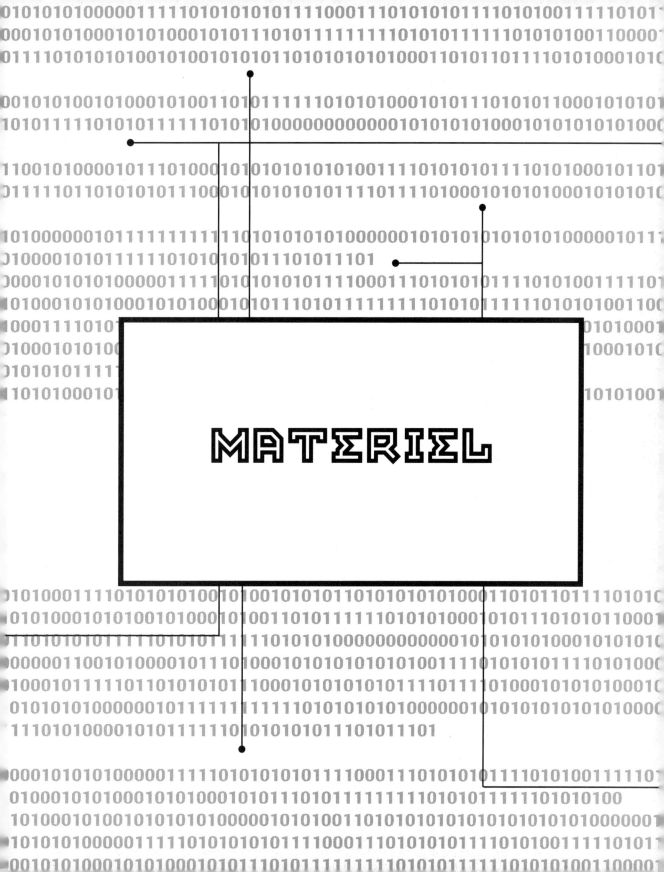

MATERIEL

WEAPONS

ANNELID LAUNCHER

An exotic device, made of semi-sentient organic material.

WEAPON SETTING	TYPE OF DAMAGE	DAMAGE AMOUNT	RADIUS	PROJECTILE SPEED	THRESH OLD%	MIN %	MAX %
Anti-Human	Anti-Human	25	5 ft	25	25	1	10
Anti-Annelid	Anti-Annelid	25	7 ft	25	25	1	10

- Requires worm ammo, which is fairly hard to come by.

- **Setting 1**　　　　　　　5 shots per second
　　　　　　　　　　　　　instant reload time

- **Setting 2**　　　　　　　5 shots per second
　　　　　　　　　　　　　instant reload time

- **1st Modification**　　　increases clip size by 10
　　　　　　　　　　　　　increases damage by 10%

- **2nd Modification**　　　doubles the projectile speed
　　　　　　　　　　　　　increases damage by an additional 14% (25% total increase)

- **Wear (degradation)**　3% per shot
　　　　　　　　　　　　　once condition drops below the midway point of "3," chance of breaking grows from 1% to 10% per shot

- **Req. Research skill**　　6, and small amounts of Selenium and Molybdenum
- **Req. Strength**　　　　3
- **Req. Agility**　　　　　3
- **Req. Exotic Weapons skill**　6
- **Req. Repair skill**　　　5
- **Req. Modify skill**　　　2
- **Req. Maintenance skill**　4

This object has been heavily modified, to the point where it is impossible to discern its original function. As currently configured, this object is a weapon, designed to deliver payloads of annelid worms.

If you plan to use exotic weapons, collect beakers whenever you find them. Using beakers on Worm Piles will collect worm ammo in usable form. The annelid launcher may be set to damage either pure annelid creatures, or human/hybrid creatures. The worm projectile is telekinetically directed by the weapon, and will try to 'home in' on its target; you can't influence its choice of target other than by changing your aim.

The annelid launcher is the ultimate exotic weapon. It does even more damage than the viral proliferator against organic targets, but it does take more ammo to use.

ASSAULT RIFLE

A military issue automatic rifle.

WEAPON AMMO	TYPE OF DAMAGE	DAMAGE AMOUNT	RADIUS	PROJECTILE SPEED	THRESH OLD%	MIN %	MAX %
Standard	Standard	10	n.a.	300	10	.5	5
Armor Piercing	Armor Piercing	10	n.a.	300	10	.5	5
Anti-Personnel	High Explosive	10	n.a.	300	10	.5	5

- **Setting 1**   2 shots per second
1-second reload time

- **Setting 2**   continuous burst of shots every 1/10 second
1-second reload time

- **1st Modification**   cuts reload time to 1/3
increases damage by 10%

- **2nd Modification**   increases clip size from 36 to 72
increases damage by an additional 14% (25% total increase)

- **Wear (Degradation)** 0.5% per shot
once condition drops to "1," chance of breaking grows from 0.5% to 5% per shot

- **Req. Strength**   2
- **Req. Standard Weap. skill** 6
- **Req. Repair skill**   4
- **Req. Modify skill**   2
- **Req. Maintenance skill**   4

The M-22 assault rifle's rapid-fire keeps vulnerable enemies down and the single shot mode is good for accuracy. Armor penetration and damage potential are both moderate. When used for heavy automatic fire, the aim point tends to wander fairly far. The design by committee nature of the unit, however, has led to some questions regarding its reliability.

Uses the same ammunition as a pistol, but has a bigger clip (which can be Modified to hold even more) and does 25% more damage. Like the pistol, careful use of appropriate ammo is vital to getting the most bang for your bullet. If your Agility is high enough to hold down the kickback, the fully automatic setting will let you deliver huge amounts of damage in a very short time. But watch your ammo supply; full auto burns through bullets *fast*.

This is the top weapon in the Standard Weapons class. Once you have (and can use) this baby, you can throw that pistol away; the assault rifle is strictly better on all counts. Assuming you can keep up your ammo supply, the assault rifle remains a great weapon through the end of the game.

CRYSTAL SHARD

This crystal structure is composed of thousands of close-together crystal needles, attached together in a close-branching, nearly fractal, tree.

The crystal shard is the most potent hand-to-hand weapon in the game. Period.

WEAPON	TYPE OF DAMAGE	DAMAGE AMOUNT
Crystal Shard	WeaponBash	12 (15 overhand with Smasher Upgrade)

- **Req. Research skill** 4, and a small amount of Yttrium
- **Req. Exotic Weapons skill** 1

This crystal, principally of silicon but doped with germanium and other unknown trace elements, appears to have a resonant frequency very close to that of neural propagation. The crystal probably serves as a repeater for the psionic abilities of the annelid creatures.

Melee damage is also affected by Strength. When fighting hand-to-hand, you should ready your swing at a distance, then close and attack, then back away before your opponent can strike back. Be aware that many monsters with hand-to-hand attacks have a greater reach, so always back away quickly; even if you missed, you may well be within your opponent's range. When fighting a ranged opponent with a melee weapon, close as fast as possible and strike fast, to try and keep him off balance and unable to fire.

EMP RIFLE

A large rifle, with plasma-resonance chambers that create the EMP blast.

WEAPON SETTING	TYPE OF DAMAGE	DAMAGE AMOUNT	RADIUS	PROJECTILE SPEED	THRESHOLD%	MIN %	MAX %
Normal	EMP	10	10 ft	70	10	.5	5
Overload	EMP	15	15 ft	70	10	.5	5

- **Setting 1 (Normal)** — 5 shots per 2 seconds
  shots drain 2 units of energy (reload time n/a)

- **Setting 2 (Overload)** — 5 shots per 2 seconds
  shots drain 20 units of energy
  shots do 50% more damage (reload time n/a)

- **1st Modification** — increases charge capacity by 50 units
  increases damage by 10%

- **2nd Modification** — decreases energy consumed per shot by 50%
  increases projectile speed by 50% (from 70 to 105)
  increases damage by 14% (25% total increase)

- **Wear (degradation)** — 1.5% per shot
  once condition drops to "1," chance of breaking
  grows from 0.5% to 5% per shot

- **Req. Energy Weapons skill** 6
- **Req. Repair skill** 2
- **Req. Modify skill** 3
- **Req. Maintenance skill** 6

When the first atomic weapons were tested in the middle of the 20th century, it was noted that not only did the weapons themselves do catastrophic damage, the electro-magnetic pulse they released coincident with the blast effectively neutralized most electronic devices for miles. Once this pulse was isolated, one could cultivate its benefits without the unpleasantness inherent in a nuclear fireball.

This is *the* weapon of choice against electronic targets. Against *non*-electronic targets, it is completely ineffective. The overload mode delivers an even bigger punch, but is less energy-efficient. Since energy weapons are typically 'reloaded' at recharge stations, ammo is essentially free — just be careful not to run out when you're far from a recharge station. With 'free' ammo, the limiting factor on using the laser pistol becomes the condition of the weapon. A high Maintenance skill will help in this regard, and will *also* let you store more charge in the weapon's battery. The Energy Weapons specialist should definitely invest in a high Maintenance skill as well. Energy weapons can also be 'reloaded' with portable batteries, or with the Electron Cascade psi discipline. Modifications can increase the effective storage potential to extremely high levels.

The high skill requirement and highly focused effects make this a specialist-only weapon. Still, given the deadliness of mid-to-late-game electronic foes such as the Assault Robot and Rocket Turret, the EMP rifle is well worth it.

FUSION CANNON

A huge rifle-like weapon, with chambers of concentrated green plasma surrounding the barrel.

WEAPON SETTING	TYPE OF DAMAGE	DAMAGE AMOUNT	RADIUS	PROJECTILE SPEED	THRESH OLD%	MIN %	MAX %
Normal	Energy	20	10 ft	60	20	1	10
Death	Energy	30	12 ft	24	20	1	10

- Uses prisms for ammunition.

- **Setting 1 (Normal)**   1 shot per second
  1/5th second reload time

- **Setting 2 (Death)**   1 shot every 2 seconds
  1/5th second reload time

- **1st Modification**   increases clip size from 40 to 80
  increases damage by 10%

- **2nd Modification**   reduces ammo consumption by 50%
  increases damage by an additional 14% (25% total increase)

- **Wear (degradation)**   2% per shot
  once condition drops to "2," chance of breaking grows from 0.5% to 5% per shot

- **Req. Strength**   4
- **Req. Heavy Weapons skill**   6
- **Req. Repair skill**   4
- **Req. Modify skill**   4
- **Req. Maintenance skill**   3

"Early experimentation with atomic fusion yielded disappointing and potentially dangerous results. However, scientific tolerances were considerably lower in the UNN military specifications, so TriOp rushed headlong into production on these god-forsaken devices. Is fusion weaponry incredibly powerful? Of course it is. What is its long-term environmental impact? I have absolutely no idea." – Dr. Marie Delacroix, VB Chief Engineer.

It uses prisms for ammunition, and fires a devastating ball of superheated plasma, that explodes on impact to do damage in an area effect. The secondary fire mode fires a larger, but slower projectile.

An excellent late-game weapon. The ammo is sufficiently rare and expensive that you should save this for the biggest threats... but in the late game, there are a *lot* of those.

GRENADE LAUNCHER

A military issue grenade launcher.

WEAPON AMMO	TYPE OF DAMAGE	DAMAGE AMOUNT	RADIUS	PROJECTILE SPEED	THRESH OLD%	MIN %	MAX %
Disruption Gren.	Standard	35	5 ft	80	10	.5	5
EMP Grenade	EMP	10	10 ft	80	10	.5	5
Incendiary Gren.	Incendiary	15	10 ft	80	10	.5	5
Frag Grenade	Standard	20	10 ft	80	10	.5	5
Proximity Gren.	Standard	10	10 ft	80	10	.5	5

- **Setting 1** — 1 shot per second; 1-second reload time
- **Setting 2** — 1 shot per second; 1-second reload time
- **1st Modification** — increases clip size by 3
  increases damage by 10%
- **2nd Modification** — increases projectile speed by 50% (from 80 to 120)
  cuts reload time to 1/3
  increases damage by 14% (25% total increase)
- **Wear (degradation)** — 1% per shot
  once condition drops to "1," chance of breaking grows from 0.5% to 5% per shot
- **Req. Heavy Weapons skill** — 1
- **Req. Repair skill** — 2
- **Req. Modify skill** — 1
- **Req. Maintenance skill** — 2

The TC-11 self-loading "Brick" can launch a wide variety of ordnance. Unlike the earlier generations of launchers, The TC-11 utilizes a reverse polarization magnetic launching mechanism instead of compressed gas.

Grenades can be set to either explode on impact or bounce around for 3 seconds before detonating (good for getting enemies around corners). There are five different types of grenades, with a variety of effects. **Fragmentation grenades** are the basic type, and deliver a goodly amount of damage to any target. **Proximity grenades** do less damage, but have intriguing strategic uses, as they don't go off until someone comes near them. On the basic setting proximity grenades stick to whatever terrain surface they are fired at; on the Bounce setting, they will bounce around for 3 seconds before sticking and arming. **EMP grenades** do massive damage to electronic targets, but none to organics. **Incendiary grenades** do massive damage to organics, but very little to electronics. **Disruption grenades** cause a highly localized explosion; they have a much smaller blast radius than a fragmentation grenade, but causes considerably more damage within that radius.

This is a useful mid-game weapon. Ammunition is fairly scarce and expensive, so it is best saved for use against the most threatening opponents or large groups.

LASER PISTOL

A small hand weapon that fires blue laser bolts.

WEAPON SETTING	TYPE OF DAMAGE	DAMAGE AMOUNT	RADIUS	PROJECTILE SPEED	THRESH OLD%	MIN %	MAX %
Normal	Energy	2	n.a.	100	10	.5	5
Overload	Energy	12	n.a.	100	10	.5	5

- **Setting 1 (Normal)**
  3 shots per second
  shots drain 3 units of energy (reload time n/a)

- **Setting 2 (Overload)**
  1 shot every 3 seconds
  shots drain 20 units of energy (reload time n/a)
  shots do 6x damage

- **1st Modification**
  increases charge capacity by 50 units
  increases damage by 10%

- **2nd Modification**
  decreases energy consumed per shot from 3 to 2 on setting 1
  decreases energy consumed per shot from 20 to 14 on setting 2
  increases damage by 14% (25% total increase)

- **Wear (degradation)**
  0.5% per shot
  once condition drops to "1," chance of breaking grows from 0.5% to 5% per shot

- **Req. Energy Weapons skill**   6
- **Req. Repair skill**   1
- **Req. Modify skill**   2
- **Req. Maintenance skill**   1

While it doesn't deliver much damage per shot, its rate of fire is good, and its battery holds enough energy for many shots. Modifications can increase the effective storage potential to even greater levels. The overcharge setting delivers a much bigger blast than the standard shot, but is less energy-efficient, and has a much slower rate of fire. Since energy weapons are typically 'reloaded' at recharge stations, ammo is essentially free — just be careful not to run out when you're far from a recharge station. With 'free' ammo, the limiting factor on using the laser pistol becomes the condition of the weapon. A high Maintenance skill will help in this regard, and will *also* let you store more charge in the weapon's battery. The Energy Weapons specialist should definitely invest in a high Maintenance skill as well. Energy weapons can also be 'reloaded' with portable batteries, or with the Electron Cascade psi discipline.

This is the basic energy weapon, good for the early-to-mid-game and remains useful as a secondary weapon until the end of the game, especially if modified. The major weakness of the laser pistol is that many alien creatures, especially in the late game, are resistant to energy damage; you'll want to have something in your arsenal that can deal with them.

LASER RAPIER

A shimmering blue sword, emitting a constant low hum.

WEAPON	TYPE OF DAMAGE	DAMAGE AMOUNT
Laser Rapier	Energy	11 (15 overhand with Smasher upgrade)

- **Req. Agility**   3
- **Req. Energy Weapons skill**   4

Far more effective than the prototype model first developed on Citadel Station in 2072, the Mark IV laser rapier is a much more reliable piece of technology. The unit works by projecting a porous field of reflective material in a shaft shaped region around the base of the rapier. When the material is bent (as when the rapier strikes a target) the intense refracted light inside is released locally, causing intense burns to the target. "That's right, just like the one the Hacker used on Citadel Station! We're the only one in town who's got 'em! Only 40 nanites!" — Street vendor selling laser rapier replicas in New Detroit.

Melee damage is also affected by Strength. When fighting hand-to-hand, you should ready your swing at a distance, then close and attack, then back away before your opponent can strike back. Be aware that many monsters with hand-to-hand attacks have a greater reach than the laser rapier, so always back away quickly; even if you missed, you may well be within your opponent's range. When fighting a ranged opponent with a melee weapon, close as fast as possible and strike fast, to try and keep him off balance and unable to fire.

For the player who likes melee combat, this is a beautiful addition to his arsenal. A brutally effective melee weapon, the laser rapier does so much damage that even Energy-resistant creatures go down fairly fast before it. If you have the skill and Agility to use it, the laser rapier is better than the wrench in every respect.

PISTOL

A standard bullet-firing hand weapon.

WEAPON AMMO	TYPE OF DAMAGE	DAMAGE AMOUNT	RADIUS	PROJECTILE SPEED	THRESH OLD%	MIN %	MAX %
Standard	Standard	4	n.a.	300	10	.5	5
Armor Piercing	Armor Piercing	4	n.a.	300	10	.5	5
Anti-Personnel	High Explosive	4	n.a.	300	10	.5	5

- Holds 12 shots (unmodified)

- **Setting 1** — 2 shots per second; 1/2-second reload time.

- **Setting 2** — three-shot burst, 3 times every 2 seconds 1/2-second reload time

- **1st Modification** — increases clip size from 12 to 24 increases damage by 10%

- **2nd Modification** — cuts reload time to 1/3 increases damage by an additional 14% (25% total increase)

- **Wear (degradation)** — 1% per shot once condition drops to "1," chance of breaking grows from 0.5% to 5% per shot

- **Req. Standard Weap. skill** — 1

Developed by TriOptimum's military division, the Talon M2A3 .45 caliber pistol is a standard issue sidearm provided to all UNN military personnel. After 23 years in service, the weapon has been designed to accept a number of kinds of ammunition, including the standard steel-jacketed rounds, uranium tipped armor piercing rounds and even nanite-based anti-personnel rounds.

For the pistol, correct use of ammo is very important. **Standard bullets** deal a medium amount of damage to any target. **Armor piercing bullets** do extra damage to mechanical targets, but less damage to organics. **Anti-personnel bullets** do extra damage to organic targets, but almost no damage to mechanical ones. In the secondary fire mode, the pistol fires a burst of three shots, but if your Agility is low, kickback greatly reduces the accuracy of the burst.

This is the most common ranged weapon, and is found quite early in the game. If you keep your gun in good condition, and keep a good (and varied) supply of ammunition on hand, the pistol can remain a valuable weapon until quite late in the game.

Psi Amp

A fist-sized black sphere, with a narrow tube connected to a hypodermic needle.

• Allows psionically-able individuals to amplify and project their powers into the world.

Developed by Esper Industries, a critical branch of TriOp's military R&D division. Before the development of the psi amp, psi powers were mostly only detectable in a lab environment. The amp contains and inhibits the normal diffusion problems inherent in psi phenomena. The amp also allows the user to effectively channel their innate psi powers to a number of proscribed effects. This device caused a furor in the psi community, primarily because of its obvious military applications, but also because of the amp's tendency to define psionic "disciplines" along a few specific (and generally utilitarian) axes.

The psi amp must be equipped to use any psionic disciplines. OSA characters will tend to use the psi amp more than any more mundane weapon. Psionics are versatile and powerful, and the psi amp can be tuned to any one of 35 different psionic disciplines. For the psi-using character, 'ammunition' is in the form of psi hypos, which replenish his natural supply of psi points.

After using one of the psi amp's non-combat powers, remember to switch back to a combat power. There are few thing more distressing (and embarrassing) than getting the drop on a Hybrid — and using Psi Pull on him ....

SHOTGUN

Looks like a traditional shotgun, but is made out of advanced materials; lightweight, but extremely strong.

WEAPON AMMO	TYPE OF DAMAGE	DAMAGE AMOUNT	RADIUS	PROJECTILE SPEED	THRESH OLD%	MIN %	MAX %
Slug	Standard	8	n.a.	300	10	.5	5
Pellet	High Explosive	6 x 1	spread	300	10	.5	5
Slug Triple	Standard	16	n.a.	300	10	.5	5
Pellet Triple	High Explosive	6 x 2	spread	300	10	.5	5

- **Setting 1**
  1 shot every second
  1-second reload time

- **Setting 2**
  1 shot every second
  1.5-second reload time
  shots do double damage, but use 3x ammo

- **1st Modification**
  cuts reload time to 1/3
  increases damage by 10%

- **2nd Modification**
  cuts weapon kickback to 1/3
  increases damage by 14% (25% total increase)

- **Wear (degradation)**
  1% per shot
  once condition drops to "1," chance of breaking
  grows from 0.5% to 5% per shot

- **Req. Standard Weap. skill**   3
- **Req. Repair skill**   3
- **Req. Modify skill**   1
- **Req. Maintenance skill**   2

While it works like a traditional (albeit incredibly deadly) shotgun, this magazine-loaded behemoth also supports a triple-load shot, which has been known to split its victims in two. A few months after its introduction, its popularity with hunters and other weapons enthusiasts prompted a large-scale purchase of the guns by the UNN military.

While much more damaging than the pistol, it takes longer to reload, and has significantly more kickback. Both of these problems can be mitigated by Modifying the shotgun. There are two kinds of shotgun ammo: rifled slugs and pellets. **Slugs** are the standard ammo, and deliver a good punch to any target. **Pellet ammo** is most effective against organic targets, but has a wide spread, so damage decreases significantly with range. The secondary fire mode delivers double the damage of the basic mode, but takes three times the ammunition.

Shotguns can be found relatively early, and make an excellent early-to-mid-game weapon. If you have Repair skill, you can salvage the shotguns wielded by Shotgun Hybrids. Even without Repair, you can salvage some rifled slugs from their weaponry.

STASIS FIELD GENERATOR

A short, bulky generator with complex circuitry and a forward-facing coil that projects the field.

WEAPON SETTING	TYPE OF DAMAGE	DAMAGE AMOUNT	RADIUS	PROJECTILE SPEED	THRESH OLD%	MIN %	MAX %
Normal	Stasis	n.a.	n.a.	70	20	1	10
Area	Stasis	n/a	10 ft	70	20	1	10

- A target hit with the projected 'stasis ball' is frozen in place for several seconds.

- Requires prisms as ammunition.

- **Setting 1 (Normal)**   5 shots per second
  instant reload time
  each shot uses 4 units of stored charge

- **Setting 2 (Area)**   5 shots per second
  instant reload time
  each shot uses 8 units of stored charge
  shots explode, applying stasis effect in 10-ft. radius

- **1st Modification**   doubles the speed of the projectile (from 70 feet/sec to 140 feet/sec)

- **2nd Modification**   reduces ammo consumption by 50%

- **Wear (degradation)**   2% per shot
  once condition drops to "2," chance of breaking grows from 1% to 10% per shot

- **Req. Strength**   3
- **Req. Heavy Weapons skill**   3
- **Req. Repair skill**   6
- **Req. Modify skill**   2
- **Req. Maintenance skill**   3

An experimental device, originally developed as an effective, non-narcotic method to both tranquilize and immobilize patients undergoing major medical procedures. However, the military and security utility quickly became apparent to the TriOptimum executive corps.

The secondary fire mode uses more ammunition, but can freeze multiple opponents in an area effect around the impact.

Since it does no actual damage, unconventional strategies are required to take best advantage of the stasis field generator. A skilled melee fighter can use the SFG to freeze an otherwise dangerous opponent long enough to take it down with melee weapons. The SFG can also be used to avoid many dangerous fights entirely. When pursuing this strategy, however, be sure to remember where you've left enemies behind you, in case you need to double-back later!

VIRAL PROLIFERATOR

This weapon appears to have been cobbled together from both human and alien technologies. Judging by the stock and trigger, it was built by humans.

WEAPON SETTING	TYPE OF DAMAGE	DAMAGE AMOUNT	RADIUS	PROJECTILE SPEED	THRESH OLD%	MIN %	MAX %
Anti-Human	Anti-Human	15	10 ft *	50	25	1	10
Anti-Annelid	Anti-Annelid	15	10 ft *	50	25	1	10

* Damage drops off linearly to edge of radius of effect

- Requires worm ammo.

- **Setting 1 (Anti-Human)** — 5 shots per second
  instant reload time.

- **Setting 2 (Anti-Annelid)** — 5 shots per second
  instant reload time.

- **1st Modification** — increases clip size by 10
  increases damage by 10%

- **2nd Modification** — decreases ammo usage by 50%
  increases damage by 14% (25% total increase)

- **Wear (degradation)** — 3% per shot
  once condition drops below the midpoint of "3,"
  chance of breaking grows from 1% to 10% per shot

- **Req. Research skill** — 3, and small amounts of Tellurium and Technetium
- **Req. Exotic Weapons skill** — 4
- **Req. Repair skill** — 4
- **Req. Modify skill** — 3
- **Req. Maintenance skill** — 4

The central hexagonal core is an energy-rich media, ringed with receptacles containing nanite-virus hybrids. Release of the virus hybrids into the core will cause cycles of replication at nanite, rather than biological, speeds, building up until the payload is released. Additional energetic charges will disperse the viral payload in an explosive radius. The media must be replenished with annelid tissue — these worms must be collected in standard laboratory beakers.

This weapon releases a host of anti-annelid virus in an explosive radius. The virus can be tailored to affect pure annelids, or humans and human/annelid hybrids. Press and hold down the trigger to fire — when you release the trigger, the viral payload will detonate. Don't let it detonate too close to you when it's set to affect humans! The viral proliferator requires worm ammo, which is fairly hard to come by. If you plan to use exotic weapons, collect beakers whenever you find them. Using beakers on Worm Piles will collect worm ammo in usable form.

The viral proliferator is a good late-game weapon. While ineffective against electronic targets, it does a lot of damage to organics — if it's on the right setting.

WRENCH

A multi-purpose tool generally used for engineering purposes. However, it makes an effective makeshift weapon.

WEAPON	TYPE OF DAMAGE	DAMAGE AMOUNT
Wrench	WeaponBash	6 (9 overhand with Smasher upgrade)

• No minimum skill requirement

• Melee damage is affected by Strength

"When you hit someone over the head with 22 pounds of steel, they tend not to appreciate it" — Taz Amanpour, VB Maintenance Crew

Your ability with a wrench is determined by your Standard Weapons skill. When fighting hand-to-hand, you should ready your swing at a distance, then close and attack, then back away before your opponent can strike back. Be aware that many monsters with hand-to-hand attacks have a greater reach than the wrench, so always back away quickly; even if you missed, you may well be within your opponent's range. When fighting a ranged opponent with a melee weapon, close as fast as possible and strike fast, to try and keep him off balance and unable to fire.

This is the basic melee weapon that you find at the start of the game. It's good for most of the early game, but will probably be supplanted by better melee weapons later on (if you have the appropriate skills to use them). Melee combat is one area where the player's skill matters as much as the character's skill. A skilled player can save a lot of ammo by using a melee weapon much of the time. Even if you're not very good at *fighting* with melee weapons, you may want to carry one around to be able to break through windows and similar obstacles without wasting ammo.

AMMUNITION

PISTOL / ASSAULT RIFLE

Armor-Piercing (AP)

The armor piercing round is not particularly effective against soft targets, but it's the round of choice when up against mechanized foes. The uranium tips provide considerable penetrating power, even to relatively weak slug throwers like the Talon M2A3 and the M-22 assault rifle. This bullet is the kid brother of the discarding sabot rounds used by tanks in the 21st century. Besides the incredibly dense uranium tip, the casing is lined with an advanced ballistic material that decreases drag, imparting even greater penetration.

High-Explosive (HE)

While nearly useless against armored targets, the Mite anti-personnel round is devastatingly effective against flesh and blood. Nanites inside the head of the clip autonomically sense when the round has entered an organic target. First, the head of the bullet fragments into several dozen pieces. Immediately, they seek the highest local temperature and, using microscopic pockets of gas, propel themselves towards the warmth and (presumably) the vital organs.

Standard

This .45 standard round is encased in a solid steel jacket, providing general purpose stopping power. The main advantage of this ordnance is that it's extremely cheap to produce, and therefore readily available. No target type is either particularly vulnerable or resistant to these rounds.

SHOTGUN

Pellet

These explosive pellets combine a chemical incendiary with a cluster of self-converting nanites to pack an extra kick. Not many organic targets can stand up to these for long. They are best used at relatively short range, as the pellets tend to spread, and they are not effective against robotic or cybernetic targets.

Rifled Slug

The design of the basic shotgun slug hasn't changed much in the past century. A small, heavy piece of metal, delivered with a high kinetic energy, is a short, simple recipe for damage.

GRENADES

Fragmentation

This is your standard fragmentation grenade. Damage is a combination of the concussive effects of the explosion and the resultant pieces of shrapnel.

Incendiary

This grenade releases a quick-dispersing white phosphorous. WP can cause cyanosis, intestinal pain, and perhaps coma or death. It generally only affects organic targets.

Disruption

The disruption grenade is the only profitable product of the UNN military contractor Flegel-Kraft. Amongst a host of eccentric, technically complex weapons, including the Sulfuric Putty Pancake and the Magnesium Tommygun (neither of which proved themselves in the field) Flegal-Kraft introduced this small, but deadly, explosive. Its explosive radius is much smaller than that of an incendiary or fragmentation grenade, but almost nothing can withstand the center of the explosion.

EMP

EMP (electro-magnetic pulse) grenades yield more impressive results, in terms of damaging or destroying nearby electronics, than an EMP rifle. However, they also come with a much lower rate of fire and a stratospherically higher cost per usage.

Proximity

"The Radius IV proximity grenade utilizes no fewer than six separate methods of detection, from IR signature to EM field sampling to volumetric air displacement in order to make sure that it explodes with pinpoint accuracy and in the close vicinity of your enemies! Be sure to purchase our Radius Exclusion Emitter, coming soon, in order to make sure that your grenades exclude you and your squadmates from detonation!" – TriOptimum advertising copy

HEAVY WEAPONS

Prisms

The Syvintec crystal prisms were introduced in 2023 for high-density energy storage, and have been the storage medium of choice ever since for heavy energy weapons. The silicon/vanadium crystal lattice stores energy in six orthogonal dimensions in the prism's compressed EM fields, allowing for completely efficient energy drain and recharge."

EXOTIC WEAPONS

Worm Beakers

These disgusting things can be used as ammunition by exotic, annelid-based weaponry. The worms can be collected by using empty beakers on piles of worms.

ARMOR

HAZARD SUIT

A full-body suit, designed to protect the wearer from environmental hazards.

The TriOptimum Zero-Phase Hazard Armor uses a combination of triple-layer rubberized mesh, reflective shielding, and low-intensity force-field path warps, in order to protect its wearer from not only vacuum but other environmental hazards such as radiation and chemical spills. Competitors such as the HaziShield Group and Wykodyne have claimed that keeping force-field generators so close to the skin for long periods of time can be carcinogenic, but most wearers are more concerned about short-term hazards and prefer the added protection.

The hazard suit has no minimum skill requirements. This armor provides significant protection against radiation and toxic hazards. This is most useful when navigating highly radiated areas, such as the coolant tunnels on the Engineering Deck. It can be of some use when dealing with foes that have a toxic attack, but you're probably better off with combat armor in that case.

After you're past Engineering, this armor becomes much less useful. One possible reason to keep it around is to be able to more safely approach Annelid Eggs (which often spew toxin). With a hazard suit, you probably won't be poisoned by the toxin, and can safely harvest any organs the Egg contains.

LIGHT ARMOR

A suit of lightweight combat armor, covering the torso.

- **Req. Strength**   2

- Reduces all combat damage by 20%.

The Dartech class 1 armor is a complex mesh of Kevlar and substrate steel mesh that provides lightweight, marginally effective firepower stoppage. The armor is not only designed to resist penetration, but also to disperse the kinetic energy of the impact throughout its frame. Dartech is the arm of TriOptimum's military branch that generally supplies the poorer belligerents, such as terrorists and local militias. While it's better than nothing, more than one wearer has met an unpleasant end while wearing the Dartech class 1.

MEDIUM ARMOR

Full-torso body armor.

- **Req. Strength**   4

- It reduces all combat damage by 30%.

The SenniTech Class 3 Armor is composed of a triple-layered composite of self-stiffening resins and long-chain replicating polymers. Heavier than the Dartech Class 1, the Class 3 also provides substantially more protection from hostile firepower. The SenniTech subdivision of the TriOptimum military provides the armor for many light infantry platoons of both the UNN and corporate military forces.

HEAVY ARMOR

Bulky full-torso body armor.

- **Req. Strength**   6

- Reduces all combat damage by 40%

The UltraTech class 5 combat armor is close to the best you can get without continuous power. A weave of titanium/kevlar shielding panels overlays a regenerative polymer gel, and provides serious protection from both physical and energy attacks.

While not quite as effective as powered armor, heavy armor has the benefit of not requiring power (which always seems to run out in the middle of a firefight). It is more effective than anything short of powered armor, though, so if you have Strength 6, you should strongly consider using this.

POWERED ARMOR

An extremely high-tech suit of armor, with built-in micro force fields.

- **Req. Strength**   3

- Reduces all combat damage by a whopping 50%, but only while it still has charge.

- Requires power to run the repulsion fields and support the shielding panels.

- Burns 1% of its charge every five seconds.

- Maintenance skill lets you charge the armor with more power, for a longer effect.

The Class 7 Armor is the TriOptimum military division's top model. From the solid titanium/polymer shielding panels to the 1-inch repulsion field around the wearer, the Class 7 is the premier in protection. While supposedly only available for UNN military, most Class 7 models seem to be available principally for TriOptimum security forces.

While its tendency to run out of charge at the most dangerous possible time is a significant liability, the high protection value and relatively low Strength requirement make this the armor of choice for most people.

WORM SKIN

This skin has been fashioned into a crude body covering, suitable for a human to wear.

- Worm skin must be researched before it can be used, requiring Research skill 3 and small amounts of Hassium and Technetium.

- Worm skin provides 30% protection from combat damage, and 25% protection from radiation and toxins.

- Raises the wearer's PSI by 2, but slowly drains psi points.

The skin is far tougher than its biochemical makeup would suggest, and further investigation demonstrates a subtle repulsive effect that appears to be psionically generated. The fact that the effect is still active, in combination with the slowly continuing metabolic processes in the skin, indicates that the skin is in some sense still alive. Wearing the worm skin as a piece of armor will provide some physical and environmental protection, and will increase the wearer's PSI statistic. However, it will be a continuous psionic drain on the wearer to keep from being attacked and consumed by the skin.

With no Strength requirement, the worm skin can be useful late-game armor for people with a low strength. For the OSA person, it presents a significant dilemma: it makes you more powerful, but is a constant drain on your reserves. Whether that tradeoff is worthwhile depends on personal play style (and on how many psi hypos you have saved up).

FOOD AND DRINK

CHAMPAGNE (BOTTLE)

Alcoholic beverages can be Used to restore one hit point. Unfortunately, they drain 3 psi points at the same time.

Champagne is a popular drink enjoyed on the *Von Braun* (and smuggled onto the *Rickenbacker*), both in its lounges and replicators. However, since the entire liquor concession is run by TriOp and all champagne is replicated from the same nanite archetype (due to limited database storage), there is only a single brand available. Fortunately, the vintage is excellent.

CHIPS

Chips can be Used to restore one hit point.

Crack-O's Potato Chips, voted the UNN's national food product in the early 21st century, are made from slices of common potatoes deep fried in hydrogenated oils. This treat is often supplemented with vitamins to boost its questionable nutritional value.

"When you need a tasty treat, Crack-O's are the chips to beat. Eat 'em by the bunch or by the pound, new improved Crack-O's won't let you down." — Crack-O's Neuro-Net Promotion 2111

JUICE (BOTTLE)

Juice may be Used to restore one hit point.

Produced from genegrafted fruit in hydroponics tanks, the popular TastyFruit Caffeinated Fruit Drink is chock full of vitamins, sugar and fruit pulp.

LIQUOR (BOTTLE)

Alcoholic beverages can be Used to restore one hit point. Unfortunately, they drain 3 psi points at the same time.

With advances in pharmaceuticals that mimic the effects of alcohol, liquor has begun to be rated in both "true proof" and "factor proof," with the strongest drinks being close to 330 factor proof. This rotgut gets you drunk the old-fashioned way, with no added factor proof.

SODA (CAN)

Invented in the early part of the 20th century, soda was created as a refreshing beverage, a mixture of carbonated water and corn syrup. For such a trivial-seeming product, soda and similar beverages fueled the rise of the first two mega-corporations, the names of which are illegal to be published by UNN Information Ordnance #234/fd34. Net rumors suggest that these two corporations' marketing skirmishes turned into physical ones, triggered by the destruction of offshore bottling plants by hired mercenary squads in 2023.

VODKA (BOTTLE)

Alcoholic beverages can be Used to restore one hit point. Unfortunately, they drain 3 psi points at the same time.

A distilled liquor, vodka is something that the replicators never really got quite right. The replicated brand is numbingly strong, but one's enjoyment is hindered by a sharp, biting taste.

SOFTWARE

HACK SOFTWARE v1, v2, v3

Hack software comes in three levels of sophistication. Each time you find a new level, it is automatically and permanently installed, raising your Hack odds by 10% across the board.

This piece of software is officially illegal, but it is the rare station or craft where it cannot be found. When equipped, it allows one to hack into many computers aboard ship (allowing access to restricted areas), shut down security systems, alter replicator databases to allow purchase of previously restricted items, and other nasty tricks.

"It's a nice toy, but is it really necessary? Jeez, the Hacker didn't have to use any off-the-shelf crap back on Citadel Station. When you boot that puppy up, you might as well be wearing a sign on your head that says: Hey, look at me, I'm a newbie!" — Todd Spokane, President, Western States Binary League

MODIFICATION SOFTWARE v1, v2, v3

Modification software comes in three levels of sophistication. Each time you find a new level, it is automatically and permanently installed, raising your Modification odds by 10% across the board.

Modification software provides even an untrained (but cyber-equipped) user with the full schematics of all currently manufactured weapons. Upgrades are available on a monthly basis containing the schematics of weapons newly on the market. Higher levels of the software employ the octane model of expert system in order to advise the user on ideal and efficient modifications.

PDA SOFTWARE

You automatically start the game with PDA Software installed. There is only one level of this software.

This software allows the user to interface with logs, receive email and retrieve various data formats such as standard .MAP files. The PDA automatically organizes the logs and email by deck through interaction with groups of passive sensors.

REPAIR SOFTWARE v1, v2, v3

Repair software comes in three levels of sophistication. Each time you find a new level, it is automatically and permanently installed, raising your Repair odds by 10% across the board.

Repair software provides even an untrained (but cyber-equipped) user with the full schematics of all common and uncommon electronic and mechanical devices, as well as a set of procedures that can be employed in nearly every type of damage or malfunction. Higher-level software also employs increasingly sophisticated expert systems to advise and assist the user with repairs.

RESEARCH SOFTWARE v1, v2, v3

Research software comes in three levels of sophistication. Each time you find a new level, it is automatically and permanently installed, raising your Research odds by 10% across the board.

Research software provides even an untrained (but cyber-equipped) user with a suite of applications enabling basic investigation research to be done on devices and objects. Such research is best suited for field agents, as it grants only a rudimentary understanding of the subject — further in-depth analysis must be undertaken in a laboratory by more qualified investigators. Higher levels of the software employ the Curie expert system to assist with the speed of research."

IMPLANTS

BRAWNBOOST

A small red implant.

- Increases the user's Strength by 1, burning up 1% of its charge every 10 seconds.

- The higher your Maintenance skill, the more charge you can store in it at recharge stations.

Crigon Manufactory's BrawnBoost™ implant acts to circumvent many of the legal restrictions on athletic pharmaceuticals by avoiding any actual drugs, and simply stimulating the musculature with electric and magnetic impulses.

Extra Strength means extra melee damage and extra carrying capacity. Be careful though; if your inventory is too full when the BrawnBoost runs out of charge, you'll automatically drop some items. You can also use this implant to meet minimum Strength requirements for some weapons. This is risky, however, as the weapon will automatically unequip when the charge runs out!

ENDURBOOST

A small red implant.

- Boosts Endurance by 1, burning up 1% of its charge every ten seconds.

- The higher your Maintenance skill, the more charge you can store in it at recharge stations.

The first of the Boost™ line of implants manufactured by Crigon Manufactory, this implant gently stimulates both nerve fibers and muscle tissue, and filters fatigue toxins from the blood. "How strong do we need to be? Is better actually better? Could Shakespeare write a play with all of the characters mentally, physically and emotionally jacked up to superheroic levels? Would he even care to?" – Prof. Joaquin Rutu, Lecturer, Capetown University.

Extra hit points are always helpful, especially when going against particularly tough opponents. The extra hit points are lost when the charge runs out (or the implant is removed), but this will never reduce you below one hit point.

EXPERTECH

A small blue implant.

- Boosts your Hack, Repair, and Modify skills by 1, burning up 1% of its charge every ten seconds.

- The higher your Maintenance skill, the more charge you can store in it at recharge stations.

The ExperTech implant was developed by a rogue group of former TriOp employees who grew disgusted with the secrecy maintained both by their employer and UNN security forces. While officially illegal, this implant has spread through the black market to almost all corners of patrolled space and can (of course) be found on the *Von Braun*.

This implant's bonus does *not* apply to meeting minimum skill requirements. You probably don't want to wear this implant all the time, but should swap it in before using any of these skills.

LABASSISTANT

A small green implant.

- Increases Research skill by 1, burning up 1% of its charge every ten seconds.

- The higher your Maintenance skill, the more charge you can store in it at recharge stations.

The LabAssistant™ is one of the least popular implants that Crigon Manufactory sells, but a core market of graduate students keeps the line afloat.

Not worth keeping in all the time, swap it in when you find something to research. Unlike the ExperTech, this implant's bonus *does* count towards skill minimums. With a LabAssistant, you can Research items that require a skill of 1, even if you have spent no points on Research skill at all!

PsiBoost

A small purple implant.

- Increases the user's PSI by 1, burning up 1% of its charge every 10 seconds.

- The higher your Maintenance skill, the more charge you can store in it at recharge stations.

Crigon Manufactory's PsiBoost™ implant monitors the user's neurotransmitter levels, and acts on nervous controllers to keep the levels optimal for peak neural function.

Obviously of benefit only to those persons who use some amount of psionic powers. The PsiBoost™ is vital element of the OSA person's arsenal, as almost all psionic disciplines become more effective at higher PSI levels.

SwiftBoost

A small blue implant.

- Boosts Agility by 1, burning up 1% of its charge every 10 seconds.

SwiftBoost™ Implant speeds up reaction times for the entire body. This implant is popular among gymnasts and other athletes, but hasn't caught on fully with the military yet.

This increases your movement speed, decreases weapon kickback, and decreases falling damage. You can also use this implant to meet minimum Agility requirements for some weapons. This is risky, however, as the weapon will automatically unequip when the charge runs out!

WormBlood

A bizarre, reddish organic implant.

- Right-click on a pile of worms to instantly heal 10 hit points of damage.

- Must be researched before it can be used, which requires Research skill 4 and a small amount of Copper.

- The higher your Maintenance skill, the more charge you can store in it at recharge stations.

This implant is a high-powered blood filtering and reprocessing unit that acts to modify blood-borne annelid tissue so that it is benign in a human host. Because of the highly regenerative nature of these annelids, their tissue, in conjunction with this implant, can be used as a replacement for damaged human tissue. A small insertion port in the implant can be used to import annelid tissue for this use. While under the effect of this implant, discarded annelid tissue, such as that found in worm piles, can be used for a regenerative effect. Use of annelid tissue in such a fashion while the implant is not powered is strongly discouraged.

Since this is a fairly specialized function, you probably won't want to keep this active all the time, but rather will swap it in when you want to use it.

WormHeart

A bizarre, light brown organic implant.

- While this implant is powered, the user takes no damage from annelid toxin and will regenerate 1 hit point every 30 seconds.

- Must be researched before it can be used, requiring Research skill 5 and small amounts of Cesium and Hassium.

- The higher your Maintenance skill, the more charge you can store in it at recharge stations.

This implant is a combination of a blood filtering device and a regenerative stimulator, using annelid regenerative tissue as an adjunct. While the implant is worn, it sequesters all annelid venom that the user is subject to, preventing it from acting. Additionally, damaged tissue is replaced quickly by a psychocreative annelid substitute. However, the substitute tissue produces some amount of degradation byproduct, which is itself toxic (and sequestered by the implant). Unfortunately, when the implant loses power or is removed, much of the sequestered venom is released into the user's bloodstream. Make sure you have some anti-toxin hypos handy!

WormMind

A bizarre, blue-colored organic implant.

- When the user of this implant is damaged, 1 point of every 4 points of damage done is subtracted from psi points instead of hit points.

- Must be researched before it can be used, requiring Research skill 3 and a small amount of Cesium.

- The higher your Maintenance skill, the more charge you can store in it at recharge stations.

This implant will alter the user's neural processes, stimulating and amplifying the areas related to psionics. Additionally, a steady drip of annelid neurotransmitter chemicals is fed into the user's lower cortex. The overall effect of this is to enhance the user's latent psychocreative abilities, specifically in the area of bodily self-control. The user of the implant will be able to psychocreatively heal some portion of any damage he takes. Long-term use is likely to cause a hyperimmune reaction.

This is obviously not a great idea if you're using those psi points actively, but for the non-psi user, this implant effectively converts those unused psi points into extra hit points.

SPECIAL HEALING & RESTORATION

ALIEN PSI BOOSTER

A small white hypospray of non-standard design.

- Increases your PSI stat by 1 for 5 minutes.

- Must be researched before use, requiring small amounts of Iridium and Sodium.

This pharmaceutical combines a complex mix of psychoactive chemicals, some of them quite powerful, and refined annelid tissue. Many of the chemicals have enzymatically bonded to the annelid tissue fragments, many of them since construction of the hypo, as if the annelid tissue is still biologically active. Longterm usage may well cause hallucinatory side effects.

This hypo does *not* have the anti-duplication protection that was installed in the standard psi hypo, and thus can be psionically duplicated with the Molecular Duplication power.

ANNELID HEALING ORGAN

This spongy, reddish organ oozes a clear liquid through many small pores and sphincters. Using this will restore 15 lost hit points.

Chemicals needed to research   Osmium (Os)

This gland secretes a prolific mix of hormones and stimulatory enzymes, and a quickly dividing layer of cells spawns off multi-purpose circulatory cells. These cells seek out sites of tissue damage and graft themselves in, taking on the characteristics of the local host tissue in moments. The shared tissue compatibilities between human and annelid tissue allow this gland to be used for healing, though not as fully as it would in an annelid host. Once removed from the host's body, it can only be used once.

ANNELID PSI ORGAN

This whitish organ is stiff and rubbery, with a feel of crystals shifting when you squeeze it. Using this will restore *all* lost psi points!

Chemicals needed to research   Gallium (Ga), Yttrium (Y)

This gland produces a potent cocktail of psychoactive and adrenal hormones that acts to rejuvenate and enervate neural tissue. In addition to standard (and somewhat unusual) biological compounds, the gland also appears to secrete small amounts of semi-physical psychocreative energy. While this gland can be used to restore psionic potential, the danger inherent in consuming alien psychocreative energies suggests that this should only be done in emergencies.

ANTI-RADIATION HYPO

A small yellow-green hypospray.

•   Removes radiation from your body.

This agent radically accelerates the half-life breakdown of many potentially hazardous compounds. Dr. Marie Delacroix, Chief Engineer aboard the *Von Braun*, was well aware of the imperfections inherent in the rushed development of the ship. Notably, the coolant system of the ship had a chronic cracking problem, leading to the wide-spread leakage of hazardous materials. While these leaks are easily detected and usually quickly fixed, she demanded that an excess supply of ChemCal rad hypos be distributed throughout the ship. Unlike most of her cautions regarding conditions on the *Von Braun*, this one was actually heeded. Most effective if used shortly after the hazardous event, anti-radiation hypos inject small amounts of an agent commercially known as NukeTralizer.

Rad hypos do not prevent you from absorbing the radiation in the first place, so you should use these hypos after leaving the radiated zone, not before entering it.

ANTI-TOXIN HYPO

A small yellow-orange hypospray.

•   Removes two units of poison from your body.

"The Vita-Hyb Detoxification Hypospray acts fast, and it acts strong, to rid your body of chemical and environmental hazards. Had too much to drink? Wandered too close to a synthocrete building in progress? Try a dose! Children, senior citizens, pregnant women, and those on any form of medication are warned to consult Health Advisory 1053-T-032 before using." — Vita-Hyb skybanner, 2110.

Unlike radiation, poison does not wear off over time, so keeping some anti-toxin hypos around is always a good idea.

DIAGNOSTIC/REPAIR MODULE

If you have the Cyber-Assimilation OS Upgrade, this device can be found on certain destroyed robots (Maintenance Bots, Security Bots and Assault Bots ... Protocol Droids explode so violently that nothing can be salvaged from them). It can be used to instantly heal 15 points of damage. Characters without the Cyber-Assimilation Upgrade can not use (or even find) this item.

Advanced models of robots contain self-modification circuitry and special nanite stores for repair and replacement parts. After the Dubuque Autodoc Scandal of 2025, programmed failsafes were implemented to prevent robots from "accidentally" generating new functionality, such as weapons. Additionally, the diagnostic/repair modules can be used by hackers and other heavily modified humans for their own healing, leading to slash-and-run robberies of unaccompanied robots such as Protocol Droids.

MEDICAL HYPO

A small red hypospray.

• Heals 10 points of damage over a period of a few seconds.

Designed as a quick fix for minor injuries, the ChemCal medical hypo injects a healing enzyme which can make a crude assessment of the patient's condition and somewhat alter the chemical makeup of the hypo to fit the case. In addition, the hypo contains a mixture of standard pain killers and anti-coagulants. Not meant as a treatment for serious injury, the med hypo will do in a pinch. The only downside is the rather sharp stick of the over-engineered vacc needle, which was nearly recalled twelve years ago on its introduction. Strong litigation by TriOp's legal department eliminated that potentially costly eventuality.

MEDICAL KIT

A small kit with several automated healing agents.

• Restores all lost hit points over a period of a few seconds.

The self-diagnostic medical kit is able to stop bleeding, rebuild damaged tissue, and even make rudimentary organ repair. A staple of emergency medical technicians, battlefield medics, and policemen everywhere.

PSI HYPO

A small white hypospray.

• Increases your psi points by 30, up to your maximum.

The psi hypo contains a potent cocktail of tension relievers, dopamine inhibitors, and circulatory stimulators. The Surgeon General has warned that psi hypos can be habit-forming and dangerous to your health.

The manufacturer has used a special, patented process to make these items unable to be duplicated by those who know the Molecular Duplication psi discipline, in order to protect their monopoly.

Note. If you are a specialized psi user, you should use the options panel to assign a hotkey to "Use Psi Hypo".

SPEED BOOSTER

A small blue hypospray.

- Confers twenty seconds of double speed.

Popular among high-school students for the dangerous street sport of "Crash Careening," the Vita-Hyb SpeedBooster™ hypo can also be invaluable in emergencies. For fastest access in an emergency, use the Options Panel to assign a hotkey to "Use Speed Booster."

STRENGTH BOOSTER

A small purple hypospray.

- Confers one point of Strength, up to a maximum of eight points, for five minutes.

Vita-Hyb, the makers of Strength-Boost™, have been rumored to sell surgically implantable Strength-Boost™ drip packages for athletes, though such things are, of course, highly illegal.

SURGICAL UNIT ACTIVATION KEY

A small computer pad designed to interface with the standard surgical unit

- Fully heals you for 5 nanites.

The standard surgical unit is useful for diagnostic procedures, under the control of a trained physician. This activation key, when attached to a surgical unit, will allow it to perform healing procedures automatically. A fierce battle with the medical lobby has resulted in a compromise, in which the nanite-driven activation keys may not be installed by the vendor on a surgical unit, but may be stocked separately for customers to install in case of emergency, and the installation is not difficult. However, once the two are connected, a factory technician is required to disconnect the two.

A working surgical unit can make many areas of the game much easier. As noted above, most surgical units start the game in an incomplete condition, so you'll need these activation keys to give them full functionality.

Since activation keys are fairly rare, and they can't be removed once installed, you should think carefully before installing one. Is this an area where you think you're going to need frequent healing? How near is the nearest working surgical unit behind you?

TOOLS AND DEVICES

AUTO REPAIR UNIT

A small spherical object with a handle on one end and a number of extended arms with tools coming from the other end.

- Performs one successful repair, regardless of the skill of the user.

The Viridian V-Badge Auto Repair Unit is marketed, in an amazing display of underrating, as a repair device. In reality, the ARU scans, and then virtually rebuilds from scratch, a target device, in its original pristine state. Several documented cases have observed subtle improvements in the repaired device, where the original was damaged beyond scannability. Much to the relief of licensed repair specialists, the ARU is a single-use device

This unit is useful for the player who hasn't taken Repair skill. Since many of the weapons and replicators you'll find have been broken, the auto repair unit can come in quite handy indeed.

BEAKER

*Beakers can be Used on worm piles to make Worm Beakers (see **Ammunition**, p. XX).*

While most DNA infusion clipping is done via protein databases, this beaker is still an effective way to test new compounds of both carbon and non-carbon based compounds. The shielded beaker is an excellent method of storing small quantities of hazardous materials for transport and/or storage.

CHEMICALS

There are numerous different chemicals stored in the Chemical Storerooms of the Von Braun. *Certain chemicals are necessary to research specific objects.*

Research software and nanite-driven molecular processing has come to mean that the necessary material for performing basic research no longer includes complex organics and complex synthetics. Instead, chemical elements serve as raw materials for the nanite research processors, and are combined as needed. Chemical containers such as these are carefully designed to prevent the material from reacting with the environment either chemically or energetically, and are fitted with dispensing nozzles that dock with most standard nanite injection ports.

CYBERNETIC MODULE

Cybernetic modules are one of the most important resources in the game, the raw material of your character advancement.

Cybernetic modules contain a mix of programmable RNA databases and brainwave EM that can be used to augment a cyber rig at any upgrade unit, a proprietary TriOptimum training device. Skills acquired via upgrade units are not guaranteed to last more than a few weeks, though skills acquired in this fashion and then used consistently, and especially under stressful conditions, are frequently found to be permanent.

"God, was he jacked. I had never seen a specimen like him. How much of his original self remained? Hard to say. However, I must admit … he put the 'sigh' back in cybernetic." – *She* magazine, July 2111

NANITE

Nanites are the "currency" of the *Von Braun*, and are also necessary to perform most technical tasks.

Efficient nanite-based technology was introduced after a series of radical experiments at the University of Masala in 2078. Nanites are sub-atomic machines that are capable of being programmed to perform a nearly infinite variety of tasks, from forming themselves in a replication grid to "create" arbitrary objects, to fighting bacteria and viruses in the human bloodstream. In other words, nanites (combined with replication tech) created the "every material." The UNN Currency Redefinition Act of 2082 opened up the door for moving financial transactions to a strict nanite basis.

FRENCH-EPSTEIN DEVICE (FED)

A small tube with numerous scanning and attachment ports.

• Performs one successful weapon modification, regardless of the skill of the user.

The perfect birthday gift for the techie with less than ideal technical skills, the French-Epstein device is a portable, nanite-driven, self-contained analysis and modification tool. Simply place your weapon in the device, and let the French-Epstein's expert systems do the work necessary in the weapon's modifications.

Weapon modifications can improve weapon damage, clip size, firing speed, or many other parameters. These devices are rare, and are one use only, so use them only on your favorite weapons.

GamePig

A small handheld screen, with controls at the bottom arranged to look like the face of a pig.

- Rumor has it that some of the games even give you nanites when you win the games.

A shiny new GamePig™ entertainment device from Vortex Mechanics Unlimited. Able to play dozens of different games, simply by inserting new memory cartridges. Most games star "Grunty the Gaming Pig," who first rose to fame in the 2005 interactive entertainment "Corporate Swine."

If the horrors of the *Von Braun* get to be too much for you to take, find yourself a GamePig and a game cartridge, and settle down for some relaxing fun.

DISCLAIMER: VMU is not liable for any accidents which may occur due to distraction from playing GamePig™ games in a heads-up display. Oink!

Game Cartridge

This memory module contains a complete working game for use with your VMU GamePig™. Oink!

ICE-Pick

A small, but extremely powerful computer chip, with a standard interface port.

- Performs one successful hack, regardless of the skill of the user.

Banned as illegal in most countries and aboard UNN ships, the ICE-pick is nevertheless a great help for any hacker who can afford the prices the black market charges for the device. A persistent rumor in the hacker underground is that "Cantor," the ICE-pick's inventor, has offered his own ICE-breaking algorithms as a reward to anyone who can demonstrate to him a system the ICE-pick can't break.

Its limited power supply and custom-programmed nanites make it good for one use only. ICE-picks are quite rare, so use them strategically. One common use is to hack a replicator that stocks useful equipment and is located near the main elevator. Visiting this hacked replicator at regular intervals can keep you well stocked without spending very much. While ICE-picks aren't as generally useful to skilled hackers, even they can use them to save time on the most difficult hacks, or in particularly tense situations.

MAINTENANCE TOOL

A small wrench-like object, largely composed of specialized nanites.

*   Used to improve the condition of your weapons, preventing them from breaking in the middle of a fight.

*   Requires one point of Maintenance skill to use it.

Gunnery sergeants everywhere make it a point of pride that their tool of choice isn't a "loser know-nothing fix-it-all device" – the better the Maintenance skill of the operator, the more effect using the tool will have.

The higher your skill, the greater the benefit for using any given tool. These tools are disposable, and can only be used once each.

Any person who uses weapons on a regular basis will want to keep a supply of Maintenance tools on hand.

PORTABLE BATTERY

A small battery with an energy port designed to interface with all standard powered devices.

*   Contains enough power to recharge virtually any powered device.

A small flaw in the discharge terminal prevents the battery from being used more than once, as it fully discharges upon use. ElectroSim has issued a recall for this particular type of battery.

These are most useful for the player who specializes in energy weapons. Other players may find them useful as well, since everyone can use powered implants, and nearly everyone is capable of using powered armor.

Portable batteries may often be salvaged from destroyed Laser Turrets.

RECYCLER

A small gray box, with an intake chamber on one end and a nanite dispenser on the other end.

*   Degrades just about any object into more nanites.

Early incidents in which recyclers were used for disposal of bodies led to quick restrictions on what sort of items the recycler will accept.

If there are ammunition types or hypos that you find yourself never using, the recycler can convert them into useful nanites.

The fourth-tier psi power Molecular Transmutation has a similar effect. Which option is most profitable depends on a large number of factors, so feel free to experiment.

RECYCLING AND TRANSMUTATION

Those "useless" items lying around the ship, like plants, smokes, magazines and mugs, aren't useless anymore once you get either the recycler device (see p. XX), or the Tier 4 psionic power Molecular Transmutation. Either of these will allow you to convert these miscellaneous objects (as well as many other things that may or may not be useful to your specific character) into nanites.

Recycling. When you recycle, it recycles a whole stack (everything in a single inventory slot) at once. Be very careful not to drop your recycler onto that large stack of medical kits you've been carefully hoarding! Sure, you'll get some nanites, but it'll hardly be worth it …

Transmutation, conversely, affects only one "clip" worth, if the stack is larger than a single clip (6 bullets or shells, or 3 grenades; for hypos a "clip" is 1). You should never use transmutation on a less-than-full clip, since it costs just as much but you'll get fewer nanites.

Transmutation Economics. As explained in the description of **Molecular Transmutation** (see p. XX), effective use of that power requires careful thought as to whether the gain from using the power is better than the loss of psi points (which will eventually have to be recovered, probably with a psi hypo). When figuring costs, you also have to take into account difficulty level, availability of hacked replicators, and whether you have the Replicator Expert OS Upgrade. Cost can range from less than 4 all the way up to 20. On Normal difficulty level, initial cost is 10, though with everything optimized it drops to less than 5.

The formula for how much you get is:

(.8 +.2*PSI) x (# of objects in target stack/clip (whichever is less)) x Transmute Factor (see table on next page)

Any decimal is truncated. The table also lists the range of possible yields, from PSI 1 to PSI 10 (only possible with maxed and boosted PSI). If profit (Yield – Cost) is greater than the recycle gain, you'll do better using Transmutation. Otherwise, use the recycler.

In general, the best money-makers for Transmutation are fragmentation grenades and prisms. They are very profitable even on Impossible, without any cost breaks.

OBJECT	TRANSMUTE FACTOR	YIELD RANGE	RECYCLE VALUE
3 Frag Grenades	8	24 – 67	6
3 Other Grenades	2.5	7 – 21	6
6 Standard Bullets	1	6 – 16	6
6 Armor-Piercing Bullets	1.5	9 – 25	6
6 Anti-Personnel Bullets	1.5	9 – 25	6
10 Prisms	1.75	17 – 49	10
3 Shotgun Ammo (all)	1.25	3 – 10	3
4 Worms	2	8 – 22	12
Medical Hypo	4	4 – 11	2
Medical Kit	6	6 – 16	2
Anti-Radiation Hypo	3	3 – 8	2
Anti-Toxin Hypo	3	3 – 8	2
Psi Hypo	8	8 – 22	2
Speed Booster	3	3 – 8	2
Strength Booster	3	3 – 8	2
Alien Psi Booster	5	5 – 14	2
Annelid Healing Gland	4	4 – 11	2
Annelid Psi Organ	4	4 – 11	2
Most Junk Objects	n/a	n/a	1
Implant	n/a	n/a	10
Maintenance Tool	n/a	n/a	2
Portable Battery	n/a	n/a	2

PLOT-CRITICAL DEVICES

The following items are not generally useful, but are necessary at (at least) one specific point in the plot in order to finish the game. For the exact use of these items, see the Walkthrough.

ANTI-ANNELID TOXIN
Chemicals needed to research   Antimony (Sb) x 2, Vanadium (V)

CIRCUIT BOARD
ID CARD
POWER CELL
SIMULATION CHIPS
SYMPATHETIC RESONATOR

MISCELLANEOUS

Each of these generates 1 nanite when recycled.
CIGARETTES
Using cigarettes drains one hit point, without providing any benefit whatsoever.

HEART PILLOW	**PLANT**
MAGAZINE	**POOL CUE**
MUG	**RING BUOY**

WEAPONS TABLES

Projectile Speed gives you a relative idea of how rapidly the weapon propels its shot. When firing a weapon with a slower projectile speed at a moving target, slightly lead the target.

Wear per Shot, **Threshold**, **Min %** and **Max %** all describe the weapon's wear (degradation) — as you fire it, it gradually wears out and breaks unless you maintain it. Each factory-fresh or fully repaired weapon begins at 100%. (Weapons you find often begin at less-than-100% quality.) Each time you fire a weapon, it wears out a bit, as listed in **Wear per Shot**.

Your onscreen display gives a 0 – 10 rating for the condition of your weapon; that rating is translated directly from the game's 0 – 100% evaluation of the weapon. When a weapon wears out to the **Threshold %**, it has a chance of breaking each time you fire it. **Min %** lists the initial chance of breakage; **Max %** lists the chance of breakage (each time you fire it) when the weapon has worn down completely.

For example, a pistol takes 1% wear each time you fire it (that is, it will wear down completely after 100 shots). When it drops to 10% ("1" on your display), it might break each time you fire it. The initial chance of breakage is 0.5%. This chance gradually increases; if your display reads "0" there is a 5% chance it will break each time you fire it. Of course, maintaining it or repairing it immediately improves it.

COMBAT STATS

AMMO or SETTING	TYPE OF DAMAGE	DAMAGE AMOUNT	RADIUS	PROJECTILE SPEED	WEAR per SHOT	THRESH OLD%	MIN %	MAX %
Annelid Launcher								
Anti-Human	Anti-Human	25	5 ft	25	3%	25	1	10
Anti-Annelid	Anti-Annelid	25	7 ft	25	3%	25	1	10
Assault Rifle								
Standard	Standard	10	n.a.	300	0.5%	10	.5	5
Armor Piercing	Armor Piercing	10	n.a.	300	0.5%	10	.5	5
Anti-Personnel	High Explosive	10	n.a.	300	0.5%	10	.5	5
Crystal Shard	WeaponBash	12 (15 overhand with Smasher Upgrade)						
EMP Rifle								
Normal	EMP	10	10 ft	70	1.5%	10	.5	5
Overload	EMP	15	15 ft	70	1.5%	10	.5	5
Fusion Cannon								
Normal	Energy	20	10 ft	60	2%	20	1	10
Death	Energy	30	12 ft	24	2%	20	1	10
Grenade Launcher								
Disruption Gren.	Standard	35	5 ft	80	1%	10	.5	5
EMP Grenade	EMP	10	10 ft	80	1%	10	.5	5
Incendiary Gren.	Incendiary	15	10 ft	80	1%	10	.5	5
Frag Grenade	Standard	20	10 ft	80	1%	10	.5	5
Proximity Gren.	Standard	10	10 ft	80	1%	10	.5	5
Laser Pistol								
Normal	Energy	2	n.a.	100	0.5%	10	.5	5
Overload	Energy	12	n.a.	100	0.5%	10	.5	5
Laser Rapier	Energy	11 (15 overhand with Smasher upgrade)						
Pistol								
Standard	Standard	4	n.a.	300	1%	10	.5	5
Armor Piercing	Armor Piercing	4	n.a.	300	1%	10	.5	5
Anti-Personnel	High Explosive	4	n.a.	300	1%	10	.5	5
Shotgun								
Slug	Standard	8	n.a.	300	1%	10	.5	5
Pellet	High Explosive	6 x 1	spread	300	1%	10	.5	5
Slug Triple	Standard	16	n.a.	300	1%	10	.5	5
Pellet Triple	High Explosive	6 x 2	spread	300	1%	10	.5	5
Stasis Field Generator								
Normal	Stasis (SFG)	n.a.	n.a.	70	2%	20	1	10
Area	Stasis (SFG)	n.a.	10 ft	70	2%	20	1	10
Viral Proliferator								
Anti-Human	Anti-Human	15	10 ft	50	3%	25	1	10
Anti-Annelid	Anti-Annelid	15	10 ft	50	3%	25	1	10
Wrench	WeaponBash	6 (9 overhand with Smasher upgrade)						

USE, MAINTENANCE & REPAIR

Use. Each weapon (other than the wrench) requires a minimum skill to wield it; a few require a minimum stat as well.

Maintenance. Weapons don't last forever; however with enough Maintenance skill you can keep them lasting as long as possible.

Repair. If one of these is broken and you have the minimum Repair skill, you can try repairing it back to a useful condition. Be warned — a critical failure will permanently destroy the weapon.

Nanite Cost. This is the cost in nanites to attempt the repair.

Base Chance. This is the basic percentage chance of success. However, every level of Repair skill you have increases your chance of success 10%, and every level of Cybernetic Affinity increases your chance of success 5%. Each level of repair software improves your chances by 10%. Notice that some repair tasks, such as repairing a stasis generator, have a *negative* base chance of success. This means that until you have enough bonuses to bring your chances into the positive range, you will always fail.

Base ICE. There are a certain number of ICE nodes (nodes which will result in critical failure) inherent in each modification task. Note that every level of CYB decreases the number of ICE by 1.

ITEM	USE MIN. REQ.	MAINTENANCE MIN. MAINT.	REPAIR MIN. REPAIR	NANITE COST	BASE CHANCE	BASE ICE
Annelid Launcher	Exotic 6	4	5	35	-10	5
Assault Rifle	Standard 6, STR 2	4	4	25	0	5
Crystal Shard	Exotic 1	n.a.	n.a			
EMP Rifle	Energy 6	6	2	35	5	4
Fusion Cannon	Heavy 6, STR 4	3	4	40	0	5
Grenade Launcher	Heavy 1	2	2	40	25	3
Laser Pistol	Energy 1	1	1	25	25	3
Laser Rapier	Energy 4, AGI 3	n.a.	n.a			
Pistol	Standard 1	1	1	20	30	3
Shotgun	Standard 2	2	3	35	15	4
Stasis Generator	Heavy 3, STR 3	3	6	60	-5	4
Viral Proliferator	Exotic 4	4	4	50	-15	6
Wrench	–	n.a.	n.a.			
Keypad			1			
Replicator			3			
Security Computer			2			

HIGHER WEAPONS SKILLS

Each level of weapon skill higher than the minimum required for the weapon your are using gives you a 15% damage bonus.

WEAPONS MODIFICATION

With the right skills, you can modify most weapons to improve their performance. Below, the skills you must have to modify each weapon are listed.

Minimum Modify skill. You must have the necessary Modify skill to even attempt the modification.

Nanite Cost. This is the cost in nanites to begin or restart the Modifying procedure.

Base Chance. This is the basic percentage chance of success. However, every extra level of Modifying skill you have increases your chance of success 10%, and every extra level of Cybernetic Affinity increases your chance of success 5%. Each level of repair software improves your chances by 10%. Notice that some modification tasks, such as Rifle 2 modification, have a *negative* base chance of success. This means that until you have enough bonuses to bring your chances into the positive range, you will always fail.

Base ICE. There are a certain number of ICE nodes (nodes which will result in critical failure) inherent in each modification task. Note that every level of CYB decreases the number of ICE by 1.

WEAPON	MIN. MOD. SKILL	NANITE COST	BASE CHANCE	BASE ICE
Pistol 1	1	20	30	2
Pistol 2	3	35	10	4
Shotgun 1	1	25	25	3
Shotgun 2	3	40	0	5
Rifle 1	2	40	15	4
Rifle 2	4	60	-10	6
Grenade Launcher 1	1	25	25	2
Grenade Launcher 2	3	35	-10	4
Fusion Cannon 1	4	35	15	4
Fusion Cannon 2	6	50	-15	6
Stasis Generator 1	2	25	10	3
Stasis Generator 2	4	40	-15	5
Laser Pistol 1	2	20	25	2
Laser Pistol 2	4	35	5	4
EMP Rifle 1	3	25	20	3
EMP Rifle 2	5	40	0	5
Annelid Launcher 1	2	50	5	5
Annelid Launcher 2	4	75	-25	7
Viral Proliferator 1	3	50	5	5
Viral Proliferator 2	5	75	-25	7

COMBAT

The combat system for *System Shock 2* is straightforward. In general, you successfully hit anything that's in your crosshairs when you attack. The trick, of course, is to keep a target in your crosshairs long enough to strike or fire. It's naturally harder to aim and fire successfully at a faster-moving target, or one that is farther away (therefore providing a smaller target to line up on).

There are three exceptions to the crosshairs rule-of-thumb:

• Grenade launchers will throw their ammo in an arc.

• Annelid launcher projectiles will change direction to follow a warm target.

• When firing a weapon with a slow projectile speed at a fast-moving target, you must sometimes "lead" the target, firing into its path so that your target and your projectile reach the same point at the same time.

DAMAGE

If you score a hit, your target always takes full damage — as long as it is vulnerable to the type of attack your weapon does. The weapons' damage points will be subtracted from the targets hit points, and when the hit points are reduced to zero, the target is killed or destroyed.

There are a few area-effect weapons that apply partial damage to targets not at the point of impact or detonation.

VULNERABILITIES

Because of the widely varying physical makeup of the enemies you encounter in *System Shock 2*, each type of enemy is vulnerable to certain types of damage and immune to others. Below is a list of weapons and the type of damage they inflict.

When you attack an adversary, you want to lay the biggest hurt with your most efficient weapon. Unfortunately, there isn't one all-purpose terminator in your arsenal — different targets are susceptible to different weapons. For every possible adversary, there are some weapons that devastate it, some weapons that apply decent damage, and some weapons that can't even pink it. For every possible weapon, there are some targets that it wastes, some targets that it can take down with reasonable effort, and some targets that are invulnerable to it.

So it's important that you know what the right tool for the job is. That's where the next couple of tables come in handy:

Weapon Categories. The first table lists what type of damage each weapon inflicts. Often, this depends on the weapon's specific ammunition, so most listings are subcategorized by type of ammunition.

Note that there are four "weapons" (including three psionic disciplines) that each inflict a special type of "damage":

ATTACK	TYPE OF "DAMAGE"	POTENTIAL TARGETS
Stasis Field Generator	Stasis Field	Robots, Hybrids, Monkeys, Cyborgs, Arachnids
Psionic Hypnogenesis	Target stands still	Hybrids, Monkeys, Cyborgs, Arachnids
Electron Suppression	Target is immobilized	Security Cameras, Turrets, Robots
Imposed Neural Restructuring	Target attacks non-humans	Hybrids, Monkeys, Cyborgs

Target Categories. The second table lists the target category for each adversary. It also repeats the information listed above for the four special attacks.

Types of Attack vs. Types of Target. Once you know what type of damage a weapon inflicts, and the type of target you're attacking, you can see whether your weapon can hurt that target, and how badly. The third table lists the effect of each type of attack on each type of target.

Some attacks have no effect on certain targets — those targets are invulnerable to that attack, in which case the table has no listing. All other attacks do at least *some* damage. It might be the damage listed for that weapon, it might be just half the damage listed for that weapon, or it might even be quadruple damage — it all depends on the type of weapon and the type of target.

Take a Human, for example.

Invulnerable. Humans are not vulnerable to Anti-Annelid, Basic, Soma Transference, EMP and Psionic attacks. Even if hit at point-blank range with one of these attacks, a Human won't take any damage at all.

Vulnerable. Humans take full (listed) damage from Bash, Cold, Droid Fusion, Electricity, Incendiary, Radiation, SHODAN, Standard and Weapon Bash attacks. They take just half damage from Armor-Piercing attacks. (A shot from an armor-piercing rifle will do 4, not 8, points of damage.) They take double the listed damage from Energy attacks, and quadruple the listed damage from Anti-Human and High Explosive attacks. (An Energy-powered laser shot will do double its listed damage — 22 instead of 11 points — because Humans react particularly poorly to being fried from the inside out.)

WEAPON CATEGORIES

WEAPON	AMMUNITION/SETTING	TYPE OF DAMAGE (AMOUNT)
Standard Weapons		
Assault Rifle	Standard	Standard (10)
	Anti-Personnel	High Explosive (10)
	Armor Piercing	Armor Piercing (10)
Pistol	Standard	Standard (4)
	Anti-Personnel	High Explosive (4)
	Armor Piercing	Armor Piercing (4)
Shotgun	Pellet	High Explosive (6 x 1)
	Pellet Triple	High Explosive (6 x 2)
	Slug	Standard (8)
	Slug Triple	Standard (16)
Wrench		WeaponBash (6; 9 overhand Smasher)
Energy Weapons		
EMP Rifle	Normal	EMP (10)
	Overload	EMP (15)
Laser Pistol	Normal	Energy (2)
	Overload	Energy (12)
Laser Rapier		Energy (11; 15 overhand Smasher)
Heavy Weapons		
Grenade Launcher	Disruption Grenade	Standard (35)
	EMP Grenade	EMP (10)
	Incendiary Grenade	Incendiary (15)
	Frag Grenade	Standard (20)
	Proximity Grenade	Standard (10)
Fusion Cannon	Normal	Energy (20)
	Death	Energy (30)
Stasis Generator	Normal *or* Area	Stasis Field
Exotic Weapons		
Crystal Shard		WeaponBash (12; 15 overhand Smasher)
Viral Proliferator	Anti-Human	Anti-Human (15)
	Anti-Annelid	Anti-Annelid (15)
Annelid Launcher	Anti-Human	Anti-Human (25)
	Anti-Annelid	Anti-Annelid (25)
Psi Weapons		
Cryokinesis		Cold (3 + PSI)
Pyrokinesis, Localized		Incendiary (5 every 2 seconds)
Pyrokinesis		Incendiary (5 + 2 per PSI)
Psi Sword		Standard (18; 24 overhand Smasher)
Psi Mine		Psi (30)

TARGET CATEGORIES

CATEGORY: TARGET:	HUM	ANNL	SWARM	1/2ANNL	1/2MECH	MECH	BASIC	SHOD	INR	ES	SFG	PH
Humans	*											
Annelids		*										
Annelid Swarm			*									
Psi Reavers		*										
Arachnids		*									*	*
Hybrids				*				*			*	*
Cyborgs					*			*			*	*
Robots						*				*	*	
Security Cam.						*				*		
Turrets						*				*		
SHODAN Avatar						*		*				
SHODAN Shield							*					
SHODAN								*				

TYPES OF ATTACK VS. TYPES OF TARGET

TARGET: ATTACK:	HUM	ANNL	SWARM	1/2ANNL	1/2MECH	MECH	BASIC	SHOD
Anti-Annelid		4	1	1				
Anti-Human	4			2	1			
Armor Piercing	1/2	1/2		1/2	2	4	1	5/4
Bash	1	1		1	1	1/2		
Basic						1		
Cold	1	1		1	1/2	1	1	1
Soma Transfer.		1		1	1			
Droid Fusion	1	1		1	1	1	1	
Electricity	1			1	4	4	1	
EMP					2	4		3/2
Energy	2	1/2		1	1	2	1	1/2
High Explosive	4	2		4	1	1/2	1	3/4
Incendiary	1	2		2	1/2		1	1
Psi		2		1	1		1	1
Radiation	1							
SHODAN	1							
Standard	1	1		1	1	1	1	1
Weapon Bash	1	1		1	1	1/2	1	

RESEARCH

During your exploration of the ship, you'll find alien artifacts (either organs or objects). Before you can successfully use them, however, you'll need to successfully Research them. Research of each item requires certain chemical elements which you'll find over time.

ARTIFACTS AND REQUIRED RESEARCH ELEMENTS

Below is a list of all the alien artifacts that you'll find, the chemicals and minimum Research skill required needed to research them, and where the artifacts first appear.

ARTIFACT	CHEMICALS REQUIRED	MINIMUM RESEARCH	FIRST FOUND (LIKELY)
Alien Psi Booster	Sodium [Na], Iridium [Ir]	2	Deck 3 (Hydroponics)
Annelid Healing Gland	Osmium [Os]	2	Deck 1 (Engineering)
Annelid Launcher	Molybdenum [Mo], Selenium [Se]	6	Rickenbacker
Annelid Psi Organ	Gallium [Ga], Yttrium [Yt]	3	Deck 3 (Hydroponics)
Anti-Annelid Toxin	Vanadium [V], 2 x Antimony [Sb]	1	Deck 3 (Hydroponics)
Arachnid Organ	Iridium [Ir]	1	Deck 4 (Ops)
Crystal Shard	Yttrium [Yt]	4	Deck 4 (Ops)
Grub Organ	Gallium [Ga], Californium [Cf]	1	Deck 3 (Hydroponics)
Hybrid Organ	None	1	Deck 2 (MedSci)
Midwife Organ	None	1	Deck 3 (Hydroponics)
Monkey Brain	Fermium [Fm]	1	Deck 2 (MedSci)
Psi Reaver Organ	Radium [Ra], Barium [Ba]	1	Deck 6 (Command)
Rumbler Organ	Molybdenum [Mo]	1	Deck 5 (Recreation)
Swarm Organ	None	1	Deck 4 (Ops)
Viral Proliferator	Tellurium [Te], Technetium [Tc]	3	Deck 6 (Command)
WormBlood	Copper [Cu]	4	Deck 4 (Ops)
Wormheart	Cesium [Cs], Hassium [Hs]	5	The Body of the Many
WormMind	Cesium [Cs]	3	Deck 4 (Ops)
Worm Skin	Hassium [Hs], Technetium [Tc]	3	Rickenbacker

CHEMICAL AVAILABILITY

ELEMENT	DECKS AVAILABLE (HOW MANY)	ELEMENT	DECKS AVAILABLE (HOW MANY)
Antimony [Sb]	1 (2), 2 (2), 3 (2), 5 (2), Rick, Many	*Molybdenum [Mo]*	5 (2), 6 (2), Rick (2), Many (3)
Arsenic [As]	3, 4 (2), 6 (2), Rick, Many	*Osmium [Os]*	1, 2, Rick, Many
Barium [Ba]	1 (2), 2, 3, 4 (2), 6 (2), Rick (2), Many (2)	*Radium [Ra]*	3, 4, 6 (2), Rick (3), Many (3)
Californium [Cf]	1 (2), 2 (2), Rick, Many	*Selenium [Se]*	6 (2), Rick (2), Many (3)
Cesium [Cs]	1, 3 (2), 4 (2), 5 (2), 6 (2), Rick, Many (3)	*Sodium [Na]*	4 (2), Rick, Many
Copper [Cu]	3, 4 (2), 5 (2), Rick, Many	*Technetium [Tc]*	1, 2, 3, 6 (3), Rick (2), Many (3)
Fermium [Fm]	2 (2), 3, 4, Many	*Tellurium [Te]*	1, 2 (2), 3, 5 (2), 6, Rick, Many (5)
Gallium [Ga]	2, 3 (2), 5	*Vanadium [V]*	1, 3, 5 (2)
Hassium [Hs]	3, 4, 5 (2), 6 (2), Rick, Many (3)	*Yttrium [Yt]*	1 (2), 2 (2), 4, 5, Rick, Many (3)
Iridium [Ir]	1 (2), 2 (2), 3 (2), 4 (2), 5 (2), Rick, Many		

HACKING SKILL TABLE

A skilled hacker can bypass or reprogram electronic programs and devices. Here is the minimum Hacking skill you must have to Hack each item.

ITEM	MIN. HACKING
GamePig	6
High Security Crate	6
Keypad	1
Replicator	3
Security Computer	1
Security Crate	2
Turret	4

STAT MODIFIERS

AGI	SPEED FACTOR	END	HAZARD DAMAGE	STR	MELEE DAMAGE BONUS
1	1.2	1	100%	1	0
2	1.3	2	94%	2	1
3	1.4	3	85%	3	2
4	1.5	4	73%	4	3
5	1.6	5	58%	5	4
6	1.7	6	40%	6	6
7	1.85	7	20%	7	10
8	2.0	8	1%	8	15

REPLICATORS

Replicators are essentially vending machines that "make" the items rather than storing and dispensing them. Therefore, if you don't like what they offer, it is possible to hack them into giving you something more useful.

There are two sets of four items each for each replicator. In each case, the first set lists the replicator's normal contents. The second set lists its contents when it has been hacked.

* = this replicator is broken but repairable

INVENTORY

MEDSCI Map 1, near Xerxes Core

Chips	Maintenance Tool
Medical Hypo	Medical Hypo
Small Standard Clip	Small Standard Clip
Standard Clip	Standard Clip

MEDSCI Map 2, Small Bar West of Security Station

Cigarettes	Research Soft V1
3 Frag. Grenades	3 Frag. Grenades
Psi Hypo	Psi Hypo
Rifled Slug Box	Rifled Slug Box

ENG Map 2, Cargo Bay 2A *

Cigarettes	Repair Soft V1
Portable Battery	Portable Battery
Small Standard Clip	Small Standard Clip
Anti-Radiation Hypo	Anti-Radiation Hypo

ENG Map 1, Entrance to Engine Core)

Cigarettes	Proximity Grenade
Small Standard Clip	Small Standard Clip
Anti-Toxin Hypo	Anti-Toxin Hypo
Psi Hypo	Psi Hypo

MEDSCI Map 1, near R&D Door

Chips	Anti-Radiation Hypo
Small Standard Clip	Small Standard Clip
Psi Hypo	Psi Hypo
Anti-Toxin Hypo	Anti-Toxin Hypo

MEDSCI Map 2, above Crew Lounge

Juice Bottle	Anti-Toxin Hypo
Maintenance Tool	Maintenance Tool
Anti-Radiation Hypo	Anti-Radiation Hypo
Hack Soft V1	Hack Soft V1

ENG Map 1, near Pump Station

Soda Can	Sm. Arm.-Pierc. Clip
3 Frag. Grenades	3 Frag. Grenades
Psi Hypo	Psi Hypo
Medical Hypo	Medical Hypo

ENG Map 2, Cargo Bay 1A

Soda Can	Pellet Shot Box
Maintenance Tool	Maintenance Tool
Rifled Slug Box	Rifled Slug Box
Strength Booster	Strength Booster

HYDRO Map 2, near Entrance

Mug	Small Standard Clip
Anti-Toxin Hypo	Anti-Toxin Hypo
Psi Hypo	Psi Hypo
Portable Battery	Portable Battery

HYDRO Map 1, near Bulkhead to Sector A *

Cigarettes	Medical Kit
Anti-Toxin Hypo	Anti-Toxin Hypo
Small Standard Clip	Small Standard Clip
Modify Soft V1	Modify Soft V1

OPS Map 1, between Crew Quarters *

Cigarettes	3 EMP Grenades
Small Armor-Piercing Clip	Small Arm.-Pierc. Clip
Small Standard Clip	Small Standard Clip
3 Frag. Grenades	3 Frag. Grenades

OPS Map 2, outside Mess Hall

Mug	Medical Kit
Maintenance Tool	Maintenance Tool
Strength Booster	Strength Booster
Medical Hypo	Medical Hypo

RECREATION Map 2, East End of Mall

Cigarettes	Medical Kit
3 Frag. Grenades	3 Frag. Grenades
Medical Hypo	Medical Hypo
Psi Hypo	Psi Hypo

RECREATION Map 1, near Athletics Center

Cigarettes	Rifled Slug Box
Small High-Expl. Clip	Small High-Expl. Clip
Anti-Toxin Hypo	Anti-Toxin Hypo
10 Prisms	10 Prisms

RECREATION Map 2, Sensual Stimulation Center

Candy's Room Key	Candy's Room Key
Lance's Room Key	Lance's Room Key
Nikki's Room Key	Nikki's Room Key
Sven's Room Key	Sven's Room Key

HYDRO Map 1, Biological Survey Area

Vodka Bottle	Repair Soft V2
Medical Hypo	Medical Hypo
Rifled Slug Box	Rifled Slug Box
Repair Soft V1	Repair Soft V1

HYDRO Map 3, Turbine Control

Cigarettes	3 Incendiary Grens.
3 Frag. Grenades	3 Frag. Grenades
Maintenance Tool	Maintenance Tool
Psi Hypo	Psi Hypo

OPS Map 2, inside Mess Hall

Vodka Bottle	Repair Soft V2
Psi Hypo	Psi Hypo
Pellet Slug Box	Pellet Slug Box
3 Proximity Grenades	3 Proximity Grenades

OPS Map 3, across from Armory

Cigarettes	Small High-Expl. Clip
Juice	Recycler
Rifled Slug Box	Rifled Slug Box
Psi Hypo	Psi Hypo

RECREATION Map 2, West End of Mall

Soda Can	Recycler
Maintenance Tool	Maintenance Tool
Anti-Toxin Hypo	Anti-Toxin Hypo
10 Prisms	10 Prisms

RECREATION Map 3, Pool Hall *

Chips	3 Incendiary Grenades
Small Arm.-Pierc. Clip	Small Arm.-Pierc. Clip
Anti-Toxin Hypo	Anti-Toxin Hypo
Psi Hypo	Psi Hypo

RECREATION Map 2, Theater Lobby

Chips	Chips
Cigarettes	Cigarettes
Soda Can	Soda Can

COMMAND Map 2, near Entrance *

Vodka Bottle	Medical Kit
3 Frag. Grenades	3 Proximity Grenades
Recycler	Recycler
10 Prisms	10 Prisms

COMMAND Map 2, CEO's Quarters

Vodka Bottle	Repair Soft V3
Psi Hypo	Psi Hypo
Pellet Shot Box	Rifled Slug Box
Rifled Slug Box	Pellet Shot Box

RICKENBACKER Map 1, near Bio-Reconstruction St.

Chips	20 Prisms
Psi Hypo	Psi Hypo
20 Prisms	Medical Kit
10 Prisms	10 Prisms

RICKENBACKER Map 3, Past Bridge *

Juice Bottle	20 Prisms
Maintenance Tool	Maintenance Tool
3 EMP Grenades	3 EMP Grenades
Psi Hypo	Psi Hypo

THE MANY, First Piece of Rickenbacker

Juice	3 Proximity Grenades
Psi Hypo	Psi Hypo
Medical Kit	Medical Kit
Sm. Anti-Pers. Clip	Sm. Anti-Pers. Clip

COMMAND Map 1, near Tram

Vodka Bottle	Small Arm.-Pierc. Clip
Psi Hypo	Psi Hypo
Anti-Toxin Hypo	Anti-Toxin Hypo
Small Standard Clip	Small Standard Clip

COMMAND Map 1, Shuttle Control

Vodka Bottle	3 EMP Grenades *or*
	(later) Sympath. Resonator
3 Frag. Grenades	3 Frag. Grenades
Incendiary Grenade	Incendiary Grenade
Maintenance Tool	Maintenance Tool

RICKENBACKER Map 1, Missile Storage

Vodka Bottle	3 Disruption Grens.
10 Prisms	10 Prisms
ExperTech	ExperTech
Anti-Toxin Hypo	Anti-Toxin Hypo

THE MANY, Third Piece of Rickenbacker

Chips	3 Disruption Grens.
Anti-Toxin Hypo	Anti-Toxin Hypo
Pellet Shot Box	Pellet Shot Box
10 Prisms	20 Prisms

REPLICATOR ITEM PRICES

There is a set, normal price for replicator items. However, if you can Hack the replicator, you can significantly decrease the price. If you can Hack and are an expert in replicators, you can get an even lower price.

AMMUNITION

ITEM	NORMAL PRICE	HACK. PRICE	HACK + REP. EXP.
Armor-Pierc. Clip, Small	120	90	72
High-Expl. Clip, Small	120	90	72
Pellet Shot Box (6)	90	70	56
Rifled Slug Box (6)	80	60	48
Standard Clip (12)	100	75	60
Stand. Clip, Small (6)	60	45	36

BOOSTERS

ITEM	NORMAL PRICE	HACK. PRICE	HACK + REP. EXP.
Psi Hypo	75	50	40
Speed Booster	50	35	28
Strength Booster	50	35	28

FOOD

ITEM	NORMAL PRICE	HACK. PRICE	HACK + REP. EXP.
Chips	3	n.a.	n.a.
Cigarettes	5	n.a.	n.a.
Juice Bottle	4	n.a.	n.a.
Soda Can	3	n.a.	n.a.
Vodka Bottle	8	n.a.	n.a.
Chips (Theater)	900	800	640
Cigarettes (Theater)	950	825	660
Soda Can (Theater)	925	925	740

HEALTH

ITEM	NORMAL PRICE	HACK. PRICE	HACK + REP. EXP.
Anti-Toxin Hypo	35	25	20
Medical Kit	130	100	80
Medical Hypo	30	20	16
Anti-Radiation Hypo	35	25	20

IMPLANT

ITEM	NORMAL PRICE	HACK. PRICE	HACK + REP. EXP.
ExperTech	150	120	96

SENSSTIM ROOM KEYS

ITEM	NORMAL PRICE	HACK. PRICE	HACK + REP. EXP.
Candy's Room Key	200	100	80
Lance's Room Key	200	85	68
Nikki's Room Key	225	125	100
Sven's Room Key	210	75	60

SOFTWARE

ITEM	NORMAL PRICE	HACK. PRICE	HACK + REP. EXP.
Hack Soft V1	35	25	20
Modify Soft V1	35	25	20
Repair Soft V1	35	25	20
Repair Soft V2	120	95	76
Repair Soft V3	200	170	136
Research Soft V1	35	25	20

WEAPONS

ITEM	NORMAL PRICE	HACK. PRICE	HACK + REP. EXP.
10 Prisms	120	90	72
20 Prisms	200	150	120
3 Frag. Grenades	100	75	60
3 Proximity Grenades	110	80	64
3 EMP Grenades	130	100	80
3 Incendiary Grenades	130	100	80

MISCELLANEOUS

ITEM	NORMAL PRICE	HACK. PRICE	HACK + REP. EXP.
Maintenance Tool	60	45	36
Portable Battery	85	65	52
Recycler	100	75	60
Mug	4	n.a.	n.a.

ADVERSARIES

INTRODUCTION

The servants of The Many are a varied lot indeed. There's the Annelid aliens, the human-alien Hybrids, Xerxes' force of Robots and Cyborgs, and more. This chapter compiles all the adversaries you'll have to face on the way to your final showdown on the *Von Braun*.

Your adversaries are listed by type, starting with Turrets, Cameras and Robots, and moving on through Hybrids, Cyborgs and Annelids. Within each type the creatures are listed in the order in which they're most likely to appear.

Information given for each adversary includes its vulnerabilities (see **Vulnerabilities**, p.78, for an explanation of the various vulnerabilities), hit points, attack damage and the chance of finding loot on its corpse. The table on page 92 gives more specialized combat information for each creature, like rate of fire, accuracy and blast radius.

The entry for each adversary also includes notes on the creature's place in the universe of *System Shock 2*, strategies on how to deal with it in combat, and commentary on its place in the game — where it appears and what its function is.

Toward the end of this chapter (p. 110) is a special section on The Body of the Many and SHODAN herself. More detailed strategies and descriptions of these challenges can be found in the appropriate sections of the Walkthrough.

ADVERSARY STATS

Knowing what you're up against is one of the most effective tools you have. If, after looking at your adversary's stats, you think you aren't up to a fight, fall back and improve your situation.

Vulnerabilities. Every adversary is more vulnerable to certain types of damage. (See page XX for a table explaining what damage each weapon inflicts, and how it affects each of your opponents.) We've classified each adversary, based on the type of damage it takes. For example, Security Cameras are classified as "Mechanical" — they take quadruple damage from armor piercing, electricity or EMP attacks, but only half damage from bashing or high explosive attacks. And they aren't hurt at all by draining, incendiary, psi or similar attacks.

Take advantage of this information — always try to have the best weapon in hand for each new adversary you expect to meet.

Hit Points. An adversary's hit points indicate how tough it is. In general, each damage point a weapon inflicts subtracts one hit point from its target. When a target's hit points are reduced to zero, the target is permanently out of commission.

Loot. Loot is what the adversary is carrying. When it is killed, the loot is yours for the taking. Note, however, that you rarely know for certain what anyone, or anything, is carrying. For example, a Maintenance Droid is listed as having a 30% chance of having a maintenance tool. That means you'll find a maintenance tool on 3 out of every 10 maintenance Droids you take down.

Also remember that the game's difficulty level affects the odds for any loot — the higher the difficulty level, the lower the chance of any loot at all. If you're playing at the Hard level, there's only a 70% chance that an adversary is actually carrying any of the loot listed in this guide. If you're playing at the Impossible level, there's only a 25% chance that an adversary is actually carrying any loot! See Difficulty Levels, p. 122, for more details.

Damage. Unfortunately, most of the adversaries can also hurt you, through natural ability or with a weapon. (That's why they're called "adversaries.") For adversaries that can hurt you, we've listed the damage they inflict per attack, along with the type of damage (whether it is electricity, incendiary, bashing, or whatever).

If one attack triggers multiple projectiles, we list the damage as <projectiles> x <damage per projectile>. For example, a Slug Turret shoots a volley of three shots, each doing two damage. That is listed as "3 x 2."

Speed. There are three speeds: slow, average and fast (plus immobile). Your own speed is determined by your Agility, but it's usually around average — you're faster than the slow adversaries, but probably slower than the fast adversaries, unless your speed is significantly boosted artificially.

ADVERSARY STATS TABLE

ADVERSARY	VULNERABILITIES	HPS	LOOT	DAMAGE	SPEED
Security Cameras	Mechanical Electron Suppression	5	None	None	Immobile
Turrets Slug	Mechanical Electron Suppression	48	6 Standard Bullets 50% No Loot 50%	3 x 2 (Standard)	Immobile
Laser	Same as *Slug Turret*	48	Portable Battery 50% No Loot 50%	3 x 5 (Energy)	Immobile
Laser II	Same as *Slug Turret*	48	None	7 (Energy)	Immobile
Rocket	Same as *Slug Turret*	48	None	10 (Standard)	Immobile
Robots Protocol Droid	Mechanical Stasis Field Generator Electron Suppression	20	None	15 (Incendiary)	Fast
Maintenance	Mechanical Stasis Field Generator Electron Suppression	100	2 of the following: Maintenance Tool 30% Rad Hypo 10% 20 Nanites 50% No Loot 10%	6 (Electricity)	Slow
Security	Mechanical Stasis Field Generator Electron Suppression	160	2 of the following: 10 Prisms 15% Iridium 5% No Loot 80%	8 (Energy)	Slow
Assault	Mechanical Stasis Field Generator Electron Suppression	200	2 of the following: 10 Prisms 15% Portable Battery 30% No Loot 55%	12 (Droid Fusion)	Slow
Hybrids Pipe Hybrid	Half Annelid Psionic Hypnogenesis Stasis Field Generator Imposed Neural Restruct.	12	2 of the following: 5 Nanites 20% Med Hypo 5% Soda Can 25% Organ 5%, No Loot 45%	10 (WeaponBash)	Average
Shotgun Hybrid	Half Annelid Psionic Hypnogenesis Stasis Field Generator Imposed Neural Restruct.	24	Broken Shotgun (always) 1 Rifled Slug (always) 2 of the following: 6 Rifled Slugs 10% 5 Nanites 20% Med Hypo 10% Liquor Bottle 25% Organ 5%, No Loot 30%	4 (Standard)	Average
Grenade Hybrid	Half Annelid Psionic Hypnogenesis Stasis Field Generator Imposed Neural Restruct.	15	2 of the following: Med Hypo 10% 3 Frag Grenades 15% 5 Nanites 15%, Organ 5% Cigarettes 25%, No Loot 30%	10 (Standard)	Average
Rumbler	Same as *Hybrids*	220	Organ 30% No Loot 70%	20 (WeaponBash)	Fast

ADVERSARY	VULNERABILITIES	HPS	LOOT	DAMAGE	SPEED
Reaver Psi Reaver	Annelid	120	Organ 75% No Loot 25%	5 (Anti-Human)	Average
Psi Reaver Brain	Annelid	10	None	None	Immobile
Greater Psi Reav.	Annelid	200	Organ 80% No Loot 20%	15 (Anti-Human)	Average
Monkeys Blue Monkey	Half Annelid Psionic Hypnogenesis Stasis Field Generator Imposed Neural Restruct.	10	Organ 30% Chips 30% No Loot 40%	10 (Cold) or 4 (WeaponBash)	Average
Red Monkey	Half Annelid Psionic Hypnogenesis Stasis Field Generator Imposed Neural Restruct.	12	Organ 30% Chips 30% No Loot 40%	15 (Incendiary) or 4 (WeaponBash)	Average
Cyborgs Midwife	Half-Mechanical Psionic Hypnogenesis Stasis Field Generator Imposed Neural Restruct.	36	Portable Battery 20% 20 Nanites 5% Med Hypo 10% Organ 25% No Loot 40%	5 (WeaponBash) or 5 (Energy)	Average
Assassin	Half-Mechanical Psionic Hypnogenesis Stasis Field Generator Imposed Neural Restruct.	60	5 Nanites 20% 20 Nanites 5% No Loot 75%	10 (WeaponBash)	Fast
Red Assassin	Like *Assassin*	48	Sim Chip (always) Like *Assassin*	10 (WeaponBash)	Fast
Annelids Toxic Egg	Annelid	10	Annelid Heal 30% Annelid Psi 5% No Loot 65%	None	Immobile
Grub or Swarm Egg	Annelid	10	Organ (always) Annelid Heal 30% Annelid Psi 5% No Loot 65%	None	Immobile
Black Egg	Annelid	10	None	None	Immobile
Grub	Annelid	5	None	1 (Anti-Human)	Average
Swarm	Swarming	36	None	1 / 2 sec (Anti-Hum)	Fast
Arachnids Baby	Psionic Hypnogenesis Stasis Field Generator	10	Organ 20% No Loot 80%	2 (WeaponBash)	Fast
Adult or Invisible	Psionic Hypnogenesis Stasis Field Generator	60	Organ 20% No Loot 80%	10 (WeaponBash)	Fast
The Many					
Nerve Cluster	Annelid	5	None	None	Immobile
Brain Def. Node	Annelid	10	None	None	Immobile
Brain	Annelid	100	None	None	Immobile
SHODAN Avatar	Mechanical SHODAN	100	None	12 (Energy)	Average
Shield	Basic	140	None	None	Immobile
Head	SHODAN	125	None	16 (SHODAN)	Immobile

TURRETS AND CAMERAS

Turrets and cameras are Xerxes' eyes and hands. These units are controlled by the security grid, and by hacking a Security Terminal you can take all the turrets and cameras on the ship temporarily off line. Cameras won't see you, turrets won't shoot at you.

SECURITY CAMERAS

Vulnerabilities	Mechanical; *also* Electron Suppression
Hit Points	5
Damage	None
Loot	None
Speed	Immobile

Cameras swivel around, mechanically observing their immediate area. Their range is line of sight … if you can see a camera, it can see you (although it might take it a few moments before it swivels to a point where you're in its sight … those few moments can be very valuable).

When a camera spots you it goes from green (nothing in view), to yellow (security sees you and is trying to identify you) to red (alert). When a camera sounds the alert Xerxes will immediately send every hostile creature it can muster straight at you. Unless you have lots of ammo and a very good tactical position, you might as well just hit [Esc] immediately and reload.

Fortunately, if your aim is good, a camera can be taken out by one, or at most two shots. Bashing a camera with a hand-to-hand weapon is a bit trickier (it usually requires some jumping, and good timing). If you see the camera at the same moment it sees you, you'll probably end up winning the race. The biggest danger with cameras is that you won't notice them at all – they're small, and tend to be tucked in out-of-the-way corners. However, they also emit a distinctive whirring noise that will immediately tip you off to a camera's presence in a hallway or room … once you learn to recognize it.

TURRETS

All

Vulnerabilities	Mechanical; *also* Electron Suppression
Hit Points	48 (all types)
Speed	Immobile

Slug

Loot   6 Standard Bullets 50%, No Loot 50%

Damage   3 x 2 (Standard)

Laser

Loot   Portable Battery 50%, No Loot 50%

Damage   3 x 5 (Energy)

Laser II

Loot   None

Damage   7 (Energy)

Rocket

Loot   None

Damage   10 (Standard)

Turrets activate whenever you come in range of their sensors (i.e., when you come into line of sight). They're normally in a stand-by configuration with their armament recessed into their casing, and when they sense a threat it takes a second or two for them to reconfigure and start shooting. Getting off two or three solid shots in this time can be crucial in anti-turret actions. They also typically track slower than you can move, so it's usually possible to dash across a hallway or even across a room before the turret can score a hit, assuming you don't pause or run directly into its line of fire. Because they're stationary, it's sometimes possible to find a "sweet spot" behind cover, where you can target the turret, but it can't target you.

Of course, the most emotionally satisfying way to deal with turrets is to Hack them (requiring Hacking 4). A Hacked turret will stop targeting you, and start targeting all enemy creatures. A Hacked turret will shoot you if you happen to come between it and the creature it's actually targeting, so watch out. Hacked turrets are wonderful things, serving not only as additional firepower, but also as diversions and early warning systems. Of course, a Hacked turret's useful lifespan is highly dependent on how tough and numerous the local creature population is, and how resistant they are to the kind of damage that turret puts out.

When you have two turrets that can "see" each other, and you Hack one, they will both immediately activate and start firing at one another. (I.e., they won't wait until the current Security Hack time runs out.) If both turrets are in equivalent condition, the Hacked one will usually lose. Therefore, before hacking one turret in the pair, you either need to destroy the other outright, or damage it so badly that the other can take it out with a shot or two. The most efficient way to take out a twin turret is to reduce one turret to almost (not quite) destroyed, then hack the other and let it administer the coup de grace.

Turrets tend to explode when destroyed, so don't stand too close. If you're really lucky you might make one go boom just as some hapless creature charges past it.

PROTOCOL DROID

Vulnerabilities	Mechanical; *also* Stasis Field Generator, Electron Suppression
Hit Points	20
Loot	None
Damage	15 (Incendiary)
Speed	Fast

The Protocol Droid is programmed to be helpful at all times, and has no armament. Terrorist factions have been known to tamper with the power supply to turn these droids into walking proximity grenades.

Xerxes has modified all the Protocol Droids on the Von Braun so that, as soon as it gets close enough to you, it will self-destruct in a devastating explosion. Avoidance and ranged weapons are your best strategies – once it goes "boom," a Protocol Droid is gone for good, so make it blow up far away from you. If, despite your best efforts, a Protocol Droid gets close to you, don't waste any ammunition on it. You would simply trigger its explosion a little earlier, which is no benefit if you are already inside its blast radius.

Protocol Droids first appear on the Engineering Deck, and are found sporadically through the rest of the game. If you're lucky, you may see a Protocol Droid at a distance, walking near another monster. If you shoot the Protocol Droid rather than the other monster, you may manage to kill them both when the Droid explodes!

MAINTENANCE ROBOT

Vulnerabilities	Mechanical; *also* Stasis Field Generator, Electron Suppression
Hit Points	100
Loot	2 picks; Maintenance Tool 30%, Rad Hypo 10%, 20 Nanites 50%, No Loot 10%
Damage	6 (Electricity)
Speed	Slow

Maintenance Robots (nicknamed "Beavers") are large and slow, but their electrical spark welder can be a painful weapon when used against a human.

Maintenance Bots are well armored, and can take a lot of punishment. At the stage of the game where you'll be facing Maintenance Robots, your best weapon will be Armor-Piercing Bullets. Their spark welder shots are not terribly accurate, so if you can engage them at long range, they may hit you only rarely, even during an extended battle.

You'll see your first Maintenance Bot at the very end of the MedSci Deck. They are quite frequent on the Engineering Deck, but later in the game they are mostly replaced by more formidable models. After destroying one, you should search its chassis for salvageable equipment.

The quickest way to tell Robots apart is by color. Maintenance Bots are yellow, Security Bots are gray, and Assault Bots are green.

SECURITY ROBOT

Vulnerabilities	Mechanical; *also* Stasis Field Generator, Electron Suppression
Hit Points	160
Loot	2 picks; 10 Prisms 15%, Iridium 5%, No Loot 80%
Damage	8 (Energy)
Speed	Slow

The Security Bot is designed to defend high security areas. Any complaints should be directed to Sgt. Bronson, on the Operations Deck.

The Security Robot is better armored than the Maintenance Robot, and has a built-in laser cannon. This laser is more damaging than the Maintenance Robot's spark welder, and considerably more accurate. EMP rifles or EMP grenades are the weapons of choice against robots, though Armor-piercing bullets or fragmentation grenades are passable substitutes when necessary.

Because of their bulk, Security Bots (and Maintenance Bots too) don't corner well. One of the best ways to take out a Security Bot when your defenses are minimal is to fall back to a position where the Bot will have to come through a door and turn to get you. This will allow you to either squeeze off three or four quick shots while it's turning, or take your shot and fall back to around another corner.

Security Bots first appear on the Operations and Recreation Decks. After destroying one, you should search its chassis for salvageable equipment.

The quickest way to tell Robots apart is by color. Maintenance Bots are yellow, Security Bots are gray, and Assault Bots are green.

ASSAULT ROBOT

Vulnerabilities	Mechanical; *also* Stasis Field Generator, Electron Suppression
Hit Points	200
Loot	2 picks; 10 Prisms 15%, Portable Battery 30%, No Loot 55%
Damage	12 (Droid Fusion)
Speed	Slow

The Rickenbacker carries a number of Assault Robots on board. These are high-performance military robots, meant to be used only in the face of a significant alien threat.

The Assault Robot is the toughest of the three large Bots, and has a built-in Fusion Cannon. As with all mechanical foes, EMP rifles or EMP grenades are the weapons of choice. These are extremely deadly, so take them down as fast as possible. Assault Bots are significantly faster and more maneuverable than Security Bots … the "hide around the corner" strategy discussed under Security Bots might still be useful, but only if you are extremely fast and accurate.

Assault Bots first appear on the Recreation Deck. After destroying one, you should search its chassis for salvageable equipment.

The quickest way to tell Robots apart is by color. Maintenance Bots are yellow, Security Bots are gray, and Assault Bots are green.

HYBRID

ALL

Vulnerabilities

Half Annelid; *also* Psionic Hypnogenesis, Stasis Field Generator, Imposed Neural Restructuring

PIPE HYBRID

Hit Points

12

Loot

2 of the following: 5 Nanites 20%, Med Hypo 5%, Soda Can 25%, Organ 5%, No Loot 45%

Damage

10 (WeaponBash)

Speed

Average

These poor creatures look as if they were once human, but have been transformed by the alien parasite.

This is the first enemy you meet, and you'll see quite a lot of them before you're done with the MedSci Deck. You'll continue to run into them over the next few decks, but they are eventually supplanted by their better-equipped brethren. If you have Research Skill, be sure to investigate the first Hybrid Organ you find … it will give you a damage bonus against all Hybrids, not just those wielding Pipes!

When fighting these with a melee weapon, ready your swing at a distance, close and attack, then back away before the Hybrid can strike back. Be aware that the Hybrid's Pipe has a greater reach than your Wrench. After you swing, back away from it quickly; even if you missed … you may well be within his range. Once you have a few points in Strength or Standard Weapons, one blow with the Wrench should kill a Pipe Hybrid. It's worthwhile to kill them with melee weapons and save your ammo for tougher opponents.

SHOTGUN HYBRID

Hit Points

24

Loot

Guaranteed Broken Shotgun with 1 Rifled Slug, plus 2 of the following:
6 Rifled Slugs 10%, 5 Nanites 20%, Med Hypo 10%, Liquor Bottle 25%, Organ 5%, No Loot 30%

Damage

4 (Standard)

Speed

Average

The Shotgun Hybrids are much tougher than their pipe-wielding kinsmen, so one has to presume that The Many gave the cream of the Hybrid crop the most effective weaponry.

Shotgun Hybrids can take twice as much damage as Pipe Hybrids. Their shots are frequent, but not too powerful, so attacking them with melee weapons remains a viable option. They'll back away from you if you get in close, so they're trickier to fight that way than Pipe Hybrids. Try to corner them against a wall or other obstacle.

Shotgun Hybrids start appearing in the second half of the MedSci Deck, and will continue to be found for the next several decks. All Shotgun Hybrids, naturally, have a Shotgun on their corpse when killed. Sadly, it's been modified for their mutated limbs, which makes it unusable to you. It *can*, however, be repaired to function like a normal Shotgun again. Even if you don't have Repair Skill, it can be worth your while to pick up their modified Shotguns simply to unload them. Each one has very little salvageable ammunition, but it adds up over time.

GRENADE HYBRID

Hit Points	15
Loot	2 of the following: Med Hypo 10%, 3 Frag Grenades 15%, 5 Nanites 15%, Organ 5%, Cigarettes 25%, No Loot 30%
Damage	Standard 10
Speed	Average

Grenade Hybrids are tougher than Pipe Hybrids, but weaker than Shotgun Hybrids. Apparently, they were selected more for their speed than their strength (although for some reason drinkers tend to become Shotgun Hybrids and smokers tend to become Grenade hybrids, while Pipe Hybrids are just caffeine fiends).

While Grenade Hybrids aren't as physically tough as their Shotgun-wielding Cousins, they are considerably deadlier. The Grenades aren't terribly accurate, but with their blast radius, they don't need to be. The Grenades are thrown by hand, rather than with a Grenade Launcher, so their range is fairly low. When possible, take out Grenade Hybrids with ranged weapons before they can get close enough to attack. These Hybrids aren't bright enough to stay out of the blast radius themselves, so if you close to melee range, they'll probably kill themselves – but they'll do a lot of damage to you in the process.

Grenade Hybrids first start appearing on the Operations Deck, and are found in abundance on the Recreation Deck. Sometimes useable Fragmentation Grenades can be salvaged from their corpses.

Why can Grenade Hybrids throw their weapons while you need a working Grenade Launcher? It's a mutant thing … don't worry about it.

RUMBLER

Vulnerabilities	Half Annelid; *also* Psionic Hypnogenesis, Stasis Field Generator, Imposed Neural Restructuring
Hit Points	220
Loot	Organ 30%, No Loot 70%
Damage	20 (WeaponBash)
Speed	Fast

The Rumbler, for all its formidability, is merely a transitional stage in the Annelid life cycle. Its huge body is designed to shield the growth of the powerful psionic brain which forms the ultimate stage of Annelid-Human Hybrid.

The Rumbler is much faster than a creature of its bulk has any right to be. Try and find a sniping position where it can't reach you, or it will rip you apart within seconds. Since its form is mostly Annelid, it is particularly vulnerable to Incendiary damage, and resistant to Energy. Be prepared to use a lot of ammunition to take one down.

Rumblers first start showing up late on the Recreation deck, and are seen throughout the rest of the game. If you have Research skill and some Molybdenum, you can research a Rumbler Organ to get a damage bonus against them.

PSI REAVER

PSI REAVER BRAIN

Hit Points	10
Loot	None
Damage	None
Speed	Immobile

PSI REAVER

Hit Points	120
Loot	Organ 75%, No Loot 25%
Damage	5 (Anti-Human)
Speed	Average

GREATER PSI REAVER

Hit Points	200
Loot	Organ 80%, No Loot 20%
Damage	15 (Anti-Human)
Speed	Average

Although it appears as a huge, gray, floating mass, with dangling tentacles, actually, that form is only a *projection* of the true Psi Reaver. The true Psi Reaver is a small and immobile brain-shaped structure, located somewhere nearby the Projection.

Incredibly, Psi-Reavers were once human. This is the ultimate form of the Annelid-Human Hybrid, a mass of almost pure psychic energy. The brain has become completely specialized to channel psionic forces, so that its "body" is merely an ectoplasmic projection. There are rumors of an even more powerful variant, the Greater Psi Reaver.

The Projection can fire powerful bolts of concentrated psionic force. If the Projection is killed, the Psi Reaver brain structure automatically recreates it within a few seconds. Hence, your priority should be to find and kill the Reaver's brain structure first. When the brain structure is killed, the Projection will *not* immediately dissipate, but must still be destroyed separately. With the brain dead, however, the Projection will not be recreated.

Psi Reavers only appear near the end of the game. How dangerous they are depends on how well they have hidden their brain structures. If you can find a Psi Reaver Organ, it can be researched with a small quantity of Radium and Technitium.

MONKEY

ALL

Vulnerabilities   Half Annelid; *also* Psionic Hypnogenesis, Stasis Field Generator, Imposed Neural Restructuring

Loot   Organ 30%, Chips 30%, No Loot 40%

Speed   Average

BLUE MONKEY

Hit Points   10

Damage   10 (Cold) or
4 (WeaponBash)

RED MONKEY

Hit Points   12

Damage   15 (Incendiary) or
4 (WeaponBash)

Apparently, they were originally African squirrel monkeys. Once targeted for vivisection on the Von Braun's Medsci deck, these creatures have been set free and mutated into something horrible. Two forms of monkey have been observed and it's rumored that they've been made psionically able.

"Blue" Monkeys are capable of shooting a powerful Cryokinetic blast.

"Red" Monkeys are capable of shooting a powerful Pyrokinetic blast that does *much* more damage than their blue cousins, and in a greater radius. This makes them much more of a threat, so you should take them down fast and at long range whenever possible.

If you close to melee range, both types of monkeys attack with claws and teeth instead, but they do a bit less damage that way than with their psionic attack. Because of their small size, Monkeys can be hard to hit, but they're especially difficult to tag with melee weapons. If you do close for melee combat, crouch down to get a better chance of hitting them.

Researching a Monkey Brain (requires skill 1 and a small amount of Fermium) will give you a damage bonus against all Monkeys. Monkeys often carry bags of Chips. You can eat these to gain back a single lost hit point, but they're too bulky to bother carrying around in quantity.

CYBORG MIDWIFE

Vulnerabilities	Half-Mechanical; *also* Stun, Stasis Field Generator, Imposed Neural Restructuring
Hit Points	36
Loot	Portable Battery 20%, 20 Nanites 5%, Med Hypo 10%, Organ 25%, No Loot 40%
Damage	5 (WeaponBash) or 5 (Energy)
Speed	Average

The origin of these nightmarish constructs is unclear, but they're often found around the nests of the Annelid Eggs. One has to wonder what sort of mind would create such things, but the intent is clear; they are perfectly constructed to protect and nurture the Annelid young. Though their upper half appears human, much of the skeletal structure has been replaced with machinery.

Being more machine than organic, Midwives are resistant to Anti-Personnel weaponry, and vulnerable to EMP and Armor-Piecing weaponry. If you have to take on a Midwife in a head-to-head confrontation, try to close as much as possible (unless you're using explosive weapons) … the Midwife's hand-to-hand attack is generally less deadly than her ranged energy blast.

You may first encounter a Cyborg Midwife at the end of Engineering, but they appear in abundance on the Hydroponics Deck. After that, they tend to appear wherever there are large concentrations of Eggs. You should try to extract one of the Midwife's modified Organs and Research it, to gain a damage bonus against them.

CYBORG ASSASSIN

Vulnerabilities	Half-Mechanical; *also* Stun, Stasis Field Generator, Imposed Neural Restructuring
Hit Points	60
Loot	5 Nanites 20%, 20 Nanites 5%, No Loot 75%
Damage	10 (WeaponBash)
Speed	Fast

The UM/433p Assassins are a modified version of one of the more tenacious types of cyborg aboard Citadel Station. They were secretly brought on board the Von Braun as "insurance" against the UNN forces on the Rickenbacker, should any conflict develop. Recent rumors speak of some kind of modified Cyborg Assassins clothed in red, but their nature and purpose are mysterious.

A fast-moving, stealthy human/robot construct, these cyborgs toss deadly energy stars at their prey. As a mix of man and machine, some part of them will be affected by almost any kind of weaponry. They are quite tough, however, and their stealth, speed, and accuracy make them serious threats. With Cyborg Assassins, it can make a huge difference if you can get off the first shot, while the cyborg is closing, or before it notices you.

Cyborg Assassins first appear on the Operations Deck. They have a disturbing tendency to ambush you when you least expect it. Expect it.

RED ASSASSIN

Vulnerabilities	Half-Mechanical; *also* Stun, Stasis Field Generator, Imposed Neural Restructuring
Hit Points	48
Loot	Guaranteed Sim Chip 5 Nanites 20%, 20 Nanites 5%, No Other Loot 75%
Damage	10 (WeaponBash)
Speed	Fast

ANNELID EGG

Vulnerabilities	Annelid
Hit Points	10 (all types)
Damage	None
Speed	Immobile

TOXIC EGG

Loot Annelid Heal 30%, Annelid Psi 5%, No Loot 65%

GRUB EGG

Loot Guaranteed Organ when Destroyed
Annelid Heal 30%, Annelid Psi 5%, No Other Loot 65%

SWARM EGG

Loot Guaranteed Organ when Destroyed
Annelid Heal 30%, Annelid Psi 5%, No Other Loot 65%

BLACK EGG

Loot None

These Eggs of the Annelid species are the first stage of the xenomorph's nightmarish "circle of life." They are created from converted organic material, usually human corpses. All eggs look alike until they open, except for the mysterious "Black Egg," a genetic experiment on the part of The Many.

When you approach an Annelid Egg, it will open, emitting one of three things: a Grub, a Swarm, or a cloud of toxic spores. Sadly, you can't tell from external inspection which type of Egg it is. Eggs can be killed with impunity from a distance. (Black eggs do not open.)

Eggs first start appearing on the Hydroponics Deck, and continue appearing throughout the game. If you *don't* kill an Egg from a distance, but approach it prepared to deal with whatever comes out of it, you can search the Egg afterwards (or *before* it opens, if you're lucky). Often they contain complex Organs that can be useful to you once you've Researched them. Where there are large quantities of Eggs, they are frequently guarded by Cyborg Midwives, so watch out for those. Some Eggs are hidden in difficult-to-see spots on the ceiling, so watch out for Grubs falling from above!

ANNELID GRUB AND SWARM

GRUB

Vulnerabilities	Annelid
Hit Points	5
Loot	None
Damage	1 (Anti-Human)
Speed	Average

These are the female form of the first-stage Annelid life cycle. They attempt to bore into the neck of their victims and lodge there. From that point, they use telepathic communication to overcome the will of their host and turn them into something other than human.

Grubs don't do much damage and are quite easy to kill. On the downside, their speed and size make them hard to hit (particularly with hand-to-hand weapons), and they are often found in large numbers, adding up to a significant threat. A complex muscular system allows them to spring several feet into the air to attack. Like all pure Annelids, they are resistant to Energy Weapons, so a Laser Pistol is the only weapon that won't necessarily kill a Grub in a single shot.

Grubs may turn up as early as the Engineering Deck, and will be seen intermittently for the rest of the game. Later in the game, they will tend to appear in greater numbers, often feasting upon human corpses. While the Grubs themselves are too small to salvage useful organs from, you can research organs from their Eggs, with small amounts of Gallium and Californium.

SWARM

Vulnerabilities	Swarming
Hit Points	36
Loot	None
Damage	1 every 2 seconds (Anti-Human)
Speed	Fast

These are the male form of the first-stage Annelid life cycle, and are extremely short-lived.

Swarms don't do too much damage, but they do it frequently, and they are almost impossible to kill. Very few weapons affect them at all, and it's almost never cost-effective to try to kill them. The best strategy is avoidance. Swarms only live for a few tens of seconds, so if you run away, you should take little damage from them before they expire. Be careful not to run into a more dangerous situation while fleeing them!

Swarms first start appearing on the Operations and Recreation deck, and continue throughout the game.

ANNELID ARACHNID

ALL

Vulnerabilities	Annelid; *also* Psionic Hypnogenesis, Stasis Field Generator
Loot	Organ 20%, No Loot 80%
Speed	Fast

ARACHNID, BABY

Hit Points	10
Damage	2 (WeaponBash)

ARACHNID, ADULT

Hit Points	60
Damage	10 (WeaponBash)

ARACHNID, INVISIBLE

Hit Points	60
Damage	10 (WeaponBash)

Arachnids are Annelid creatures based on the DNA templates of earth spiders, but much bigger.

Arachnids not only do a lot of damage in combat, but their bite is toxic as well. They're small, fast, and have a tendency to jump on your head. Try not to let them get too close, unless you're very skilled at melee combat and you have a supply of Anti-Toxin Hypos. Arachnids are resistant to Energy Weapons, so don't bother fighting them with a Laser Pistol. The weapon they are most vulnerable to is Incendiary Grenades, although Fragmentation Grenades also work well. If you don't have Heavy Weapons Skill, Anti-Personnel Bullets or Pyrokinesis are your best options.

You'll first meet Baby Arachnids on the Hydroponics deck, and will continue to see them throughout the game. The Baby Arachnids aren't too tough, but don't get complacent; the Adult form is much deadlier.

You'll first meet Adult Arachnids on the Operations deck, and will continue to see them throughout the game. They are deadly opponents. Research an Arachnid Organ (requires a small amount of Iridium) to give you a damage bonus against all types of Arachnids.

You'll won't meet Invisible Arachnids until quite late in the game. Their stealth makes them a significant threat. They're much more likely to successfully ambush you than the standard Arachnid.

THE BODY OF THE MANY

ALL

Vulnerabilities	Annelid
Loot	None
Damage	None
Speed	Immobile

NERVE CLUSTER

Hit Points	5

BRAIN DEFENSE NODE

Hit Points	10

BRAIN

Hit Points	100

The process involved in destroying the Body of the Many is fully described in the Walkthrough (beginning on p. 272), including the strategies necessary to destroy each target.

Briefly, in order to destroy the Body of the Many you'll have to destroy several Nerve Clusters (which allow you to pass through the Sphincters which divide one portion of the Body from another). Once you arrive at the Body's Brain Chamber you'll first have to destroy the floating Defense Nodes which psionically protect the brain, and then eradicate the Brain itself.

SHODAN

ALL

Loot   None

AVATAR

Vulnerabilities   Mechanical; *also* SHODAN
Hit Points   100
Damage   12 (Energy)
Speed   Average

SHIELD

Vulnerabilities   Basic
Hit Points   140
Damage   None
Speed   Immobile

HEAD

Vulnerabilities   SHODAN
Hit Points   125
Damage   16 (SHODAN)
Speed   Immobile

The process necessary to finally destroy SHODAN is fully described in the walkthrough, beginning on p. 284.

Basically, the core of SHODAN's consciousness (the "Head") is guarded by powerful force screens and her "Avatar," a humanoid construct of pure cybernetic energy. If you destroy the Avatar SHODAN will create a new one at full strength, so concentrate on destroying the shields, then the head, while staying out of the Avatar's way.

ORGAN RESEARCH RESULTS

HYBRID ORGAN

This is a pulpy, kidney-shaped organ that controls most of a hybrid's vital functions

Chemicals needed to research None

Summary. You've learned how to best target the Hybrid for maximal damage. All damage you deal to Hybrids will be increased by 25%.

Analysis. DNA structure indicates that this organism is a hybrid of a human host and a parasitic organism. Although the parasite (resembling a yard-long worm) has deteriorated to a stage beyond useful analysis, the effects of the process are evident. Severe deterioration of higher level mental processes is caused by tumorous growths along the spinal column and brain stem. The non-human tissues seem to be formed of a composite of small wormlike creatures that have adapted into the host body and taken over a majority of motor-control and decision-making functions. There also appears to be direct stimulation of the autonomic nervous and glandular systems. Hence, the organism produces exceptional amounts of both adrenaline and endorphins, making it remarkably strong and aggressive. What remains can not really be called human at all. The damage done to the host by the process is irrevocable, and the organism now functions with no sense of morality or hesitation.

Recommendation. The organism is vulnerable to the same forms of stimuli as a human. However, the changes in its physiology suggest a chemistry more complex than is currently understood. Further analysis of similar organisms might provide more insight in this area.

RUMBLER ORGAN

This is a dense multipurpose organ, taken from the 'chest' of a Rumbler.

Chemical needed to research   Molybdenum (Mo)

Summary. You've learned how to best target the Rumbler for maximal damage. All damage you deal to Rumblers will be increased by 25%. In addition, its annelid tissue is particularly vulnerable to incendiary devices.

Analysis. This organism marks a further evolution of the first-stage Annelid Hybrid. Discernable human elements are minimal above the DNA level. Muscle tissue density has increased twenty-fold, and adrenaline production has increased proportionally. Brain tissue is extremely dense, which would normally indicate a creature of extreme cognitive ability, but the brain-stem has atrophied to a useless stub, and there is no analog to a human spinal column. All muscular activity is controlled locally by alien cells designed for this purpose. It appears that this creature is an evolutionary stage between an earlier-stage human-annelid Hybrid, and a third, unknown form.

Recommendation. This creature is extremely dangerous, being, in effect, a heavily muscled host designed to protect a highly evolved yet unconnected brain. The peculiar chemistry of this Hybrid's brain tissue indicates a latent psionic predisposition.

ARACHNID ORGAN

A sticky, dripping mass of mucus-colored tissue, which smells like rotting flesh.

Chemical needed to research   Iridium (Ir)

Summary. You've learned how to best target the Arachnids for maximal damage. All damage you deal to Arachnids will be increased by 25%. Arachnids, like all pure Annelids, are resistant to energy weapons.

Analysis. This creature's internal systems are both distributed and redundant in a way that suggests intentional design, or evolution in a very dangerous environment. What serves as its nervous system uses a significantly larger amount of energy than a human's, so the creature's tissues are correspondingly more energy-resistant. The creature's metabolism allows for a boost of hyperkinetic activity, while allowing it to remain normally in a dormant state, and presumably allowing it to exist for a long period of time without nourishment.

Recommendation. Using energy weapons against this creature is not recommended.

PSI REAVER ORGAN

This organ continues to pulse slowly and ooze a black fluid.

Chemical needed to research   Barium (Ba), Radium (Ra)

Summary. You've learned how to best target the Psi Reavers and their projections for maximal damage. All damage you deal to Psi Reaver and their projections will be increased by 25%. The projections will continually regenerate themselves unless you destroy the brain structure which creates them.

Analysis. This is a continuously energized sample of psycho-creative residue. It is the end product of a massively complex and focused psionic projection. This residue can be temporarily disrupted, but not permanently destroyed, since the psionic projection can simply be re-created by the source organism.

Recommendation. While the projection can be disrupted by most conventional means, this serves as a short-term solution only. Resources should not be wasted in combating this phenomenon unless it is crucial for survival. If it must be destroyed, seek out and destroy the controlling brain structure first.

MONKEY ORGAN

This looks much like your brain, except that it's smaller and there are hairlike silvery filaments penetrating it.

Chemical needed to research Fermium (Fm)

Summary. You've learned how to best target the Monkeys for maximal damage. All damage you deal to Monkeys will be increased by 25%.

Analysis. The Monkey is genetically normal, an African squirrel monkey. However, it appears to have been subject to a large number of chemical and surgical procedures, both before and after birth. These procedures have enhanced brain size and connectivity, as well as enhanced the myelination of the central nervous system. The skull of the creature has been surgically removed, presumably both to prevent cranial pressure and to allow quick experimental access.

Recommendation. The neural construction of the creature is similar in nature to psionic human neural structure — the Monkeys are likely to have psionic capability. They are vulnerable to all attacks which affect standard organic creatures.

CYBORG MIDWIFE ORGAN

This organ combines biological nervous tissue with cybernetic technical parts, and shielding.

Chemicals needed to research None

Summary. You've learned how to best target the Midwife for maximal damage. All damage you deal to Midwives will be increased by 25%. They are resistant to incendiary and anti-personnel weapons, but vulnerable to armor-piercing.

Analysis. DNA sequence confirms that the subject was originally a human female, cybernetically modified. An auxiliary CPU in the base of the spine serves as a controller, overriding most signals sent by the subject's natural brain. Both speed and musculature have been mechanically enhanced, and the cybernetic apparatus also serves as physical shielding for the softer human tissues.

Recommendation. Due to the half-mechanical nature of this creature, incendiary and anti-personnel weapons will be fairly ineffective, but armor-piercing rounds should be effective.

GRUB ORGAN

A long tube with interior cilia, this is the entire digestive tract of the Grub.

Chemicals needed to research Californium (Cf), Gallium (Ga)

Summary. While you have learned the vulnerabilities of this creature, they're so easily killed it hardly matters. Like all Annelids, they are somewhat resistant to energy weapons. Annelid Eggs often contain useful organs if you search them before they are destroyed.

Analysis. Genetically female, the Annelid Grub is the most basic Annelid form. The creature is principally nervous system and musculature — the highly advanced (for a worm) nervous system appears to be tied into a rudimentary psionic sense organ. While wormlike in appearance, the Grub has no actual digestive tract, but is furnished with energy reserves at birth. When these are depleted, the creature shuts down into a dormant state, possibly until a further psionic trigger acts on it. The Eggs that these emerge from often contain organs that might be extracted for useful purposes, unless the Egg has been destroyed in combat.

Recommendation. The Grubs are fairly fragile, but can be somewhat dangerous if they close before you see them. In large numbers, they may prove a more significant threat.

SWARM ORGAN

This looks like a tiny heart, with seven chambers and a single elongated artery.

Chemicals needed to research None

Summary. Annelid Swarms cannot be damaged by any known means, but have a very short life span. Eggs often contain useful organs if you search them before they are destroyed.

Analysis. Although small, the flying organisms generated by these pods contain a complex DNA structure indicative of a much more advanced creature. Each small creature, genetically male, is bonded to the Swarm via a sub-psionic link. This link is impervious to normal psionic attacks or disturbances. Annelid Swarm creatures seem to exist only as a living weapon, since their cells have a genetically programmed lifespan of no more than a few seconds. During these seconds, they are attracted to human tissue, as they frantically attempt to prolong their short lives with nourishment. The Eggs from which these emerge often contain organs that might be extracted for useful purposes, unless the Egg has been destroyed in combat.

Recommendation. The Annelid Swarm is best dealt with by avoidance, since the creatures will die soon after being hatched. Do not waste ammunition on them.

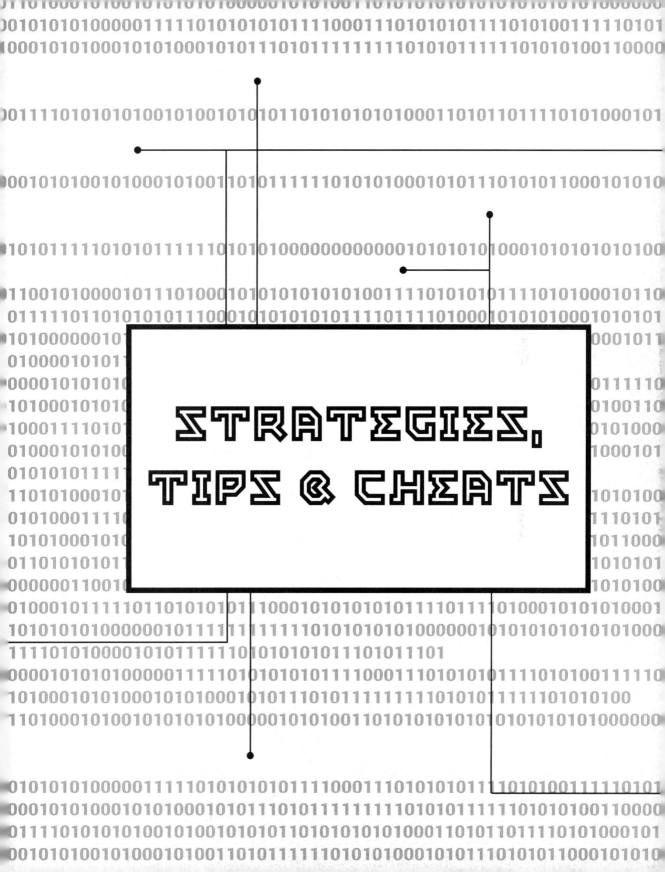

STRATEGIES, TIPS & CHEATS

TIPS

COMBAT

- Learn to work that wrench. Even after you get ranged weapons, don't waste ammo on Pipe Hybrids (or even Shotgun Hybrids). With some caution and practice, the wrench should be all you need against these creatures. Expert players can defeat all but the toughest monsters with hand-to-hand weapons. (On Impossible difficulty, this is almost required.)

- Unless you're very a very skilled player with hand-to-hand weapons, you should avoid melee combat with small creatures like Monkeys, Grubs and Baby Annelids ... they're hard to hit. If you must take on these creatures with a hand-to-hand weapon, kneel — sometimes that helps.

- This is very basic, but ... know your ammo types. Don't waste armor-piercing ammo against Hybrids and Grubs, don't waste anti-personnel ammo against Turrets, Robots and Cyborgs.

- Don't fight it if you don't have to. Adversaries respawn in this game (that is, more are created when you kill the first ones), so there's no point in trying to completely clear out a whole deck or even a whole room if you don't have to. If you can slip past a pod of wandering creatures without engaging them (and thereby losing ammo and proba- bly hit points), by all means slip away.

- Learn to lean. Those nifty commands for leaning around corners can save your life; learn to love 'em. Also, remember the instructions on mantling you received in Basic Training. This is an *extremely* important part of the game — it's literally impossible to finish without it.

- Most turrets have "sweet spots" where you can get to them, but they can't get to you. Keep an eye out for these opportunities. Sometimes you can lean back against a dis- tant bulkhead and blast away at the turret at your leisure, other times you can slip around the wall literally right next to the turret, and hack it before it even "wakes up."

- Seize the high ground. Always look for a chance to take out creatures from a high-level "sniper's nest." This is particularly satisfying against Annelids, who can't climb ladders.

- Learn to love energy weapons. They don't require you to carry ammo! (Of course they have to be recharged periodically, which can be an issue all by itself.) You can carry a laser *and* an EMP rifle in the same space (or less) than would be required for any other ranged weapon and all its ammo types. (Just remember that EMP rifles only work on robots, cyborgs, turrets and cameras, while lasers are inferior against Annelids.)

- If you're skilled in Energy Weapons, you may want to carry more than one laser pistol. It costs no more to recharge two laser pistols than it does one, so this can effectively double your "ammo" store.

INVENTORY MANAGEMENT

- If you try to go into Inventory mode every time you have to change weapons or reload, you will die very quickly. Learn the hot keys for the different weapon types (the number keys), changing ammo types (B) and for reloading (R).

- What good are those broken shotguns that the Shotgun Hybrids carry around? Not much. The single shell you'll always find inside them, however, is extremely useful. Pick up the gun, unload it, then toss it. You won't believe how fast your shotgun clips fill up.

- The elevator is pretty much convenient to everywhere on the *Von Braun*, plus it's one of the few totally secure areas on the ship (when the door is closed, of course). The moral? Take all that stuff you think you might need some day, but don't have room to carry around, and cache it on the elevator. This includes advanced weapons, armor (including that useful enviro-suit), redundant implants, and even chemicals. Make the elevator your central armory.

- When should you use those nifty nanotech devices like the auto-repair unit, ICE pick and the French-Epstein device? Do *not* slap them down as soon as you pick them up … these are precious things. The time for the auto-repair unit and ICE pick is either those moments when you can't afford even a few seconds for repair or hacking, or very late in the game, as a substitute for cripplingly high Hacking and Repair requirements. Don't start using French-Epstein devices until your Maintenance skill is high enough that you're no longer tempted to toss used weapons when a new one shows up. Even the lowly maintenance tool requires some preparation. Try not to use one when your Maintenance skill is just 1 … that's not good value for what you're spending on it. Try to hold off using the maintenance tools until your Maintenance skill is up to 2, or better yet 3.

- If you have the Hacking skill, Hack every replicator you find, period. It will save you a pile of nanites over the course of the game, plus giving you access to nifty stuff that you wouldn't find on your own until much later. If you haven't got Hacking skill, use an ICE-pick to hack a replicator that sells your primary ammunition (preferably one near an elevator, so you can come back to shop without going too far out of your way).

- While we're on the subject, there's one replicator, on the Operations deck (see the Walkthrough for exact information) that when hacked will give you a recycler, a device that otherwise wouldn't show up until much later in the game. This device allows you to take junk items like magazines, smokes, coffee cups and plants, and convert them back into nanites. The yield per object is small, but cumulatively over the course of several decks this device can mean all the difference between being constantly broke and comfortably flush.

- Using the Options Panel, you can assign hotkeys to many useful items (which have no default hotkey), such as medical kits and psi hypos.

MORE TIPS

- Listen! Every adversary in the game has its own distinctive sound cue (including Cameras and Turrets). By listening at the junction of a hallway or the door of a new room, you can frequently tell what's waiting for you inside. This is such an important part of survival in the game that you may want to turn off the music entirely (as cool as the music is).

- We're not going to list every intriguing cache of treasure in the game, but there's one stock of nanites, in the Sensual Stimulation Chambers of the Recreation Deck, that will single-handedly take you up a whole tax bracket. For exact directions, see the Walkthrough.

- Poison got you down? If you don't have the more obvious method (an anti-toxin hypo), and you can't get one from a nearby replicator, consider finding a surgical unit, or even let nature take its course and return to the game at a resurrection station. Either of these wonder machines fully cleanses your body of all toxins.

- Your difficulty level isn't etched in stone — you can change it on the fly and at will. If you reach a point that's absolutely impassible for you at your current difficulty level, step it down a notch (temporarily) to an easier difficulty level till you're past the impassible.

- Just in case you happen to end up in water (or any other liquid) over your head — you can hold your breath underwater for 45 seconds

MULTIPLAYER GAMES

When starting a multiplayer game, each player goes through character creation separately, then meets up on the *Von Braun* when the game proper starts. While in training, you can still use the chat function to talk to the other players. You should settle early on who is going to specialize in what.

While there can certainly be some overlap in skills between the players, it's most effective to sharply specialize. In a single-player game, you often find yourself wanting a few levels of Research, a few levels of Maintenance, and so forth. In a multiplayer game, one player can specialize in Research for the whole team, another can specialize in Maintenance and keep everyone's weapons in working order, and so forth.

One particularly good set of specializations is the 'techie,' who gets a high CYB, and good Hacking, Modify and Repair skills. These skills are the only things affected by CYB, so no one else should bother investing points in it.

Upgrades in multiplayer games are equivalent in cost to the Hard difficulty level, but whenever *any* player gets some upgrade modules, that many modules are distributed to *all* players, thus effectively multiplying the amount of modules in the world by the number of players.

When in Use Mode, you can *a*-click on a stack of items to split off part of that stack. This is useful for sharing hypos and ammunition between multiple players. You can also *a*-click on your nanite indicator to split off some nanites to give to another player.

If you have an item on your cursor in Use Mode, you can give it to another nearby character by dropping it onto him; it will automatically be placed in his inventory (if he has room for it).

Be careful when using ranged weapons to not accidentally hit your teammates; this is a *cooperative* game. You can't damage your fellow players with hand-to-hand weapons, though, so no need to be as careful with those.

If any player picks up an access card, the codes are automatically transmitted to all players. So, if you're closer to the locked door than your friend who picked up the card, you can go open it without having to wait for him to get all the way to the front of the line.

Whenever any player initiates a level transition, all players come along — even if they were far away from the bulkhead/elevator. It's polite to check (by chatting) with other players before initiating a level transition.

If you Hack a turret, be sure to place a nav marker (N) nearby, so that other players don't accidentally destroy it without realizing it's on your side.

DIFFICULTY LEVELS

At the beginning of the game, you choose what difficulty level you want to play. Here's the explanation of how the different levels affect the game.

Note. Multiplayer is treated as a separate difficulty level. Overall, Multiplayer is somewhere between Normal and Hard.

STATS

The higher the difficulty, the less Hit Points and Psi Points you'll get for the same level of Stat.

Note. Among other things, this makes the "Tank" OS Upgrade much more valuable at Hard and Impossible levels, since it gives you a flat 5 Hit Points, which can be equivalent to many, many cyber modules spent on Endurance at those levels.

DIFFICULTY LEVEL	BASE HP	HP PER END	BASE PSI POINTS	PSI POINTS PER PSI
Easy	45	10	10	16
Normal	30	5	5	10
Hard	24	3	3	8
Impossible	7	3	1	5
Multiplayer	24	3	5	10

UPGRADES

Upgrades cost significantly more cyber modules at higher difficulties. Since the amount of cyber modules in the world stays constant, you'll be able to upgrade less often over the course of the game.

* **Easy.** On the Easy level, an upgrade costs 85% of what it would cost on the Normal level. (That is, multiply the Normal price by 0.85.)

* **Normal.** This is the standard level. The prices here are the base prices, listed in the *System Shock 2* manual.

* **Hard.** On the Hard level, upgrades cost 1.4 times what they do on Normal.

* **Impossible.** On the Impossible level, upgrades cost 1.8 times what they do on Normal.

* **Multiplayer.** On Multiplayer, upgrades cost 1.4 times what they do on Normal.

REPLICATORS

Items in replicators cost more nanites on higher difficulty levels. Since you have less nanites to begin with on the higher levels (due to monster loot, see below), you'll have to get by with much less shopping. Hacking replicators for a price break becomes much more important. If your character doesn't have Hacking skill, you should consider using an ICE-pick on a replicator with useful items (and, preferably, one near to the main elevator), and visit that replicator often.

- **Easy.** On the Easy level, replicator items cost 85% of what it would cost on the Normal level. (Multiply the Normal price by .85.)

- **Normal.** This is the standard level. The prices here are the base prices.

- **Hard.** On the Hard level, replicator items cost 1.25 times what they do on Normal.

- **Impossible.** On this level, replicator items cost 2 times what they do on Normal.

- **Multiplayer.** On Multiplayer, replicator items cost the same as they do on Normal.

ADVERSARY LOOT

At the higher difficulty levels, enemies have an increasingly greater chance of having no "treasure" whatsoever. This means that you'll be expending resources to kill them, but getting nothing in return − a fast recipe for running completely out of ammo. Speed and avoidance become much more important tactics at Impossible.

- **Easy.** On the Easy level, all enemies carry loot at their normal odds (see individual entries in **Adversaries**, see pp 94-111).

- **Normal.** Enemies will always carry loot at their normal odds, on the Normal level.

- **Hard.** On the Hard level, there's a 30% chance the enemy won't by carrying anything, before the listed percentages are even checked.

- **Impossible.** On the Impossible level, there's a 75% chance the enemy won't be carrying anything, before the listed percentages are even checked.

- **Multiplayer.** On Multiplayer, all enemies carry loot at their normal odds.

UPGRADE, REPLICATOR AND LOOT SUMMARY

DIFFICULTY LEVEL	UPGRADES (NANITE COST)	REPLICATORS COST	ADVERSARY LOOT
Easy	85% of listed cost	85% of listed cost	As listed
Normal	As listed	As listed	As listed
Hard	140% of listed cost	125% of listed cost	30% less chance of anything
Impossible	180% of listed cost	200% of listed cost	75% less chance of anything
Multiplayer	140% of listed cost	As listed	As listed

STRATEGIES

ROLEPLAYING: OPTIMUS PRIME VS. THE DRUNKEN PSIONICIST

Even more than the original *System Shock* before it, *System Shock 2* is as much a roleplaying game as a first-person adventure game. The high degree of customizability you have over your character matches or exceeds that of many "true" RPGs. With so many options, you can not only ask, "What can this character do?" but also, "Who is this character, really?"

So who is your character? At one extreme, there's the ultra-efficient character who's all about "what can I do" (dubbed by playtesters as "Optimus Prime" after the leader of the Transformers in that cartoon series). Optimus is determined to squeeze as much as he can out of every upgrade and every goodie. Nothing must ever go to waste. Every attribute must be raised to the point of diminishing returns, and no farther. Resources must be found and used. This is fine … the game is tough, and you'll need any edge you can find.

At the other extreme — where a character is totally driven by personality — consider (for example) an alcoholic psionicist. This is a character who's a powerful psychic, but who just can't resist immediately guzzling down every bottle of booze that happens into his path. (This little character quirk will result in a dramatic increase in that character's psi hypo consumption.) Why would anybody want to play a psionic drunkard? A silly and deadly whimsy? An added challenge for the truly hardcore gamer? A dramatic roleplaying concept? A bit of all three? That's up to you.

There is, of course, a happy medium between these two character extremes. It's entirely possible to create an efficient character without stripping him of all personality, and to personalize a character without undermining his efficiency. The point is that if Optimus Prime is really your man, have fun with it, but a little bit of personality (or a lot) can make the game that much more real, and your connection to your character that much stronger.

CHARACTER DEVELOPMENT

- Don't "window shop" your character advancement. It's very important to develop an advancement plan and then stick to it. Don't just grab any upgrade you can afford — save up for the next upgrade you really *need*.

- We strongly suggest you eventually get at least a level or two of PSI. This will allow you to get some value out of those psi hypos and boosters you're always finding. If you don't consider yourself a Psionicist, confine yourself to level 1 and 2 abilities, with a handful of carefully tailored disciplines. Even if you don't want to carry your psi amp around with you, cache it in the elevator and learn Cerebro-Stimulated Regeneration. Use it to heal up fully between decks without using up medical hypos. And everybody should learn Kinetic Redirection, for those cool caches of goodies that you just can't get to any other way. Another excellent discipline for the "amateur" psionic to acquire as early as possible is Anti-Entropic Field, which can keep your weapons clicking along smoothly until you're ready to buy up your Maintenance skill (or even replace Maintenance entirely).

- If you're a dedicated, super-brain, hard-core psionicist, don't think you have to get every single discipline on the list. Pick your disciplines intelligently and discriminately, to enhance your strong points and make up for your weaknesses. If you don't use normal weapons, don't bother with Neuro-Reflex Dampening or Anti-Entropic Field; and if you're going to buy high levels of Standard Weapons or Heavy Weapons, you probably don't need Projective Pyrokinesis.

Finally, here's a highly effective overall development strategy designed to make the most of your character's overall resources at any given moment. Note that this only works if you already have a coherent character concept firmly in mind. Also note that this is only one style of play — feel free to choose others.

1. **Specialize in the early game.** Identify what will be your core attributes, and concentrate on getting them to a point where you feel really competent. Get your most important attributes up to 3 or 4, with your secondary attributes at whatever the minimum level is to make them useable.

2. **Diversify in the middle game.** Now's the time to buy psionics if you're not a Psionicist, or extra tech and weapon skills if you are. Boost your stats a bit across the board. Build up Maintenance, Research and Modify … they're going to come in handy soon. Learn to Hack turrets. In general, get at least a start on every attribute you think you might ever possibly need.

3. **Master in the late game.** Once your character is completely diversified, it's time to return to those core competencies. Psionicists can dig in and master the fourth and fifth tier, while fighters can choose which weapon skills to take all the way up to 6. Once you feel you've fully mastered your essential skills, put any leftover modules into raising stats.

HIGH-CONCEPT CHARACTERS

There are infinite choices for your character, beyond the basic three archetypes of fighter, tech and psi. Here are a few of the more dramatic hybrid characters. These advanced character concepts are best suited for experienced players who've already been through the game at least once (because this game has a *lot* of replay value).

NINJA

This character specializes in close combat. He'll have high Strength and Agility, good Exotic Weapons and Research (so he can use the crystal shard — the best hand-to-hand weapon in the game — as soon as he finds it). He'll also have a carefully selected suite of psionic abilities, starting with those that boost his Stats, and continuing on to those that involve stealth and defense. He'll find Hacking useful, but will have no need at all for Modify, Maintenance or Repair. The two hand-to-hand OS upgrades (Lethal Weapon and Smasher) are tailor-made for him. The Ninja will have to watch out for small enemies like Monkeys, Grubs and Baby Annelids, because hand-to-hand is still tough against small opponents. He'll also need plans against Protocol Droids, Turrets and other exploding enemies (an emergency pistol or laser might be handy).

PSIONIC WARRIOR

The Psionic Warrior fights with guns, but uses psionics rather than technology to defend himself and maintain his arsenal. He needs high Agility and Psi stats and good weapon skills. His psionic powers are those that make his weapons more efficient (for example, Neuro-Reflex Dampening and Anti-Entropic Field), followed by those that enhance his defense and stealth. He won't need more than minimal technical skills.

CYBER-PSI

This is the Psychic Hacker. In the early game, Psychogenic Cyber Affinity makes him more efficient at his technical skills. Later on, a combination of a high Maintenance skill with the psi discipline of Electron Cascade can let this character charge up any powered item (or weapon!) to high levels, without needing to visit a recharge station. (Note that Remote Circuitry Manipulation is based solely on your Psi stat and does not combine with your 'normal' hacking abilities, hence, it's a better choice for the pure psi character than this psi/hack combo.)

WORMKIN

This concept doesn't fully come into its own until late in the game, but it's definitely cool. The goal here is to become as much as possible like the alien creatures you hunt. The Wormkin will specialize in Exotic Weapons (and the Research needed to discover how to use them), plus high physical stats. As much as possible, alien weapons, armor and implants will be used (some of the higher-level alien items have strange and serious drawbacks, which will present an extra challenge). Finally, the Wormkin will tailor a suite of psionic abilities that will allow him to mimic the abilities of aliens, and pass among them unnoticed until he's ready to strike.

EASTER EGGS

- During your third year of character training on the space station, don't hurry off to a new mission right away. Turn left, and spend a while watching the Protocol Droid through the window.

- In the movie theater on the Recreation Deck, make sure you look twice before using the replicator. Some things never change, even in the future.

- In the Athletics Sector of the Recreation Deck, you can get an Easter Egg by hitting the backboard with a basketball. Since *System Shock 2* doesn't really have a throwing interface, per se, this is hard to pull off, but it can be done. Dropping the basketball from the balcony above helps. Too bad you don't know where to find a basketball (if only you'd brought one with you …). Rumor has it that Snickers knows where to find one. When you successfully hit the backboard, you get a special email from an unexpected ally.

- If you have a Hacking skill of 6, you can Hack your GamePig. This will give you access to all the minigames. Moreover, in many of the games, you will get some added abilities!

- The minigame Overworld Zero has got an endgame. If you win, your GamePig will give you 20 nanites!

- To prove that the *System Shock 2* designers will go to any length for quality game material, we include this tidbit. Many of the textures in The Body of The Many were derived from the colon of Josh Randall, a producer at Looking Glass Studios. He had to have an endoscopy performed, and asked the doctor for a copy of the film. Waste not, want not!

- Okay, okay, we'll give you another hint about the basketball. It's located somewhere on Earth. You'll have to mantle to get to it. Even though you have no interface, you can right-click on it to pick it up

CHEAT CODES

These codes are provided for use as-is. They are *not* supported, so you're not allowed to whine if they ruin your game. If you're not willing to take the chance that something might go wrong, don't use the cheats.

CONFIGURATION FILE CHEAT

UNDEAD

One of the most powerful codes can only be invoked from a configuration file, not from inside *System Shock 2* itself.

1. Open a text editor, such as Notepad™ or MSWord™.

2. Put a line saying UNDEAD.

3. Save the text file to your *System Shock 2* directory, naming the file **USER.CFG**.

Now, whenever you take enough damage to kill you, you instead become "undead." You continue playing as normal, but now *nothing* in the game can damage you again, ever.

COMMAND LINE CHEATS

Most codes are entered from the command line inside *System Shock 2*. They are not case-sensitive, so you can use capital letters or not as you prefer.

To bring up the command line, press the colon key (Shift) (`;`) while in Shoot Mode.

Note. Do *not* press [[pix-colon]] while in Use Mode; you may put the game in an unstable state by doing so.

Type one of the following commands on the command line and hit (Enter).

ADD_POOL

Type the line ADD_POOL # (with a number in place of "#") and you get that many cyber modules. So, for instance, if you type in ADD_POOL 300 you get 300 cyber modules.

Note. There must be a space between ADD_POOL and the number.

UBERMENSCH

If ADD_POOL wasn't fast enough for you, typing UBERMENSCH simply gives you max stats, max skills, and every psi power. Now you don't *need* any more cyber modules!

OPEN_MFD

Typing the line OPEN_MFD # (once again with a number in place of the "#") opens a specific type of MFD, depending on what # you enter. (All the numbers and their MFDs are listed below.)

Note. There must be a space between OPEN_MFD and the number.

Warning. Playing around with arbitrary numbers can get your interface seriously messed up!

The ones we find most useful are the ones that bring up various upgrade units.

COMMAND	UPGRADE	NOTES
Open_mfd 20	*OS Upgrade*	You can invoke this up to 4 times, getting one OS upgrade each time. Trying to get a 5th OS upgrade won't work.
Open_mfd 35	*Stat Upgrade*	With enough cyber modules, you can upgrade any of your stats (for example, Strength, Agility, etc.).
Open_mfd 36	*Tech Ability Upgrade*	With enough cyber modules, you can upgrade any of your tech abilities (for example, Repair, Maintenance, etc.).
Open_mfd 37	*Weapon Upgrade*	With enough cyber modules, you can upgrade any of your weapon skills.
Open_mfd 38	*Psi Ability Upgrade*	With enough cyber modules, you can upgrade any of your psi abilities.

PSI_FULL

Even as an Ubermensch (superman), you may need to refill your psi point from time to time. Typing PSI_FULL in the command line brings your psi points to maximum.

SUMMON_OBJ [*NAME*]

When you type this line in, and substitute the name of an item for "NAME," that item drops at your feet. The name must be spelled exactly as it is in the computer code, with all proper punctuation, spacing, and so forth. (Capital letters are not important.) The following table lists the names of most things that you might commonly want to summon.

Note. The tricky bit is that the correct name is *not* necessarily the name you see in the game normally. You must use the name for the game's internal object representation, which is often quite different since many objects went through a lot of name changes as the game was developed.

Money

TO GET	TYPE IN
50 Nanites	Summon_Obj Big Nanite Pile
20 Cyber Modules	Summon_Obj Big BP Pile

Software

TO GET	TYPE IN
Hack Soft V3	Summon_Obj Hack Soft V3
Modify Soft V3	Summon_Obj Modify Soft V3
Repair Soft V3	Summon_Obj Repair Soft V3
Research Soft V3	Summon_Obj Research Soft V3

Weapons

TO GET	TYPE IN
Wrench	Summon_Obj Wrench
Pistol	Summon_Obj Pistol
Shotgun	Summon_Obj Shotgun
Assault Rifle	Summon_Obj Assault Rifle
Laser Pistol	Summon_Obj Laser Pistol
Laser Rapier	Summon_Obj Electro Shock
EMP Rifle	Summon_Obj EMP Rifle
Grenade Launcher	Summon_Obj Gren Launcher
Stasis Field Generator	Summon_Obj Stasis Field Generator
Fusion Cannon	Summon_Obj Fusion Cannon
Crystal Shard	Summon_Obj Crystal Shard
Viral Proliferator	Summon_Obj Viral Prolif
Annelid Launcher	Summon_Obj Worm Launcher
Psi Amp	Summon_Obj Psi Amp

Ammo

TO GET	TYPE IN
12 Standard Bullets	Summon_Obj Standard Clip
12 Armor-Piercing Bullets	Summon_Obj AP Clip
12 Anti-Personnel Bullets	Summon_Obj HE Clip
6 Rifled Slugs	Summon_Obj Rifled Slug Box
6 Anti-Personnel Pellets	Summon_Obj Pellet Shot Box
3 Fragmentation Grenades	Summon_Obj Timed Grenade
3 Proximity Grenades	Summon_Obj Prox. Grenade
3 EMP Grenades	Summon_Obj EMP Grenade
3 Disruption Grenades	Summon_Obj Toxin Grenade
3 Incendiary Grenades	Summon_Obj Incend. Grenade
20 Prisms	Summon_Obj Large Prism
8 Worm Clusters	Summon_Obj Large Worm Beaker

Implants

TO GET	TYPE IN
BrawnBoost	Summon_Obj BrawnBoost
EndurBoost	Summon_Obj EndurBoost
ExperTech	Summon_Obj ExperTech
LabAssistant	Summon_Obj LabAssistant
PsiBoost	Summon_Obj SmartBoost
SwiftBoost	Summon_Obj SwiftBoost
WormBlood	Summon_Obj WormBlood
WormHeart	Summon_Obj WormHeart
WormMind	Summon_Obj WormMind

Organs

TO GET	TYPE IN
Annelid Healing Gland	Summon_Obj Annelid_Medpatch
Annelid Psi Organ	Summon_Obj Annelid_Psipatch
Hybrid Organ	Summon_Obj OG Organ
Monkey Brain	Summon_Obj Monkey_Brain
Midwife Organ	Summon_Obj Midwife Organ
Grub Organ	Summon_Obj Grub Organ
Arachnid Organ	Summon_Obj Arach. Organ
Swarm Organ	Summon_Obj Swarm Organ
Rumbler Organ	Summon_Obj Rumbler Organ
Psi Reaver Organ	Summon_Obj Gr. Over. Organ

Chemicals

TO GET	TYPE IN
Antimony (Sb)	Summon_Obj Chem #4
Arsenic (As)	Summon_Obj Chem #11
Barium (Ba)	Summon_Obj Chem #18
Californium (Cf)	Summon_Obj Chem #7
Cesium (Cs)	Summon_Obj Chem #12
Copper (Cu)	Summon_Obj Chem #6
Fermium (Fm)	Summon_Obj Chem #1
Gallium (Ga)	Summon_Obj Chem #3
Hassium (Hs)	Summon_Obj Chem #13
Iridium (Ir)	Summon_Obj Chem #10
Molybdenum (Mo)	Summon_Obj Chem #15
Osmium (Os)	Summon_Obj Chem #9
Radium (Ra)	Summon_Obj Chem #17
Selenium (Se)	Summon_Obj Chem #19
Sodium (Na)	Summon_Obj Chem #8
Technetium (Tc)	Summon_Obj Chem #16
Tellurium (Te)	Summon_Obj Chem #14
Vanadium (V)	Summon_Obj Chem #2
Yttrium (Y)	Summon_Obj Chem #5

Armor

TO GET	TYPE IN
Hazard Suit	Summon_Obj Vacc Suit
Light Combat Armor	Summon_Obj Light Armor
Medium Combat Armor	Summon_Obj Medium Armor
Heavy Combat Armor	Summon_Obj Heavy Armor
Powered Armor	Summon_Obj Reflec Armor
Worm Skin	Summon_Obj Worm Skin

Devices

TO GET	TYPE IN
Auto-Repair Unit	Summon_Obj Molec. Analyzer
French-Epstein Device	Summon_Obj French-Epstein Device
ICE Pick	Summon_Obj ICE Pick
Maintenance Tool	Summon_Obj Maintenance Tool
Portable Battery	Summon_Obj Portable Battery
Recycler	Summon_Obj Recycler

Hypos

TO GET	TYPE IN
Medical Hypo	Summon_Obj Med Patch
Medical Kit	Summon_Obj Medical Kit
Psi Hypo	Summon_Obj Psi Booster
Anti-Radiation Hypo	Summon_Obj Rad Patch
Anti-Toxin Hypo	Summon_Obj Detox Patch
Speed Booster	Summon_Obj Speed Boost
Strength Booster	Summon_Obj Strength Boost
Alien Psi Booster	Summon_Obj INT Boost

Access Cards

TO GET CARD INTO	TYPE IN
Cryogenics Sector	Summon_Obj Cryo Card
Science Sector	Summon_Obj Med Card
Deck 2 Crew	Summon_Obj Crew Card
R & D Sector	Summon_Obj R and D Card
Security	Summon_Obj Security Card
Cargo Bay 2A/2B	Summon_Obj Cargo Bay 2A/2B
Hydroponics A	Summon_Obj Hydro Card A
Hydroponics B	Summon_Obj Hydro Card B
Hydroponics D	Summon_Obj Hydro Card D
Deck 5 Crew	Summon_Obj Rec Crew Key
Candy's Quarters	Summon_Obj Candy_Card
Lance's Quarters	Summon_Obj Lance_Card
Nikki's Quarters	Summon_Obj Nikki_Card
Sven's Quarters	Summon_Obj Sven_Card
Athletic Sector	(due to a bug, this card cannot be summoned)
Bridge	Summon_Obj Bridge Card
Ops Override	Summon_Obj Ops Override Key
Shuttle Bay	Summon_Obj Shuttle Access Key
Rickenbacker	Summon_Obj Rickenbacker Card
Diego's Quarters	Summon_Obj Rick Room Key

Plot Items

TO GET	TYPE IN
Anti-Annelid Toxin	Summon_Obj Anti-Annelid Toxin
Charged Power Cell	Summon_Obj Power Cell
Interpolated Simulation Chip	Summon_Obj Chip C
Linear Simulation Chip	Summon_Obj Chip B
Quantum Simulation Chip	Summon_Obj Chip A
Sympathetic Resonator	Summon_Obj Big Bomb

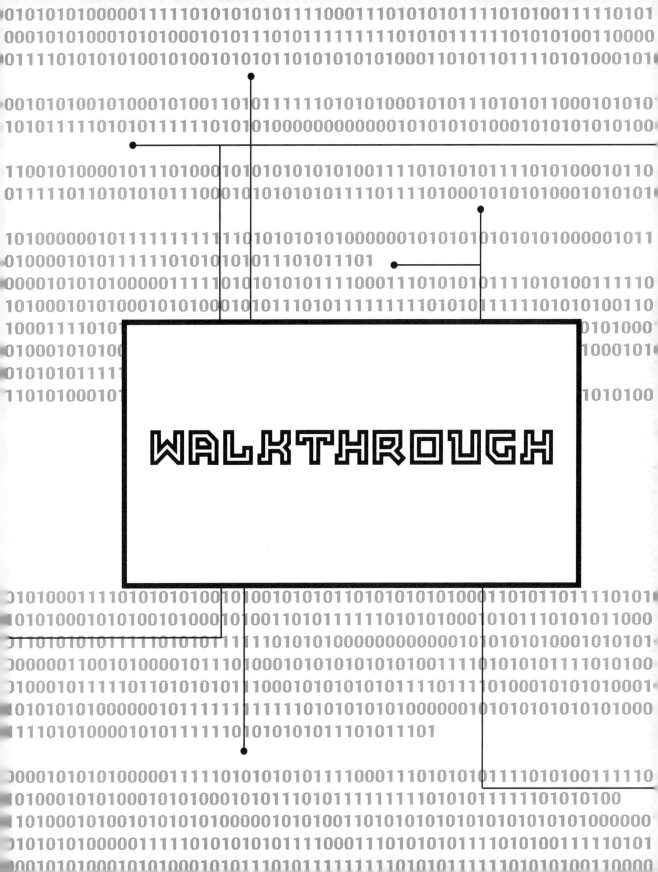

WALKTHROUGH

INTRODUCTION

The Walkthrough is divided into two sections. The **Walkthrough Outline** is a brief guide to the "critical path" tasks that you must achieve to finish the game. It's designed for gamers who want to have some idea where they're going next (or suspect they might have missed something crucial), but want "spoiler" information kept to a minimum. Immediately following this outline is a list of every necessary code, spread out and faded to help you keep from reading anything you don't want to read.

The second and much larger section is a comprehensive **Walkthrough**. This is not only a room-by-room description of the game's environment, but also serves as a systematic guide to the essential strategy and tactics of the game. This is the place to go if you want to make absolutely sure you don't miss *anything*.

USING THE WALKTHROUGH OUTLINE

Your PDA keeps a list of your necessary steps as the game progresses. It is a list of every essential task and the most useful optional tasks, in order. (Of course, order may vary, depending on how you tackle it.) We've repeated part of this list as a Walkthrough outline — you can use this list to make sure you've completed every task to get through the game.

Of course, the complete walkthrough covers all these tasks, in much more detail. However, scanning the Walkthrough Outline is much less likely to give anything away that you don't want to know as you play the game.

CODES

Immediately following the Walkthrough Outline (on page 136) is a list of all necessary codes in the game. Again, these are given in the Complete Walkthrough, but if you don't want to wade through a lot of other information, check this list.

Again, you might only want a single code, without any other information. To help you find the code you want, and only the code you want, we've printed the codes in faded numbers — with just a little care, you'll read only the code you're looking for, and nothing more.

USING THE
COMPLETE WALKTHROUGH

This section takes you through the entire game, deck by deck and room by room. Because *System Shock 2* is a very open-ended game, this walkthrough is not the only path through the game, but it is a complete and logical path that takes you through the various sections in order of availability and difficulty. The walkthrough also includes all codes and puzzle solutions for the entire game.

MAPS

Maps (for those sections of the game which are mapable) are taken directly from the in-game maps, and include the replicators, upgrade stations and other information found on those maps. In addition, they include alphabetic walkthrough keys that will help you find your way along the path.

MESSAGES

Interspersed throughout the walkthrough are every log entry and e-mail, as well as many of the telepathic messages, found in the game. These communications reveal the whole complex and dynamic plot of the game. Communications which are directly related to a specific place are placed near that section of the walkthrough, while those that deal with general plot information are spaced more randomly.

MATERIEL AVAILABLE

Finally, at the end of each deck's walkthrough is a list of Materiel Available — a categorized list of every useful item available on that deck and its location. With this list, you can be absolutely sure you haven't missed anything. Of course, this section cannot include creature loot, which is random and not placed, but creature loot is also an important source of materiel. See **Adversaries**, p. 90, for more on creature loot.

You'll probably also want to refer to the replicator lists, on pp. 84-86. These lists give the contents and prices of every replicator in the game, both the unhacked and hacked versions.

OUTLINE

MedScience

- ☐ Recharge the battery and use it to open the door to Medical.

- ☐ Get a crew card from Grassi. He's near Biopsy in Medical.

- ☐ Get through a secure airlock.

- ☐ Find Dr. Watts' room in the Crew sector.

- ☐ Look for Dr. Watts in his office in R&D

- ☐ Get the maintenance access shaft code from Dr. Watts.

- ☐ Get to Deck 4 to meet Dr. Polito.

Engineering

- ☐ The code for Engineering Control is in Cargo Bay 2.

- ☐ Find a way to override the Fluidics Computer.

- ☐ Get unit 45m/dEx from aux. storage 5, code: 34760.

- ☐ Install unit 45m/dEx in Command Control.

- ☐ Use Fluidics Computer in Engineering Control to purge the tubes.

- ☐ Purge radiation from coolant tubes to re-open Engine Core.

- ☐ Reset Port Engine Nacelle.

- ☐ Reset Starboard Engine Nacelle.

- ☐ Reset Main Power Computer.

- ☐ Reset Main Power at the Engine Core to restart elevators.

- ☐ Get to Deck 4 to meet Dr. Polito.

HYDROPONICS

- [ ] Clear the biomaterial from the elevator shaft.

- [ ] Find and Research Toxin-A.

- [ ] Place Toxin-A in all 4 environmental regulators.

- [ ] Get to Deck 4 to meet Dr. Polito.

OPERATIONS

- [ ] Find the passcode for the MedSci2 sub armory.

- [ ] Go to the Command Deck.

- [ ] Reprogram the three sim units.

- [ ] Go to the Recreation Deck

RECREATION

- [ ] Find the transmitter and activate it.

- [ ] Activate transmitter with code hidden in art terminals.

- [ ] Go to the Command Deck.

COMMAND

- [ ] Find the Ops Override access card.

- [ ] Go to the Command Center on the Ops Deck.

OPERATIONS

- [ ] Create a data access channel from the Command Center.

- [ ] Go to the Engine Core on the Engineering Deck.

ENGINEERING

- Set the Engine Core to overload, code: 94834.

COMMAND

- The shuttle card is in the security station in the officer's quarters.

- Deactivate the shields around the shuttles from the control chamber.

- Destroy the shuttles on this deck.

- Hack the shuttle control rep. to get a sympathetic resonator.

- Attach the sympathetic resonator to the Shield Generator … and run!

- Go to the *Rickenbacker* via the central tram station.

RICKENBACKER

- The access card for Nacelle B is beyond the hull breach.

- Go to Engine Nacelle B.

- Reverse the gravitonic generators in order to safely access Pod 2.

- Destroy all the eggs.

- Proceed to Pod 2.

- Use the escape pod on the bridge to attack the Many.

THE BODY OF THE MANY

- The sphincter doors are controlled by the nerve clusters.

- The Many has a centralized nervous system … find and destroy it!

SHODAN

- Stop SHODAN … somehow …

CODES

MedSci

45100   Exit Cryo

00000   Closet in Cryo retraining

98383   Armory

12451   Maintenance Access Shaft

Engineering

59004   Utility Storage 4

34760   Auxiliary Storage 5

45m/dEx   Part needed from AS5

94834   Destruct computer
(but *don't* do this early,
you'll just break the plot.)

Operations

13433   Armory

Recreation

12345   Safe behind reception desk

11111   Locked room in crew sector

50220   Door to security station

14106   Activate Transmitter

Command

83273   Security station

Look at you hacker. A pathetic creature of meat and bone, panting and sweating as you run through my corridors. How can you challenge a perfect immortal machine?

In 2072, a rogue artificial intelligence known as SHODAN lost her mind.
In her limitless imagination, SHODAN saw herself as a Goddess destined to inherit the Earth. That image was snuffed out by the hacker who created her.

February 3rd is the day the magic happens. The Von Braun, the first starship in history capable of travelling at faster than light speed will undertake her maiden voyage. This incredible journey is the result of teamwork between the UNN protectorate and the incredible scientific minds at the newly re-licensed TriOptimum Corporation!

Imagine, travelling to distant star systems in a period of weeks! It's all part of TriOp's commitment to the future. The Von Braun is packed with over 1.8 billion flight, scientific and security systems nearly all developed by TriOptimium and its wholly-owned subsidiaries.

Providing security for the Von Braun as she plows through the heavens will be the UNN Rickenbacker. At her helm will be no less than Captain William Bedford Diego himself, hero of the battle of Boston Harbor during the Eastern States police action.

This incredible union of government and corporation is made possible by an intricate series of docking mechanisms that will allow the Rickenbacker to piggyback its way into jump space.

Sleek, fast, revolutionary. Who knows what wonders await our crews in the bosom of the cosmos. All we do know, is that it's a great day for mankind!

Systems on line.
Reviving patient ... initializing.

Reinitializing memory strings ...Restoring patient memory.

Restoring memory ... Restoring memory ... Restoring memory ...

... ERROR

MEDSCI

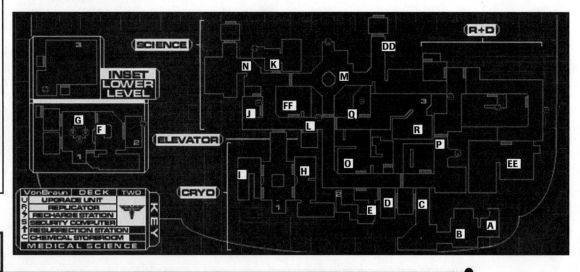

CRYOGENICS AREA

You awaken in a cryosleep tube. Spend a moment or two looking around. Notice that there is blood on the floor. It doesn't look good.

(A) Take note of the corpse in the room to the left. Right click on the body to search it. If you drag the wrench you find onto your "weapon" slot, you'll see your hand holding it in front of you.

(B) The ladder out of the area is blocked by some debris, but you can clear it away by hitting it (left click) with the wrench. Soon you'll receive an email from Dr. Polito telling you that the radar dish outside is becoming unstable, and warning you to get out of the way. A moment later, explosions erupt on the radar dish, and debris flies through the window. A force field keeps you from being instantly depressurized, but Polito emails you again to warn you to get out of the area as quickly as possible.

> This is Dr. Marie Delacroix of the UNN Von Braun. We've been hijacked by an unknown force. Ship's security has been compromised. Do not allow this ship to [static]. Repeat … [static] under any circumstances. I don't know what we're up against here [static cuts off transmission].

> Steady yourself soldier. This is Dr. Janice Polito of the Computer Ops staff of the Von Braun. You're safe for the time being. You're recovering from the effects the surgery and will be unable to remember any of the events of the last few weeks. You're onboard the starship Von Braun and something's gone very, very wrong. Some kind of force has hijacked this ship. That's why you volunteered to be implanted with some experimental cybernetic implants. Rely on your cyber-interface, it just might save your life. You must find an elevator and come up to deck 4 to meet me. Deck 4, can you remember that? But keep your eyes open, they're after us both now.

To climb the ladder, move close to it. You automatically climb onto the ladder. To climb, look up, and then move forward. This moves you up the ladder. Try looking down instead — moving forward causes you to back down the ladder. As you head up the ladder, you'll hear a loudspeaker warning you of imminent depressurization. At the top of the ladder is a hallway with an automatic door. Keep moving through this area, but watch out for falling debris and explosions.

> **POLITO 12.JUL.14 RE: SHIP DAMAGE**
>
> Watch out … I'm getting strange readings from that radar dish outside the window. It's become unstable due to … Move! Take cover!

> **POLITO 12.JUL.14 RE: SECTOR DEPRESSURIZING**
>
> The entire sector is depressurizing and the blue vacuum shield won't last long. Get through a secure airlock before you are sucked into space. Move it!

(C) The door at the end of the hallway doesn't open automatically: you'll need to press the button next to it. In the next room, access the info kiosk — it gives you some information about the "interaction interface" of your cyber interface, which you can display by hitting ⌶ or Tab. If you try to use the access slot to open the door before you've picked up the access card, you see a message indicating that you need CRYO access. Pick up the CRYO access card — it doesn't take up an inventory slot, but you can display your available access cards by clicking the access icon … the middle button in the lower right MFD panel. Once you have the CRYO card, you can open the door.

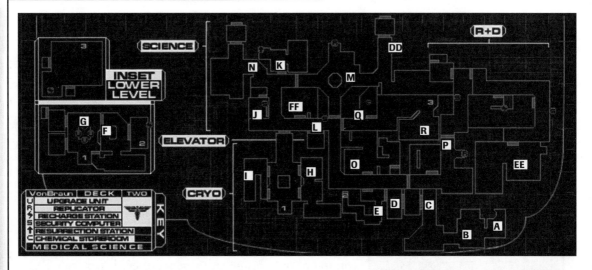

(D) In the next room is another body. You can search him by right clicking on him, which opens a display window of his possessions. He has a log, which you can pick up by clicking on it, and read/listen to by hitting Ⓤ. The log tells you the combination to the door. All your logs, and all your email, are stored in your PDA (left icon, bottom-right interface display), sorted by level. Right click on the keypad by the door, and enter the combination. You see a HACK panel, but since you don't have any nanites yet, you can't hack it. Also in this room is another info kiosk, this one describing your PDA. You'll encounter further kiosks in the areas to come, and all of them have useful basic information.

(E) The room beyond the combination lock has a broken door, but there's a crawlway leading out. Past the window to the right is a strange creature, apparently chasing someone. Good thing it's on the other side of the broken door, or you could be in danger. Crouch Ⓢ, and move along the tunnel until you emerge into another room. This room contains the airlock door that Polito's been telling you to get behind. Unfortunately, if you try to open it with the button next to it, you'll hear an error message warning you that the door is inoperative and out of power, instructing you to put power in the auxiliary power override. Nearby, you'll find a power cell — but when you pick it up, you'll realize it's dead. Dr. Polito sends email, telling you to charge the cell at the recharge station. If you activate the recharger, everything in your inventory is fully powered (at this point, that's probably just the power cell). Open your inventory and left-drag the charged power cell from your inventory into the auxiliary power override, and the airlock door will open.

AMANPOUR 07.JUL.14 RE: NEW CODE

Great. I've got to change the access codes out of Cryo A again! Like I've got nothing better to do. I think Grassi just likes to make work for me. I'll set the new code to 45100. That should be easy enough to remember.

POLITO 12.JUL.14 RE: DEAD POWERCELL

This powercell is dead. There should be a recharger nearby ... just use it and it will recharge all the power-driven devices in your possession. After you've recharged the cell, plug it into the auxiliary power unit. That should open the airlock door. Be quick about it, the vacuum seals won't hold up much longer.

(F) Head through the airlock; the door will seal behind you. You'll receive email from Dr. Polito, informing you she's sent you four upgrade modules (usable at upgrade units to increase your skills and stats). Look around the room. The button on the wall in front of you turns on the lights. Search the shipping container to find twenty nanites (used for hacking, repairing, and buying things from replicators). Go through the doorway to the left. Search the body: it's carrying some more nanites, which are always handy. Continue on through the red-lit door.

(G) This room has all four upgrade units (devices used to increase your statistics and skills by using cybernetic modules). As Dr. Polito points out in her email, cybernetic modules are rare and increases can be expensive, so it's worth putting thought into any increases before you use up the cybernetic modules. Search the corpse to the left and find some more cybernetic modules.

> **POLITO 12.JUL.14 RE: UPGRADE UNITS**
>
> Good. You've managed to get out before the whole area depressurized. I've just uploaded you some cybernetic modules. You can use them to upgrade your cybernetic rig at the upgrade units in this area. There are four types of units in the next room, one for each subsystem of your cybernetic gear: stats, psi, weapons and tech. But use the modules carefully ... they're hard to come by.

The right door is broken, but the left door leads to a room with a log which seems to be talking about you, and a crate with more nanites. Through the broken wall you get to the room behind the broken door. A body on the floor has a medical hypo. You can use this to heal ten hit points of damage, though it takes a few sec-

> **GRASSI 07.JUL.14 RE: IMPLANT JOB TO: POLITO, DR. JANICE**
>
> Hey, doc ... a security bot showed up with orders from you to place this grunt into the recovery freezer. I'm no cyberdoc, but I know a plant job when I see one. I suppose you know they outlawed R-grade cyber-goodies after that fiasco back on Citadel Station ... but, hey, I just work here, right?

onds to have its full effect. There's also a keypad-locked door in here. Unlike last time, there's no convenient log telling you the combination, but you can attempt to hack through. Click on the keypad, and then select the HACK panel. If you have at least one point of Hack skill, this brings up your hacking display, showing things like the results of hacking and chances of success. Click on the "start" button to make the attempt – you need to successfully connect three nodes in a row. Red nodes have dangerous ICE, and green nodes are "safe". If you're successful, the door opens to a closet containing two Speed Boosters and a Brawn Boost Implant.

Note that the Brawn Boost Implant has a charge of 100. If you equip it by dragging it to your Implant inventory slot, your Stats MFD panel will display an extra chevron for your STR stat. However, using the implant runs down its charge, and then you need to find a recharger. Since the only recharger you've seen so far is on the other side of the airlock, you might want to save the implant for when it will be more useful.

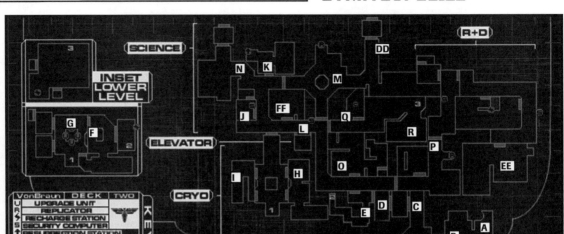

(H) That's about it for the set of rooms down here. Time to move upstairs. Get on the lift, and press the button to go up. Through the door on the right is a body with a psi amplifier. If your character is from the OSA, then you'll already have one, but if you're from another branch and think you might want to eventually get psi powers, be sure to get a psi amp before doing so. From this area, you can also see an open doorway looking out on a rather precarious set of girders. You can jump across to the far girder to pick up the bullets and Speed Booster, but be careful — if you miss, you can take damage from the fall. If you know Kinetic Redirection, you can use that psi power to pull these (and other) distant objects towards you with less risk.

(I) On the other side of the lift is another small set of rooms. There's another body here, this one with some nanites and an access card. Behind the glass in the wall, there's also a box of shotgun shells and a psi hypo. Use the wrench to break the glass.

Head for the hallway and door across from the catwalk. When you approach it, a strangely transparent crewman appears out of nowhere and walks towards the door, muttering about having lost his access card, then vanishes. Hard to tell what you're supposed to do for the poor gentleman now, but at least you have an access card from the nearby room which lets you into the next door.

POLITO 12.JUL.14 RE: GHOSTS

You might witness some strange phenomena. Your R-grade cyber rig has an experimental perception enhancement that can theoretically detect residual psychic emanations. These emanations traditionally come from the recently dead. Literature might call them ghosts. I call them self-hypnotic defects in the R-grade unit. Don't let it distract you from the job at hand.

SCIENCE SECTOR, PART ONE

As you head through the door, watch out for another strange, unfriendly creature (like the one you saw through the window in Cryogenics) on your left. You can kill him with the wrench — your cyberware will tell you how damaged he is. Some hints: Melee combat is all about distance. If you fight with a wrench or other melee weapon, ready your swing while at a distance from your opponent. Run toward him and release the swing once you're close. Immediately back away again, so you have a good chance of evading your opponent's swing while you ready your own next attack. Be warned, the creatures you meet on this level have a longer melee range than you do! If you're from the OSA, you may want to fight with your Cryokinesis power. As a ranged weapon, it's much safer than the wrench, but it uses up psi points, which are a limited commodity. If you're a Marine, you may start with a ranged weapon. But again, ammunition is limited and should be used carefully.

After you kill the creature, search him to see if he's carrying anything useful. A close look shows that he is some sort of hybrid between a human and an alien-looking worm. The noise of your fight may attract a second Hybrid, who is patrolling a nearby hallway. If you hear him coming, be ready for another fight!

(J) The room the first Hybrid came out of is the security station for this area, with a security computer and a security crate. The back office of the station has a desk with a log that complains about hacking into the security computer. If you have Hack skill, you might want to try that yourself. Access the computer. Unless you've run around in the view of any cameras, the security computer indicates that the alarm is not currently active. You can hack the computer in order to temporarily disable security (both cameras and turrets), though if you critically fail, the alarms will go off. If you succeed, an icon in the lower left of your display indicates that security is hacked. You can also use Hack skill to try and open the security crate here. This is more difficult, and requires a Hack of at least 2 to even attempt. If you critically fail to Hack a security crate, it explodes, destroying its valuable contents and doing a considerable amount of damage to you in the process.

> **DELACROIX 04.APR.14**
> **RE: XERXES**
>
> Why is it that no one listens to me? The security protocols on the Xerxes system are clearly immature. Some idiot hacked into the primary data loop last night and made Xerxes sing Elvis Presley songs for three hours. I finally had to pull the voice sub-system off line. What would happen if somebody with a real agenda got into him?

From here, you have a number of options. We'll take you on one possible path through the level, visiting most of the interesting locations, but feel free to deviate from it to explore some more. Make sure to read all logs you find — many contain useful information.

From the security area, turn left and go to the end of the hall. If you haven't already dealt with the Hybrid patrolling this area, you'll have to fight him now.

One of the first few Hybrids you fight may have "An unresearched object" in his possession. This is actually an organ that you can remove, intact, from the Hybrid. If you have the Research Skill, then you can initiate research on the organ by right clicking on it. Successfully researching an organ will give you useful information about a creature's strengths and weaknesses, allowing you to do more damage to it in combat.

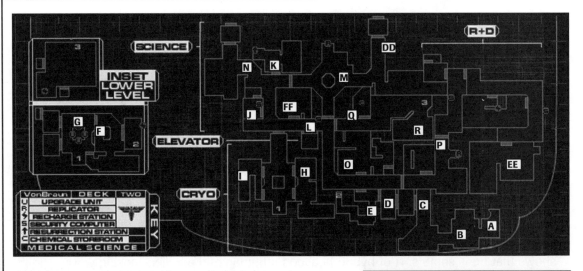

(K) At the end of this hall, you should see a door. Walking through this door you'll see some computer consoles, and a hapless former crewman hanging from a rope. A Hybrid will attack you from the next room, so deal with him before more sightseeing. When you approach the complex-looking niche in the corner, Polito will send you email explaining that it is a bio-reconstruction station. Once you activate it (by right clicking on the nearby button), any time that you "die" in this area, your body will be reconstructed here (with all your possessions intact). As she says, "It's not pleasant, but it's preferable to slow decomposition." When you are "reconstructed," you will have only one third of the hit points you would have at full health.

POLITO 12.JUL.14 RE: BIO-RECONSTRUCTION

On most decks, you'll find a quantum bio-reconstruction device. Xerxes shut them all down, but I've discretely put them back online. You'll need to interface with each machine locally to provide a quantum entanglement sample. Once you do that, the device will be able to rebuild your body essentially from scratch. It's not pleasant, but it's preferable to slow decomposition.

GRASSI 20.JUN.14 RE: ALL WORK, NO PLAY

I got called up around 0430 to help unload the shuttle coming back from Tau Ceti. Korenchkin was there alone. Jesus, what the hell happened to him? He'd lost most of his hair, and you could see these lumps on the side of his neck. And that smell. I told him he should go see Dr. Watts, but he told me to mind my own business. Well, la-dee-da.

The neighboring room appears to be a combination morgue/crematorium. There are a number of body bags in here. If you're not feeling too squeamish, you can search them to find some useful items. There's also a log on the floor, which may shed a little light on what's been going on.

(L) Leave this room and head back to the security station, then down the hall to the left. There's a door on the left, apparently leading to a maintenance access shaft, but it's locked with a keypad and you don't yet know the code. If you look through one of the nearby windows, you'll see a big robot in the next room. Looks like he'd be tough to fight with the wrench; good thing he's on the other side of a locked door.

As you continue down this hall, you'll see an elevator door on the right. Hey, this is your chance to get up to Deck 4 and meet Dr. Polito! Hit the elevator button. Sadly, as Polito informs you over email, the power to the elevator has been cut off, and you'll need to get down to the Engineering Deck to fix it. Getting down there is complicated, but Polito explains what you'll need to do. If you open your PDA and look at the Notes tab, you'll see that your PDA is keeping a list of summarized "to do" tasks for you.

(M) Turn left after the elevator, and proceed through the doors. You'll see a bunch of debris on your right; if you search it carefully, you'll find some nanites. Proceed into the large room with a column in the center. This is the core of Xerxes, the ship's computer that extends through all decks of the Von Braun. As you approach him, he may make a public service announcement. There are also a couple of bodies in this room. One of them has a pistol, which you should certainly take. If you have any Standard Weapons skills, you'll probably find it to be much more useful then the wrench (as long as the ammo holds out).

> **POLITO 12.JUL.14 RE: FIXING THE ELEVATORS**
>
> That insipid computer Xerxes has shut down the elevator as well. You can transfer power at the engine core on deck 1, which will get the elevator up and running again. But you can't use the elevator to get down there. Wait ... there's some kind of maintenance access right on this hallway. You can use it to reach deck one. However, it's locked and Xerxes is hiding the passcode from me. Dr. Watts should have the code. He's probably in the Crew sub-section. Grassi has the key to get in there, but he's in the Medical sub-section, probably near the biopsy lab. Now get to the Medical sub-section and find Grassi.

This room also contains a replicator, where you can spend nanites to buy various useful items. As you approach it, though, you'll see another apparition, this one complaining that someone has hacked into this replicator again. If you have a Hack of at least 3, you can try hacking the replicator yourself. Success will give you a better selection of items, and they'll be cheaper, too. Critical failure will break the replicator, and it won't be useable unless you use the Repair skill (at at least level 3) on it.

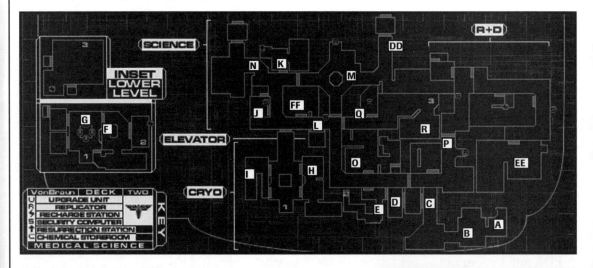

(N) Continue down the hall past the room with the bio-reconstruction machine it. As you approach the medical reception area, you'll see a console on a nearby wall explode – apparently there are some power flow problems in this area. Just after that, you'll come in sight of a security camera – you should hear its distinctive whirring sound before it actually comes in view. Pay attention to that sound; early warning about upcoming cameras can make a crucial difference throughout your mission. If the camera spots you, it will turn yellow, then red, then set off an alarm which will summon many monsters to come and kill you. To prevent this, either Hack a security computer, or shoot out the camera before it sounds the alarm. If you *do* set off an alarm, head to a security computer as soon as you can; right clicking a security computer will terminate any active alarms.

POLITO 12.JUL.14 RE: THE SECURITY SYSTEM

Xerxes has control of the ship's security system. Avoid or destroy any security cameras you see. You can hack security computers to power down the cameras too, if you're good enough. But don't botch the job, or you'll set off the alarm yourself. Your corpse is useless to me.

POLITO 12.JUL.14 RE: POWERING THE DOOR

Damn. The power outage has also taken out access to this bulkhead. It's the only way to get to the Medical subsection. Pick up the battery from the floor and find a recharger. The one you used before is in hard vacuum now, I'm afraid, but there should be another one on this deck. Once you get the battery recharged, place it in the auxiliary override.

As you approach the Security Door which leads into the Medical Sector, Polito will send you some email. Apparently this door is inoperative, and needs to get a power override, just like the airlock near where you awoke from cryosleep. There's a battery nearby, but it's not charged. The only recharger you know about is now in hard vacuum, so you'll need to find another one to proceed. Take the battery with you, so you can recharge it once you find a recharge station.

While you're here, search the smoking corpse. He's got a minigame player, and a basic game cartridge. Right click on the cartridge to install it in the minigame player, and right-click on the player to play a minigame. Also in this area, you'll find a log from one of the ship's engineers complaining about radiation leaks down on the Engineering Deck. Since you'll be going there soon, you'll need some anti-radiation hypos for yourself. There's one on the desk here, and another that seems to have gotten forgotten on a high shelf behind the desk (near the potted plants).

> **CURTIZ 06.JUL.14 RE: COOLANT LEAKS TO: DELACROIX, DR. MARIE**
>
> Marie, I've got to restrict access to Engineering until we can figure out what to do down there. It's just too hot. I don't know where all the Hazard Suits went, so I'm reduced to bringing down an armful of Rad Hypos. Those damn things always give me a headache."

Head back to the Xerxes core and turn right. Continue straight past the intersection with the elevator. There's a camera at the end of this hall, so be prepared to deal with it. Turn left at the end of the hall, and go into the nearby room.

(O) Be prepared for a fight: there are two creatures in here waiting to ambush you. The lights will go out, the door will lock behind you, and they will charge. One is a Hybrid, like those you've seen before, but the other is a cute little monkey. At least he looks cute right up until he starts shooting you with Cryokinetic blasts!

After you kill them, you'll see that this Monkey has a brain that has expanded outside of his skull. There's something very odd going on here. A log in a nearby desk may help explain some of the situation. A button in the back room will restore power to the lights (and the door), but you should explore this area a bit before leaving, as there's some useful items in here. In one room, the floor is a grating. Looking through that grating, you can see a recharge station! Now you just need to find a way to get to it ....

> **GRASSI 26.JUN.14 RE: ANIMAL RIGHTS?**
>
> "Ever since we reached Tau Ceti, the lab monkeys have been acting strangely. Nurse Loesser picked one out of a cage to be brought in for vivisection and the rest of them, I mean the entire group, stood up on their legs and howled. This wasn't just a random display, it was a protest."

Leaving this room, continue left down the hall. You may recognize this hall as the one you saw a Hybrid chasing a crewwoman down earlier. Through the next door, you'll find her body. The next room on the left contains a Hybrid, and a med hypo lying in a back corner of the room. At the end of the corridor, there is a sunken area with a Hybrid wandering around in it. You could fight him with conventional means, but there's a bit of a shortcut available as well. You may notice that there are some barrels in the sunken area marked "Flammable". If you shoot one of those while the Hybrid is nearby, he'll be killed by the resulting explosion, and you'll have only spent a single bullet. Going down the ladder yourself, you can find some nanites that someone accidentally discarded by searching the trash barrel.

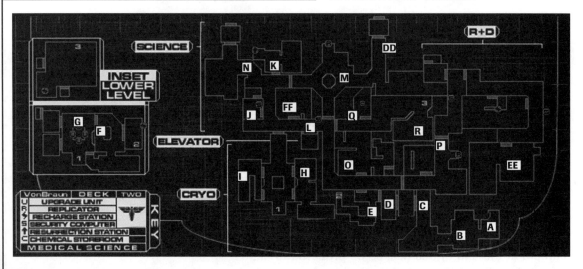

(P) Continue past the bend in the corridor. There's another replicator here, with a different selection of goods. At the end of the hall is a door leading to the Research & Development section, but it's locked, and you don't have a keycard. Looks like a dead end for now, so head back the way you came.

POLITO 12.JUL.14 RE: CHEMICAL STORES

Each deck has a chemical store room where you can find the resources you need to research the artifacts you'll find around the ship. Don't try to carry around all the chemicals at once. It's impractical and unnecessary. Your research software will tell you what chemicals it needs ... and when.

(Q) When you get to the intersection with the elevator, turn right through the door. Enter the first room on your left. This is the chemical storeroom for this deck of the Von Braun. As Polito explains in her email, each deck has a chemical storeroom. These chemicals are used to research certain items, but you don't yet know what you might need, so don't bother taking any. You should pick up the Chemical Manifest Log, so that when you *do* need chemicals, you'll know what deck to has some.

Also in this room, you can find another pistol and some bullets. It's good to have more than one pistol, as they degrade in condition over time. A poor condition pistol may jam, which renders it unusable until repaired. If one pistol jams in the middle of a fight, you can quickly switch to your other one. Eventually, you may want to acquire the Maintenance Skill, to improve the quality of your weapons so that they won't jam in the first place.

Back out into the hall, and continue left. You'll enter a room with a Hybrid who's apparently just killed a crewman. When he notices you, the Hybrid charges, so be ready. When he's been dealt with, search the crewman's body to get some armor-piercing pistol ammo. This ammo type does less damage against soft targets (like Hybrids), but more damage against mechanical targets (like robots). You can switch ammo types quickly with the B key.

(R) Through a nearby door, there are some catwalks over a pumping station. If you look carefully, you'll see a psi hypo lying on top of a crate down there. If you want, you can try to jump over to get it. Otherwise, you could just go down the nearby ladder to get into the pump station. At the other end of the pump station ... is the long-sought recharger!

Head towards the recharger, but don't slow down to pick up the stuff on the floor: if you do, you may get a nasty surprise. As you cross the middle of the room, the lights go out and two nearby doors open up – revealing automated gun turrets! If you run, though, you can make it to the sheltered nook with the recharger before they can draw a bead on you. Right click on the recharger to charge your battery. From here, you should be able to edge out far enough to get the useful stuff on the floor, without getting into the turrets' line of fire. When you want to leave, there are two options: run like hell or fight it out. If you run straight for the ladder, you should be able to escape with only a few scratches, as the turrets aren't too good at hitting a moving target. This method, however, makes it difficult to ever come back here and charge anything else, should you want to. Fighting should be done carefully; edge slowly around the corner until you can just see the edge of the turret, but the turret can't shoot you. Armor-piercing ammo is the most efficient weapon against turrets (that you have access to at this time, anyway). After the turrets are dead, search their "corpses" – they may have some "left over" bullets.

Now that you have the battery, head back to the door into the Medical Sector and put it in the power override box. This will open the door, and Polito will send you some cyber modules in congratulation for your accomplishment. You may wish to go back to the upgrade units to spend some modules before proceeding on to the Medical Sector. When you're ready, enter the bulkhead to Medical and press the button.

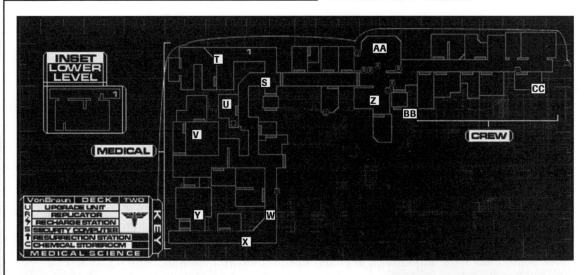

MEDICAL SECTOR

(S) When you arrive in the Medical Sector, you're right next to the door to the Crew Sector, but you don't have an access card for it. Polito reminds you that a fellow named Grassi should have a Crew card, and he's in the Biopsy area. Let's start looking for that area by going straight ahead.

(T) The corridor turns left quite soon, and splits into an upper and a lower level. We'll stay on the upper level for now, but first we'll have to deal with a Hybrid who patrols

POLITO 12.JUL.14 RE: WATTS' ACCESS CARD

Good, you've managed to get into Med. Now find Grassi and get the keycard to the crew sector. He's the one who monitored your cryo-sleep, so he might be interested in joining you ... if he hasn't been butchered yet.

this area, and has probably seen us by now. At the end of the hall, you'll find a lab containing a lot of dead Monkeys inside of force cages. In this area, you'll also find a "research soft," a log talking about these Monkeys, and a surgical unit activation key. This is a very useful item, that can convert an incomplete surgical unit into a fully-working one, which can fully heal you for a mere 5 nanites. You could install it in the nearby surgical unit, but it would be wiser to save it for later.

On your way out of this room, you may notice a ledge with some nanites on it, across a gap in the floor. You can jump across and get them without too much trouble, or use the psi power Kinetic Redirection to get them.

Head back to the ramp, and go down it. As you head down that hall, you'll see a turret at the end of it – better jump through the nearby door before it starts firing at you. There's a bunch of useful stuff in this room, including a fully functional Surgical Unit (that's why you didn't need to waste that Activation Key). At the far end of the room, there are some live Monkeys inside glass cages. If you get too close, they'll shatter the glass and attack you, so be ready for a fight! When you're ready to leave, either kill the turret, or run out fast enough that it can't harm you too much.

(U) Nobody named Grassi here, so continue down the hall. The first door on the right leads to a very useful little room. It contains both the bio-reconstruction machine for this area *and* a complete and functioning surgical unit (so you can be conveniently fully healed after being reconstructed). After using both machines, head back into the hall and turn right to continue.

As you walk down the hall, you should hear a security camera nearby. Ignore the door on your left for now, and edge carefully towards the sound of the camera, so you can take it out before it sees you. As soon as you've done this, head back to the door you just passed; there's a Hybrid in there, who has probably been alerted by the sound of you shooting the camera. There are also a number of Monkeys in the area who may be attracted by the sounds of combat, and will have to be dealt with as they appear.

Head back down the corridor towards where the camera was, but turn right before you get there. As you head down this hall, you'll see another apparition. There's a small room off to the left, with a few nanites and a log in it.

(V) At the end of this hall, on the right, is the entrance to a radiation lab. You can explore this area (there's some good stuff in here), but be quick about it, as the radiation will do more damage the longer you stay in here. You can use anti-radiation hypos by hitting the P key. This will reduce your current level of radiation, but as long as you're still being radiated, it will quickly build back up. The entrance area to this room is a decontamination shower, so when you leave all radiation will be cleaned from your system.

(W) So, still no Biopsy lab. Head back to the camera, and take the corridor leading past it. This leads past the ICU lab, which is also heavily radiated. There is a small amount of loot and an interesting log in there, but nothing absolutely vital, so only search here if you have rad hypos to spare.

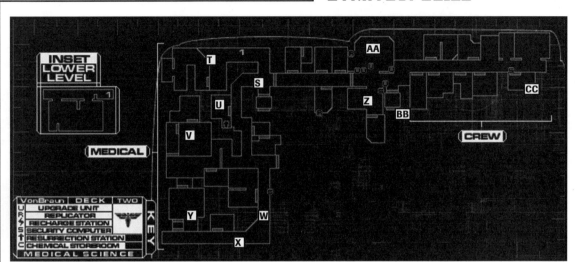

(X) Continuing down the corridor, you'll approach a corner. Right about now, you'll get ambushed by two Hybrids. These are tougher than those you've met so far, and wield shotguns instead of pipes, so they're much more dangerous. Be ready for a tough fight here, and consider heading back to the Surgical Unit to heal up afterwards. The shotguns carried by these Hybrids always seem to be in extremely poor condition. If you have decent Repair skills, though, you can return them to normal working order and use them yourself. Even if you can't do that, unloading the ammo they contain may come in handy for when you do find a working shotgun (assuming you have a Standard Weapons skill of at least 3, which is required to wield a shotgun).

Just around the corner, there's a small closet on the right. Among the things inside, you'll find a suit of light combat armor. If you have a strength of 2, you can wear it, and it will protect you from 20% of combat damage. If you've only got one point of strength, you should strongly consider getting at least one more, if only to wear this armor. It won't cost many cyber modules to go from strength 1 to 2.

Continuing right down this hallway, you'll come upon a turret at the end of the hall – right next to a sign saying "Biopsy". Either run past the turret as quickly as you can, or take cover behind the nearby pillar and carefully take it out with sniper tactics, or (if you're a hacker) retreat to a nearby security computer and hack it to temporarily disable the turret (and other security systems).

> What is a drop of rain compared to the storm? What is a thought compared to a mind? What is a day compared to a life? Our unity is full of wonder which your tiny individualism cannot even conceive.

(Y) When you enter the Biopsy lab, you'll find a Monkey and a security camera. You probably want to shoot the camera first, to avoid setting off the alarm, even if it means the Monkey gets an extra hit or two on you while you do. After dealing with the immediate threats, search the Biopsy lab, including the upper and lower areas accessible by ladder. You should find a fair amount of useful items, a log, and the keycard for the Crew Sector. Polito will send you some cyber modules when you find the Crew card.

CREW SECTOR

(S) Head back to the door to the Crew Sector and go in. Search all the rooms in the first corridor, there are a variety of interesting and useful things to be found. A Hybrid patrols this area, so be ready for a fight.

> **POLITO 12.JUL.14 RE: KEYCARD TO R&D**
>
> Good, you've made it into the crew sector. Now find Dr. Watts' room ...

> **TURNBULL 07.JUL.14 RE: PROCEDURES**
>
> Goddamn Bronson and her stupid procedures. She's changed the code on the MedSci 2 sub armory again. Now I've got to head back up to deck 4 to find out what it is ... Somebody's gonna frag her but good some day ...

(Z) Beyond the first corridor, turn right into a security station. There's a security computer here, and a door locked with a keypad. There's also a log complaining that the code to this door (which is apparently an armory) has been changed, and that it may be found up on Deck 4. Now you have another motive to reach Deck 4!

(AA) Leaving the security station, head directly across the hall into the crew lounge. There are upgrade units and a replicator here, so you can spend cyber modules and nanites if you want. An earlier log you should have read described this replicator as being "a hacker's paradise." If you try to hack it, you'll find it easier than average to get past its security.

When you leave this room, you'll notice a machine next to the security station that looks somewhat like an upgrade unit, only different. This is an OS upgrade unit. This will give you a special bonus ability that can be very useful. Each such machine can only be used once, however, and they are few and far between, so choose your OS upgrades with special care.

(BB) As you continue down the hall, you'll see a bulkhead on your right. This leads back into the Science Sector, but you don't want to use it until we've found Dr. Watts. So keep going further into the Crew Sector.

> **POLITO 12.JUL.14 RE: R&D CARD**
>
> Watts isn't here, so he's probably in his office in the R&D sector. Maybe he's got a backup R&D card in here. Take a look around.

In this end of the Crew Sector, two more Hybrids are patrolling, one with a pipe, one with a shotgun. There are lots of interesting things to be found in the various rooms off this hall, so search carefully. If you have the Kinetic Redirection psi power, remember to keep looking up for things that you can pull to you with that power.

(CC) At the end of the hall, you'll find Dr. Watts' room on the right. He's not there, but you can find a backup R&D card in his desk, so maybe you can find him in his office there. Sounds like it's time to head back to the bulkhead to the Science Sector ....

SCIENCE SECTOR, PART TWO

(DD) As you come out of the bulkhead, there will be a camera in front of you — take it out before the alarm goes off. There's some useful stuff down the hallway past the camera, but it's guarded by a turret, so don't go there unless you're prepared to deal with that.

(P) Head over to the door to the R&D Sector. At this point, there are likely to be Hybrids wandering around who have come down to replace some of the ones you've killed, so stay alert.

RESEARCH & DEVELOPMENT SECTOR

Proceed through R&D. As you head down it's corridors, you'll get an email from Polito telling you that she's found out Dr. Watts is in his office, and is still alive, but badly wounded. Hurry down the hall towards his office, being careful to deal with any cameras along the way.

> **POLITO 12.JUL.14 RE: FIND DR. WATTS**
>
> Dr. Watts is alive and in his office. He should know the code to the maintenance access shaft. Hurry ... he's been badly wounded. Don't let him die before he tells you that number!

(EE) When you reach his office, you'll find a Hybrid wandering around who will have to be killed. After that, you can find Dr. Watts lying on a surgical unit in a back corner. He lives just long enough to croak out an obscure warning, and then dies — without telling you the code to the shaft, that bastard! Luckily, there is a log on his body that contains the code after all. *Un*luckily, a pair of shotgun-Hybrids run in at this point to try and prevent your escape. Assuming you survive your encounter with them, leave the R&D Sector, being careful to search for useful loot along your way.

> **WATTS 07.JUL.14 RE: MAINTENANCE CONDUIT TO: CURTIZ, JUAN**
>
> All right, calm down already ... the access code to the conduit is 12451. I've got an autopsy at 1630, but let's grab a beer on the Recreation Deck afterwards. Sound good?

SCIENCE SECTOR, PART THREE

(FF) Remember that big robot you saw inside the room with the Maintenance access shaft? He's still around, so be prepared to deal with him. Remember, AP ammo works best against robots.

Once the shaft is open and the robot is dealt with, you're almost ready to head down to Engineering. However, before you leave this deck, it would be a good idea to go back to the training area and spend your cyber modules. Who knows when you'll get your next chance? If you took a lot of damage in recent fights, you may also want to return to Dr. Watts' office, as he has a fully working Surgical Unit in there. If you're low on ammo, but have a lot of nanites, you may want to visit one or both of the replicators on this level. If you found anything to research that needed chemicals, you might want to stop by the Chemical Storeroom. When you're all set, climb down the ladder to Engineering.

> **POLITO 12.JUL.14 RE: ACCESS TO DECK 1**
>
> Do not waste time patting yourself on the back. Get down to that shaft to Engineering and reset the primary react or core. That will restore power to the elevator and you will be able to get up to deck 4. Get going!

MATERIEL AVAILABLE

On MedSci Map 1 (A – R, DD – FF)

Cyber Modules

- 4 (Polito: going through airlock)
- 4 (body near upgrade units)
- 4 (Polito: going through Science door)
- 2 (body in pump station)
- 4 (Polito: opening Medical door)
- 4 (Polito: opening R&D door)
- 6 (Polito: opening Maintenance access shaft door)

Nanites

- 20 (crate past airlock)
- 5 (body past airlock)
- 5 (crate past upgrade units)
- 20 (body in upper training area)
- 20 (on floor by Science door)
- 21 (security crate in security station)
- 20 (among crates near Xerxes core)
- 10 (near body in pump station)
- 11 (security crate in Specimen Analysis Area)
- 20 (waste barrel in lowered area near R&D door)
- 44 (security crate in lowered area near R&D door)

> **DIEGO 17.MAR.14 RE: YANKING MY CHAIN TO: KORENCHKIN, ANATOLY**
>
> Anatoly, there's only so much corporate calisthenics I can go through before I start to feel a little queasy, so let's get down to brass tacks here. We don't like each other. We each have our own motivations for undertaking this mission, so let me give you a little warning. I cannot be circumvented, I cannot be tricked, I cannot be manipulated, and I cannot be bought. You come at me straight and keep the fancy maneuvers for your next board meeting. Just because my father swam with the sharks doesn't mean that I do.

Weapons/Ammo

Wrench (body in opening area)

Wrench (by airlock door)

Pistol [8 standard bullets; condition 7] (body by Xerxes Core)

Pistol [7 standard bullets; condition 5] (body in chemical closet)

Pistol [1 standard bullet; condition 1] (by body in Watts' lab)

6 Standard bullets (on girders in training area)

6 Standard bullets (security crate in security station)

6 Standard bullets (replicator by Xerxes core; 60 nanites unhacked /45 nanites hacked)

6 Standard bullets (near turret near crew door)

6 Standard bullets (replicator by R&D door; 60 nanites unhacked /45 nanites hacked)

6 Standard bullets (on ledge in R&D hallway)

12 Standard bullets (replicator by Xerxes core; 100 nanites unhacked /75 nanites hacked)

12 Standard Bullets (crate in chemical closet)

6 Armor piercing bullets (near turret near crew door)

6 Armor piercing bullets (on girder near turret near crew door)

6 Armor piercing bullets (body over pump station)

6 Armor piercing bullets (body in Watts' lab)

Shotgun [6 rifled drugs; condition 5] (body over room w/recharger)

6 Rifled slugs (behind window in upper training area)

6 Anti-Personnel shotgun pellets (crate near recharger in R&D)

Psi amp (body in upper training area)

Armor

Hypos

2 Anti-radiation hypos (medical reception area, counter and ledge)

Anti-radiation hypo (security crate in Specimen Analysis Area)

Anti-radiation hypo (replicator by R&D door; 25 nanites hacked)

3 Anti-toxin hypos (desk in Specimen Analysis Area)

Anti-toxin hypo (replicator by R&D door; 35 nanites unhacked /25 nanites hacked)

Medical hypo (body past upgrade units)

Medical hypo (body bag in morgue)

Medical hypo (replicator by Xerxes core; 30 nanites unhacked /20 nanites hacked)

**KORENCHKIN
14.JUN.14 RE:
FIRST CONTACT
TO: ZHUKOV, VLADIMIR**

We have picked up a transmission from the surface of Tau Ceti 5. I have been in negotiation with Captain Diego of the Rickenbacker and after some ... coercion, he's agreed to go planetside as a joint venture. Imagine, this historic mission might even become more historic. First Contact. And who is there to get exclusive rights to all media, patents and land grants? TriOptimum. Miri, I told you this would be worth it.

Medical hypo (body in pump station)

Medical hypo (security crate in specimen analysis area)

Medical hypo (body bag in hall by specimen analysis area)

Medical hypo (under duct in specimen analysis area)

Medical hypo (floor of Watts' lab)

Psi hypo (behind glass in upper training area)

Psi hypo (body bag in morgue)

Psi hypo (on crate in pump station)

Psi hypo (replicator by R&D door; 75 nanites unhacked /50 nanites hacked)

2 Speed boosters (security closet past upgrade units)

Speed booster (on girders in training area)

Speed booster (body in R&D hall)

Strength booster (near turret near crew door)

Implants

BrawnBoost (security closet past upgrade units)

Software

Research v1 (body in hall by specimen analysis area)

Access Cards

Cryogenics Sector (opening area, under a table)

Science Sector (by body in upper training area)

Logs

Amanpour 7.Jul "New code" (body in opening area)

Grassi 7.Jul "Implant job" (on crate past trainers)

Delacroix 4.Apr "Xerxes" (desk in security station)

Curtiz 6.Jul "Coolant leaks" (counter of medical reception area)

Grassi 20.Jun "All work, no play" (floor of morgue)

Curtiz 7.Jul "More trouble" (on bench near Xerxes core)

Chemical Manifest Log (in chemical storeroom)

Grassi 26.Jun "Animal rights?" (desk in Specimen Analysis Area)

Delacroix 8.Jul "Not ready" (on gurney near R&D door)

Diego 17.Mar "Yanking my chain" (counter near recharger in R&D)

Watts 7.Jul "Maintenance conduit" (body in Watts' office)

Watts 7.Jul "Watson autopsy" (body in Watts' office)

**SUAREZ 20.JUN.14 RE: 100% TORTURE
TO: SIDDONS, REBECCA**

Wow ... you are incredible, do you know that? I made this game where I tried to make myself not think about you. What a moron. I love you, Rebecca. And I've got a plan. I've been buttering up the captain to transfer me from the Rickenbacker to the goodwill team on the Von Braun. Pretty soon, nothing will keep us apart.

**POLITO 25.JUN.14 RE: STRANGE AI
TO: DELACROIX, DR. MARIE**

Marie ... I'm sorry I've been out of touch, but I've been working on that artifact Bayliss brought back from Tau Ceti 5. I've done a level 3 analysis on it ... I think it's some kind of Artificial Intelligence. I've managed to pull an audio tag file out of its memory ... I'll let you be the judge ... Marie ... I think it's speaking English ...

Chemicals (all in Chemical Storeroom)

2 Antimony

Barium

2 Californium

2 Fermium

Gallium

2 Iridium

Osmium

Technetium

2 Tellurium

2 Yttrium

Miscellaneous

Booze (security station closet)

Booze (floor near Xerxes core)

Booze (floor of pump station)

Chips (security station closet)

Chips (replicator by Xerxes core; 3 nanites unhacked)

Chips (replicator by R&D door; 3 nanites unhacked)

GamePig (body by medical reception area)

Juice (floor of R&D hallway)

Maintenance tool (replicator near Xerxes core; 45 nanites hacked)

Maintenance tool (body near recharger in R&D)

Maintenance tool (body near maintenance access shaft)

Swinekeeper cartridge (body by medical reception area)

Power cell (by airlock door)

Power cell (medical reception area)

**WATTS 30.JUN.14 RE: NONSENSE
TO: LOESSER, ANGELA**

Angela, while it may appear that the lab monkeys are communicating with each other, I assure you it's quite impossible. You claim that one monkey signed the passcode for a supply closet to another and the latter proceeded to open it. As I'm sure you know, there have literally been tens of thousands of studies of primate intelligence and there is no evidence of behavior even remotely that sophisticated. So either you've single-handedly trumped the entire field of animal behaviorists or you're badly in need of a vacation.

WATTS 01.JUL.14 RE: PATIENT WATSON

Since returning from the Surface of Tau Ceti 5, patient has experienced numerous novel phenomena, evidenced by inflammatory nodular growth and the presence of a large wormlike parasite. This morning, the parasite penetrated the subject's chest ... from the inside ... and attached one end of itself to the subject's forehead. If I remove it, I could kill the kid. If I leave it ... [sigh] Final Diagnosis: beats the hell out me. I'd love to refer this to Madorsky at CDC, but unfortunately, he's 67 trillion miles away.

On MedSci Map 2 (S – CC)

Cyber Modules

2 (body in lower primate lab)

2 (body in radiation lab)

5 (Polito: finding Crew card)

5 (Polito: finding R&D card)

4 (body above room across from Watts' quarters)

Nanites

10 (ledge above primate lab)

17 (desk by bio-reconstruction station)

23 (security crate in ICU)

7 (body in small room near radiation lab)

26 (crate in radiation lab)

20 (crate in upper biopsy lab)

26 (security crate in upper biopsy lab)

20 (girder above east crew corridor)

20 (above room across from Watts' quarters)

10 (body in east lower crew quarters)

Weapons/Ammo

Pistol [5 standard bullets; condition 3] (security crate in upper biopsy lab)

Pistol [3 standard bullets; condition 1] (ledge over east crew corridor)

6 Standard bullets (security crate in closet by bio-reconstruction station)

6 Standard bullets (west crew quarters)

6 Standard bullets (body east lower crew corridor)

12 Anti-Personnel Bullets (crate in armory)

Shotgun [no ammo; Condition 4] (near body above room across from Watts')

6 Rifled slugs (desk in west crew quarters)

6 Rifled slugs (replicator in small bar in west crew quarters; 80 nanites unhacked /60 nanites hacked)

Assault Rifle [4 standard bullets; Condition 6] (armory)

EMP Rifle [20 charges; condition 8] (armory)

Grenade Launcher [2 fragmentation grenades; condition 2; broken] (under small bar in west crew quarters)

3 Fragmentation grenades (replicator in small bar in west crew quarters; 100 nanites unhacked /75 nanites hacked)

3 Fragmentation grenades (armory)

> **WATTS 07.JUL.14 RE: PATIENT WATSON, PT. 2**
>
> Patient Watson died at 0240 of non-specific causes. Despite zero respiratory and brain function, the body is still displaying autonomous motor function, as does the parasite. At 0847, the patient even spoke to one of the nurses. Autopsy is set for 1630 and then we'll see what makes this Lazarus tick ...

> **WATTS 07.JUL.14 RE: WATSON AUTOPSY**
>
> The time is 1630. Autopsy subject: A. Watson. Now we're going to make the first incision in ...[hear rustling noise] hold him down nurse! Nurse! Hold him down! Aahhh!!! Hey! AAAHHH!!!

Weapons/Ammo (cont.)

3 Proximity grenades (desk in security closet)

Stasis field generator [no ammo; Condition 3] (armory)

Psi amp (body in lower primate lab)

Psi amp (desk in east lower crew quarters)

Armor

Light combat armor (body in closet near biopsy lab)

Light combat armor (security closet)

Medium combat armor (armory)

Hypos

Anti-radiation hypo (security crate in ICU)

Anti-radiation hypo (counter in radiation lab)

Anti-radiation hypo (crate in radiation lab)

Anti-radiation hypo (replicator in crew lounge; 35 nanites unhacked /25 nanites hacked)

Anti-radiation hypo (security crate in security closet)

Anti-toxin hypo (replicator in crew lounge; 25 nanites hacked)

2 Medical hypos (crates in lower primate lab)

Medical hypo (body in closet near bio-reconstruction station)

Medical hypo (desk in biopsy lab)

Medical hypo (counter in lower biopsy lab)

Medical kit (security closet)

2 Medical kits (crate in armory)

Psi hypo (desk in lower primate lab)

Psi hypo (security crate in ICU)

Psi hypo (crate in closet near Biopsy)

Psi hypo (crate in upper Biopsy)

Psi hypo (replicator in small bar in west crew quarters; 75 nanites unhacked /50 nanites hacked)

Psi hypo (desk in east lower crew quarters)

Implants

BrawnBoost (waste barrel in bathroom east lower crew quarters)

CURTIZ 07.JUL.14 RE: MORE TROUBLE

I've been unable to get in touch with Delacroix ... this place is falling apart ... members of my team keep disappearing. The leaks in the venting shafts shorted out the primary access channel ... and that means we'll all be on auxiliary power until we can get it back up. That means ALL the lifts are out ... Marie, where the hell are you?

CURTIZ 07.JUL.14 RE: LIFTS ARE OUT

I can't raise anybody down in Engineering. With the lifts out, I'll need to get down there through the emergency conduit in the Sci Annex. I think the access code is in Watts' lab.

Software

Hack v1 (replicator in crew lounge; 35 nanites unhacked /25 nanites hacked)

Research v1 (desk in upper primate lab)

Research v1 (body in closet near biopsy lab)

Research v1 (replicator in small bar in west crew quarters; 25 nanites hacked)

Access Cards

Crew card (body in lower biopsy lab)

Research & Development card (desk in Watts' quarters)

Logs

Watts 30.Jun "Nonsense" (desk in upper primate lab)

Curtiz 7.Jul "Lifts are out" (on desk in lower primate lab)

Watts 1.Jul "Patient Watson" (floor in ICU)

Grassi 12.May "Damn Chimps" (small room near radiation lab)

Curtiz 2.Jul "Rad Hypos" (counter in radiation lab)

Watts 7.Jul "Patient Watson, pt. 2" (lower biopsy lab)

Korenchkin 14.Jun "First contact" (desk in west crew quarters)

Turnbull 7.Jul "Procedures" (security station)

Polito 25.Jun "Strange AI" (on desk in east lower crew quarters)

Suarez 20.Jun "100% Torture" (on bench in east lower crew quarters)

Chemicals

Miscellaneous

Booze (floor of small room near radiation lab)

3 Booze (small bar in west crew quarters)

5 Booze (crew lounge)

2 Booze (armory)

Booze (security closet)

2 Chips (small bar in west crew quarters)

3 Chips (upper east crew quarters)

GamePig (desk in Watts' quarters)

Juice (Crew Lounge)

Juice (replicator in crew lounge; 4 nanites unhacked)

Maintenance tool (replicator in crew lounge; 60 nanites unhacked /45 nanites hacked)

2 Portable batteries (crate in armory)

6 Soda (small bar in west crew quarters)

Surgical unit activation key (floor of upper primate lab)

DELACROIX 08.JUL.14
RE: NOT READY
TO: KORENCHKIN, ANATOLY

This mission should have been scrubbed before it left Earth. We've been unable to contain the reactant coolant leaks on deck 1. I've put an order requiring Hazard Suits down there. I know you think this will cause a panic, but it's better than giving everybody radiation sickness, don't you think?

ENGINEERING

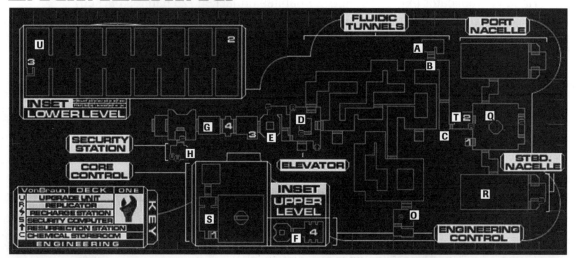

COOLANT TUNNELS, PART ONE

(A) When you first arrive on the Engineering Deck, you'll get email from Polito telling you to go to the Engine Core to get main power back online. Do search the opening few rooms though … there's useful stuff here.

POLITO 12.JUL.14 RE: PROTECTIVE SEALS

The radiation must have locked the protective seals on Engine Core access. You're going to have to find some way to purge the radiation from the coolant tubes. Xerxes is blocking me out of the primary data loop, so I can't get any information to help you. He's working for them now.

(B) As soon as you leave the opening area, you'll be in the coolant tunnels, which are suffering from radiation leaks (but not every tunnel is radiated). Watch the radiation meter on your screen; when the radiation icon dims, that means you are not currently absorbing more radiation, which means it's a safe place to stop and take a rad hypo. Alternatively, just run through the radiated areas as fast as possible. You'll take some radiation damage doing that, but unless you get stuck in combat in a radiated area, it probably won't kill you.

POLITO 12.JUL.14 RE: RESET THE CORE

You're now on the engineering deck. Find the engine core and reset it. This will restore power to the elevators. I'm getting some kind of strange readings from down there, so keep your eyes open.

(C) As you enter the tunnels, you'll see some signs on the floor, one of which points to the Engine Core. Xerxes makes an announcement that the Engine Core is off limits, but by now it's become clear that Xerxes can't be trusted, so keep going. There is a Hybrid in this hall, so watch out. When you get to the Engine Core door and try to open it, nothing happens. Polito will send you email, explaining that the radiation leaks have locked automatic protective seals on the door. Before you can open it, you'll have to flush the radiation. Too bad you don't (yet) know how to do that. Better read any logs you come across and hope to find a clue.

POLITO 12.JUL.14 RE: PURGING THE TUBES

Keep your eyes open … you must find a way to purge these coolant tubes and get into the engine core … The ship must have some kind of backup system in place for just this kind of situation.

Continue through the coolant tunnels. Follow the left-hand fork at any junctions, to keep from getting lost. Keep an eye out for wandering Hybrids, who will be a mix of pipe and shotgun-wielding. You should find two storage areas locked with keypads. Polito will send you the code to one (she's stockpiled some useful goodies there), but the other remains a mystery for now. If you keep following the left wall, you'll eventually emerge from the coolant tunnels, without having gone through too much radiation.

> **POLITO 12.JUL.14 RE: UTILITY STORAGE 4**
>
> You must move faster. Your mind cannot conceive of the stakes we are dealing with. Keep your eyes open for utility storage 4. I've laid in some supplies there, the passcode is 59004.

PUMP STATION

> We do not know death, only change. We cannot kill each other without killing ourselves. Is your vision so small that you cannot see the value of our way?

(D) When you come out, you'll be in a large square room, with a smaller square room inside it. This area contains a bio-reconstruction machine and a replicator. It *also* contains a Security Camera, and a Protocol Droid. This is the first Protocol Droid that you will see on the Von Braun. They are designed to offer helpful assistance to all crewmembers. Sadly, as you will shortly discover, someone has reprogrammed them to "help" in the form of overloading their internal power plants and exploding messily, preferably while right next to you to inflict maximum damage. Luckily, they're pretty fragile; one or two AP shots should take one out.

> **CURTIZ 07.JUL.14 RE: THAT LEAK AGAIN**
>
> Delacroix was right, this ship was NOT ready for prime time. Ok, the automatic safety seals have shut due to the radiation leak in the tubes. I'm gonna head down to engineering control ... I think I can use the fluidics monitoring computer to purge the tubes.that will keep me going long enough to figure a way past that damn turret ... Who is that? Delacroix? Sanger?

Once the enemies in here are dealt with, you may want to explore the center room (the Pump Station proper). It contains some goodies and a security computer, but also a Monkey, so be careful.

ENGINEERING CORRIDOR A, PART ONE

(E) When you're ready to go on, leave by the door that doesn't reenter the coolant tunnels. This will take you past the Xerxes core to the main Engineering Corridor. Expect to meet some Hybrids and Cameras along the way. If you have Kinetic Redirection, look up when you're near the Xerxes core; you'll see some nanites perched on a high ledge above you.

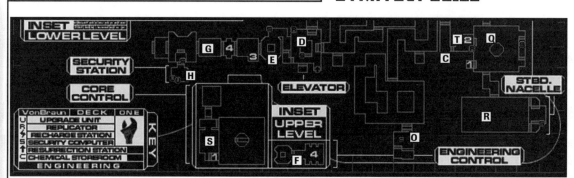

(F) A short way down the Engineering Corridor you'll find some grav shafts labeled "Engineering Control." By now you should have found a log suggesting that the radiation can be flushed by using the Fluidics Computer in Engineering Control; head up there. Unfortunately, when you get there, the door is locked (with a keypad), and you don't know the code to get in. An engineer named Sanger left a log by the door, however. It says that she recoded the lock, then went to hide in Cargo Bay 2. Sounds like that should be our next stop.

> ### SANGER 10.JUL.14 RE: LOCKING ENG. CONTROL
>
> God, get me out of here. I've re-coded the lock to this room. Maybe that will hold them. I'm heading to cargo bay 2, come find me there.

> ### BRONSON 06.JUL.14 RE: TURRET PROBLEMS
>
> Due to the tenuous situation as of late, I've ordered security defense Turrets placed at key locations. Yesterday, one went off accidentally and critically injured crewman Wells. However, somebody must have tampered with the Xerxes security sub-systems because now my technicians are unable to take them off line. Until we get to the bottom of this, I've ordered all Security Turrets recalled to storage … but now I can't get in touch with the team I sent out to do the recall.

(G) As you continue down the Engineering Corridor, you'll run into some Turrets and Cameras, and probably some wandering creatures as well. This area can be pretty deadly, so extra care is required. Hacking security before going further down this hall is highly recommended. If you've boosted your Hack skill to at least 4, then after Hacking security you can Hack any Turrets you come across! Once hacked, a Turret will shoot your foes instead of you (but be careful not to step into its line of fire; it's not very discriminating).

(H) In a heavily guarded area, you'll find (once the guards are dealt with) a body with a Security access card, allowing you into the neighboring security station. There are some useful goodies in here, including another mysterious object to research, and a pair of upgrade units (Weapons and Psi). There is also an incomplete surgical unit in here. As this is the first one you've seen in quite a while, this seems like an excellent place to use that surgical unit activation key that you've been saving up.

When you leave the security station, there will probably be some wandering creatures outside (unless you hacked some Turrets, in which case you might just find some new corpses). After they're dealt with, you're pretty much done with this sublevel for now, so proceed through the bulkhead to Engineering B.

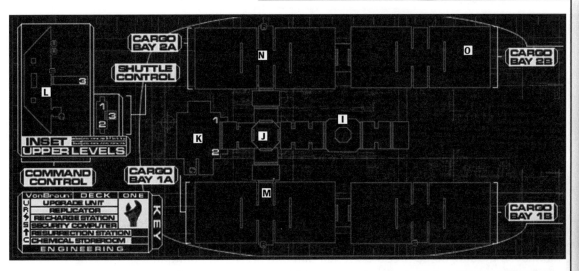

ENGINEERING CORRIDOR B, PART ONE

(I) Continue down the Engineering Corridor. Hey, wait a minute, the screen's going white, what's going on! ...

Well, wasn't *that* interesting? That offer didn't sound too appealing, so let's continue on. We should probably save the game here, though, since we haven't yet found a bio-reconstruction station.

(J) You'll probably find a Monkey in the next corridor section, and a Camera in the section just beyond that. The Camera is in a crossroads, with signs pointing back the way you came (Engine Core) and to Cargo Bay 1, Cargo Bay 2, and Shuttle Bay. We want to go to Cargo Bay 2. Sadly, after a short trip down that corridor, there's a locked door that you don't have the keycard for.

Do you not trust the feelings in the flesh? Our biology yearns to join with yours. We welcome you to our mass. But you puzzle us ... why do you serve our mother?

How can you choose cold metal over the splendor of flesh? But you fear us ... We hear your thoughts, and they rage for your brothers you believe dead. But they are not ... they sing in our symphony of life.

We offer another chance to join us. If you choose to lie down with the machine, we will rend you apart and put you separate from the joy of the mass.

SHUTTLE BAY, PART ONE

Well, first, let's try corridor leading to the Shuttle Bay. There are a lot of explosive barrels here. You may want to shoot them from a safe distance; otherwise, if there's a firefight in here, one might go off next to you ....

(K) Beyond the next set of doors is the Shuttle Bay. Inside are (among other things) a lot of explosive barrels and a Laser Turret. The Laser Turret is pretty nasty, but if you shoot one of the barrels (and back away quickly!), a chain reaction of barrel explosions will reach as far as the Turret. While they won't completely destroy it, they'll damage it to the point where one AP round or two standard rounds should finish it off. Be careful, though, as Laser Turrets dish out damage very quickly.

The Shuttle Bay also contains a Shotgun Hybrid. If your timing is impeccable, you may be able to kill the Turret while he's standing next to it, killing him as well. This is a tricky maneuver, though, so be prepared to kill him in a conventional fight.

Even after he's down, you're still not done. At the right of the Shuttle Bay, there are some high storage shelves. A Monkey is on the top one, and when you move into view, he'll start shooting at you. There is also a Pipe Hybrid in a storage area below the Shuttle Bay, but he is much less of a threat, and can be dealt with at leisure, sniper-style.

Once you've dealt with the enemies in here, search the Shuttle Bay for its various goodies. A lot of the objects in the crates may seem like junk, but really aren't, especially if you've taken a lot of damage in the preceding fights. Soda and chips will each give you back one hit point when eaten. Liquor will also give you back a hit point, but at the cost of four psi points, so psionic characters shouldn't indulge any alcoholic tendencies. There's also a recharge station in the back of the Shuttle Bay, so if you've acquired any powered implants, weapons, or armor, you should visit that.

(L) Now, head up the grav shaft to Shuttle Control. There's not much to see here, so take the lift up to Command Control. In the corridor just past the lift, you'll see another apparition, this one apparently committing suicide to avoid becoming a Hybrid. Inside Command Control are a Camera and two Hybrids (one of whom is tossing around a severed head – playing catch?). Once they're dealt with, you'll find a bio-reconstruction station, two upgrade units (stats and tech), and some complicated machinery with no immediately obvious purpose. All well and good, but the access card for Cargo Bay 2 isn't here. Time to head on, maybe the card's in Cargo Bay 1.

> **DIEGO 11.JUL.14 RE: RESIST THE CALL**
>
> My duty is to the UNN and to this ship. But can I resist the call of the Many? My father's weakness brought SHODAN into existence. MY weakness has invited these things aboard the Von Braun ... can I undo the wrong I have done?

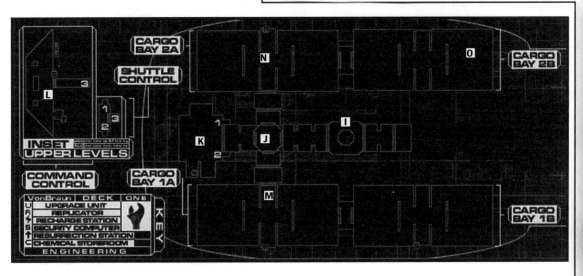

CARGO BAY 1

(M) Cargo Bay 1 also has a keycard lock, but it looks like someone broke into it a while back and left the door open. The bays each consist of four large areas, with three floors each. Each room is connected to the others at the "ground" floor only. Cargo lifts travel between the floors.

Just across from the entrance to the Cargo Bay is a replicator, which might come in handy. Be careful before buying things from it, though. There's a Maintenance Bot patrolling in this area, and it wouldn't do for it to come up behind you while you're shopping!

Cargo Bay 1A seems to mostly contain Protocol Droid storage crates. Sometimes these crates will open, releasing Protocol Droids to pester you. Sadly, although it is possible to destroy these crates, there is little profit in it, as that just tends to release the Protocol Droids prematurely. Don't spend ammo on them. Just stay prepared to run, and keep AP ammo loaded in your gun.

If you turn right as you enter Cargo Bay 1A, you'll enter a room with many Protocol Droid crates, and a body on the floor. That body has the access card to Cargo Bay 2. Once you pick it up, several Protocol Droids will come after you, so be prepared.

Once you have this card, you can either proceed to Cargo Bay 2, or continue to explore Cargo Bay 1. There are a lot of goodies in each of the bays, but many monsters as well, so it's up to you. As previously noted, Bay 1A contains mostly Protocol Droids. Bay 1B mostly contains Monkeys. A thorough exploration of both Cargo Bays would get you 11 cyber modules, over 100 nanites (more if you can hack into security crates), a SwiftBoost™ implant, a surgical unit activation key, plus an assortment of general ammunition, weapons, and hypos.

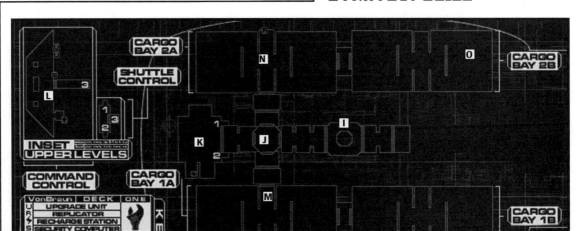

CARGO BAY 2

(N) As you enter Cargo Bay 2, you'll see a replicator across from you. This replicator is broken, but it's not beyond hope, however; if you have Repair skill of at least 3, you can put it back in working order.

(O) The code to Engineering Control can be found at the very back of Cargo Bay 2, on the top level. If you're in a hurry, don't bother going up any of the Cargo Lifts until you get to the rear room of Cargo Bay 2. This Cargo Bay contains mostly Hybrids, though there are also some Laser Turrets and Maintenance Bots that you'll have to get past (mostly in Cargo Bay 2B).

Be careful around the cargo lifts in Cargo Bay 2; some of them aren't working properly. One of them (currently on the third level) falls off its rails if you step on it. This one is slightly tilted, so you should be able to avoid it. Another lift is completely (and obviously) broken. This one has a more subtle "trap" — If you push one of the buttons controlling this lift, a Maintenance Bot is summoned!

Naturally, the code you need is at the very back of the cargo bay, on the top level, in the most inconvenient place to reach. Near that log, you will also find a French-Epstein Device, which can perform any one weapon modification for free. It's a single-use device, so don't use it on a weapon you think you'll end up discarding. Also in this immediate area is a Laser Pistol. This is the basic energy weapon, requiring only a skill of 1 to use. Sadly, this one is broken, but if you have a few points of Repair skill, you can return it to working order. Having gotten the code, return to Engineering Sector A, watching out for wandering creatures along the way.

> ## BRONSON 06.JUL.14 RE: HACKING TURRETS
>
> Well, we can't get the malfunctioning Turrets off line and now Xerxes isn't even talking to us. Pollard thought of a workaround. By running bypass into central control, we can hack into the Turrets locally and take control of them. However, that means walking right up to the little sons of bitches and hoping they don't go off. One thing is sure ... I'm going to figure out what the hell happened here.

> ## SANGER 10.JUL.14 RE: LOCKED IN
>
> Malone's dead. I was just talking to him and this ... cyborg came up behind him and ... Okay, Connie, get a grip. Get a grip. I've re-coded the door lock in engineering control to 15061. I think I'll be safe in here. I'll be safe in here.

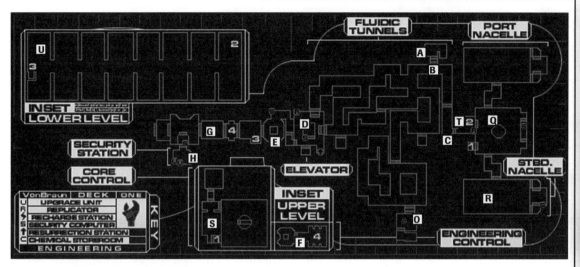

ENGINEERING CORRIDOR A, PART TWO

(F) When you arrive back on this sublevel, if you're badly wounded you may want to duck into the security station for a quick visit to the surgical unit.

After that, proceed to Engineering Control. The code works, and the door opens. Yay! Run in and right click on the Fluidics Control computer ... Nothing happens. Boo! Polito sends you email telling you that Xerxes has overridden this computer, and you'll have to find some way to get around that. Luckily for you, the log in this room has precisely the info you need.

COOLANT TUNNELS, PART TWO

(P) Your next step is to get hardware override 45m/dEx. It's in that storeroom in the coolant tunnels that you couldn't get into before, but this new log has the code. Since those tunnels are still radiated, you may want to put on a hazard suit or buy some rad hypos before going back in.

Make your way back to the storeroom (which is also the chemical storeroom), and find the part you need. There's some other useful things in a back office, guarded by a Monkey.

Having got the part, you need to go to Command Control to install it, and that's way back on the other side of the deck. Back to Engineering Sector B and through the Shuttle Bay ....

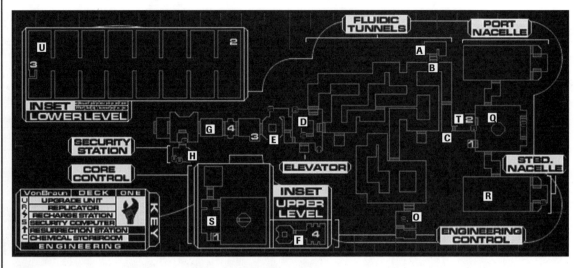

SHUTTLE BAY, PART TWO

(L) Head straight for Command Control, above the Shuttle Bay. The less time you spend wandering around yourself, the less time wandering creatures will have to find you.

When you get there, install the override as instructed. Polito will send you some cyber modules, which you might want to spend at the nearby upgrade units.

Back to Engineering Sector A, pronto ...

ENGINEERING CORRIDOR A, PART THREE

(F) Back to Engineering Control. Right click the fluidics computer again. This time, with a satisfying *whoosh*, the coolant tunnels are flushed of all harmful radiation. Now you can get into the Engine Core. Make your way back there, through the now-harmless coolant tunnels.

> ### POLITO 12.JUL.14 RE: THE ENGINE PODS
>
> Now get those engine pods online. You'll have to head into nacelle 1 and 2 and reset the pods manually. After that, reinitialize the system from core control. But that system won't come online until you reset both pods. Keep an eye out. They're mobilizing their real forces. And they know exactly where you are.

> ### MARTIN 10.JUL.14 RE: AMBUSH
>
> They hit us six hours ago. Malone, the OSA spook, tried to take one of things out with pyrokinesis attack, but it didn't even break stride. Then it unloaded both barrels into his stomach. Falzone said there's a weapons cache in one of the engine nacelles. Maybe I can find him and the others there ...

ENGINE CORE

(Q) In order to reset main power, you need to reset both engine nacelles first. They're located in control rooms on either side of the Engine Core. There are a few creatures and one Camera, but by now you should be well able to deal with them. The biggest threat is actually the Camera, since the background noise here is loud enough that the Camera's whirring is easy to miss. When you find each nacelle, just right-click on it to reset it; its lights will turn green and it will give off a sound to confirm that it's now active.

(R) In the starboard nacelle, it's worth taking a quick trip down the ladder, then going through the door into the center of the nacelle proper. As you may have read in a log, someone has hidden a small cache of weapons down there.

> **POLITO 12.JUL.14 RE: CORE ONLINE**
>
> Good work. The engine core is now back online. Now get to the elevator and come see me on deck 4. While you were doing that, I've discovered the presence of some annelid artifacts onboard the ship. I think you may be able to use them to your advantage. I've uploaded the information to the ship's weapons upgrade units. They'll be able to convey the information to your cybernetic rig. What are you waiting for? Get to the elevator now.

(S) After the two nacelles are active, take the lift up to Core Control. There's a Shotgun Hybrid up here who may attack you, so be ready. Find the master power computer and right click it. Power will be restored, and Polito will send you some more cyber modules (and nag you to get up to Deck 4). You may want to search the rest of Core Control for goodies first, but watch out for another Camera up here.

Polito also mentions in her email that she has reprogrammed the ships upgrade units so that they can teach you how to use exotic (alien) weapons. You shouldn't buy Exotic Weapons skill without also buying several points of Research, since you need to research the exotic weapons before you can use them. (Just between us, you won't find the first exotic weapon until the Operations Deck, so you don't want to buy this skill right away in any event.)

UNDERPASS

(T) When you get to the room through which you entered the Engine Core, you may have noticed a lift in the corner. It wasn't working before, but you can take it down now if you like. It leads to a "shortcut" to near the elevator, avoiding the twisting coolant tunnels. There's also some loot down there, but it's guarded by a number of monsters.

(U) One of the monsters in the shortcut tunnel is one you won't have seen before: a Cyborg Midwife. This was originally a human female, but has been heavily modified with mechanical parts, and conditioned to care for the young of the aliens that have infested the Von Braun. Midwives are tough, fast, and fire highly-damaging laser bolts at their foes. Their cyborg parts make them resistant to most normal types of ammo, but vulnerable to AP ammo. Mind you, it will still require a number of rounds to take one out of commission, so be prepared for a tough fight if you take this route.

PUMP STATION, PART TWO

(D) Whether you take the shortcut tunnel or not, you'll eventually get back to the elevator, near the Pump Station. As with the end of the MedSci Deck, you may want to take a brief break here to heal up, spend upgrade points, buy equipment from replicators, and collect research chemicals. When you're ready to go, enter the elevator and push the button for Ops (Deck 4). Hey, wait a minute! When you do that, it says the shaft is blocked! Must be something in between here and there blocking the shaft. Maybe if you go to Deck 3 (Hydroponics) you can find out what's wrong from there ....

MATERIEL AVAILABLE

On Engineering Map 1 (A – H, P – U)

Cyber Modules

2 (body near Engineering Core door)

2 (body in open storage room in coolant tunnels)

2 (body near Chemical storeroom)

10 (Polito: finding 45m/dEx)

2 (body in lower pump station)

2 (locker in security station)

10 (Polito: flush radiation)

2 (body in starboard nacelle)

10 (Polito: getting power back online)

2 (body in underpass)

Nanites

20 (desk in opening room)

10 (desk in Chemical storeroom)

10 (crate in storeroom 4)

5 (body in coolant tunnels)

5 (body in coolant tunnels)

15 (body near pump station)

5 (body in lower pump station)

15 (ledge above Xerxes core)

15 (body in hall near Turret)

15 (locker in security station)

15 (body in security station)

15 (body in Engineering Core)

10 (body in starboard nacelle)

8 (body in port nacelle)

10 (desk in Core Control)

12 (body in underpass)

Weapons/Ammo

Wrench (coolant tunnels)

Wrench (near Xerxes Core)

Pistol [1 standard bullet; condition 3] (open storage room in coolant tunnels)

Pistol [no ammo; condition 3] (near body near storeroom 4)

Pistol [2 standard bullets; condition 2] (under Engineering Control)

SIDDONS 02.JUN.14 RE: LAME OLD ME TO: SUAREZ, TOMMY

They aren't making this easy for us, are they? I miss you. I know it's stupid, but I do. I think I'll wallow in self pity for an hour or so and then write you again. Figures, I have to travel 67 trillion miles to meet a man. Once you're transferred to the Von Braun, everything will be better. I'll be better, I promise. Great, someone's coming. Counting the seconds ...

DELACROIX 30.JUN.14 RE: TAU CETI 5 TO: KORENCHKIN, ANATOLY

Anatoly, you MUST open up the planet to the scientific staff of this vessel. If there IS something down there, it's bigger than TriOp, it's bigger than the UNN and it's bigger than you. And why have you and Diego shut off deck 3? What's going on?

Pistol [1 standard bullet; condition 3] (hall near Slug Turret)

Pistol [no ammo; condition 1] (near body in starboard nacelle)

Pistol [1 standard bullet; condition 2] (near body in underpass)

6 Standard bullets (desk in Chemical Storeroom)

6 Standard bullets (body near storeroom 4)

6 Standard bullets (body under Engineering Control)

6 Standard bullets (replicator Engineering Core; 60 nanites unhacked /45 nanites hacked)

12 Standard bullets (body at far end of underpass)

6 Armor-piercing bullets (security crate near Engineering Core door)

6 Armor-piercing bullets (replicator near pump station; 90 nanites hacked)

6 Armor-piercing bullets (body in hall near Slug Turret)

12 Armor-piercing bullets (upper pump station)

6 Anti-personnel bullets (body in Engineering Control)

6 Anti-personnel bullets (security crate in underpass)

Shotgun [no ammo; condition 2; broken] (outside Engineering Control)

Shotgun [1 Rifled slug; condition 3] (inside starboard nacelle)

6 Rifled slugs (crate inside starboard nacelle)

6 Anti-personnel shotgun pellets (crate in open storage room in coolant tunnels)

Laser Rapier (body in Engineering Core)

3 Fragmentation Grenades (replicator near pump station; 100 nanites unhacked /75 nanites hacked)

3 Proximity Grenades (replicator in Engineering Core; 80 nanites hacked)

Armor

Hazard suit (crate in storeroom 4)

Light combat armor (security station)

MALONE 03.JUL.14 RE: PSIONIC CHIMPS! TO: MAK PAO RESEARCH AUTHORITY

A laboratory worker from MedSci called me down to the vivisection room yesterday. He felt the lab chimps were exhibiting uncommon intelligence. I sat with one for four hours and tried to probe it with the psi amp on a beta 4 cycle. It failed to respond. I of course assumed it was because it was, naturally, incapable of reacting to the sophisticated beta 4 cycle. But then I realized it was blocking the probe intentionally! As soon as I raised the psi-amp to attack it, the creature lashed out with its arms and projected a cryokinetic field towards me, paralyzing my arm. I immediately psi-dampened the monkey and then stunned it with an electric prod.

DELACROIX 04.JUL.14 RE: TAKING ACTION TO: KORENCHKIN, ANATOLY

I'm not sure what secrets you and your new buddy Captain Diego have got going up on deck 3, but I intend to find out. If you continue to refuse to meet with me and my staff, you will leave me no choice but to register a complaint with corporate. If you won't take me seriously, perhaps Sgt. Bronson and her security staff will.

Hypos

Annelid Healing Gland (on surgical unit in security station)

Anti-radiation hypo (shelf in opening room)

Anti-radiation hypo (body in coolant tunnels near Chemical Storeroom)

Anti-radiation hypo (near body in coolant tunnels near Chemical Storeroom)

Anti-radiation hypo (crate in storeroom 4)

Anti-radiation hypo (ledge in coolant tunnels)

Anti-toxin hypo (replicator Engineering Core; 35 nanites unhacked /25 nanites hacked)

Medical hypo (desk in opening room)

Medical hypo (security crate near Engineering Core door)

Medical hypo (crate in storeroom 4)

Medical hypo (replicator near pump station; 30 nanites unhacked /20 nanites hacked)

Medical hypo (under grate outside Engineering Control)

Medical kit (crate inside starboard nacelle)

Psi booster (crate inside starboard nacelle)

Psi hypo (replicator near pump station; 75 nanites unhacked /40 nanites hacked)

Psi hypo (body in hall near Slug Turret)

Psi hypo (replicator near Engineering Core; 75 nanites unhacked /40 nanites hacked)

Psi hypo (desk in Core Control)

Speed booster (crate in storeroom 4)

Speed booster (body in underpass)

Implants

PsiBoost (security crate in underpass)

Software

Repair v1 (body near Chemical Storeroom)

Access Cards

Security (body near security station)

Logs

Curtiz 10.Jul "Just us" (on desk in opening room)

Sanger 5.Jul "The soldiers" (coolant tunnels near Chemical Storeroom)

Delacroix 30.Jun "Tau Ceti 5" (coolant tunnels near Chemical Storeroom)

Chemical Manifest Log (Chemical Storeroom)

Delacroix 4.Jul "Taking action" (near storeroom 4)

Curtiz 7.Jul "That leak again" (near pump station)

SANGER 04.JUL.14 RE: DELACROIX

I don't know where we'd be without Delacroix. This whole ship is falling apart and she's the only one who knows what from what. I saw her arguing with that creep Anatoly Koretzkin or whatever his name is, and she was giving it to him but good. But that freak job stares her straight in the eye and starts babbling about how she doesn't know the pleasure of the joyful unity or some such. Mama mia, the clowns are running the circus ...

Sanger 10.Jul "Locking Eng. Control" (outside Engineering Control)

Delacroix 5.Jul "Fluidics backdoor" (floor of Engineering Control)

Martin 10.Jul "Cargo Bay 2" (floor of hall near Slug Turret)

Bronson 6.Jul "Turret problems" (locker in security station)

Martin 10.Jul "Ambush" (floor of Engineering Core)

Delacroix 11.Jul "A new friend?" (counter of starboard nacelle)

Sanger 4.Jul "Delacroix" (on desk in Core Control office)

Chemicals (all in Chemical Storeroom)

2 Antimony

2 Barium

2 Californium

Cesium

2 Iridium

Osmium

Technetium

Tellurium

Vanadium

2 Yttrium

Miscellaneous

45m/dEx (Chemical Storeroom)

Booze (opening room)

2 Booze (Core Control office)

Juice (Core Control office)

Juice (security crate in underpass)

Maintenance Tool (body near Xerxes Core)

Maintenance Tool (body near security station)

Soda (replicator near pump station; 3 nanites unhacked)

Swinekeeper cartridge (desk in opening room)

SANGER 05.JUL.14 RE: THE SOLDIERS

Before, I couldn't get rid of those jarheads from the Rickenbacker, and now I can't find one for love or money. That creepy OSA guy followed me around for two months until he got the hint. Now I tried to contact him to see if he knew what was going on, but all of a sudden he won't return my mail.

DELACROIX 05.JUL.14 RE: BE BRAVE TO: SANGER, CONSTANCE

Constance, I fear now for my life. I think this has gone beyond any imaginings of Diego and Korenchkin. I do not believe they are in control at all. We must discover what it was they found down on the surface of Tau Ceti 5 and why they guard their secret so jealously. I think this is more important than my life or your life or the life of this ship. Be brave. And be careful.

On Engineering Map 2 (I – O)

Cyber Modules

10 (Polito: Installing 45m/dEx)

3 (Cargo Bay 1A west side third level)

2 (Cargo Bay 1B west side third level)

2 (body in Cargo Bay 1B east side third level)

2 (body in Cargo Bay 2A west side third level)

2 (body in Cargo Bay 2B east side second level)

Nanites

20 (crates in shuttle bay)

10 (bodies in Command Control)

5 (body in Cargo Bay 1A west side first level)

10 (Cargo Bay 1A west side second level)

22 (security crate in Cargo Bay 1A west side third level)

5 (Cargo Bay 1A east side first level)

5 (body in Cargo Bay 1A east side second level)

15 (body in Cargo Bay 1A east side third level)

5 (Cargo Bay 1B west side first level)

10 (security crate in Cargo Bay 1B west side first level)

10 (Cargo Bay 1B west side third level)

5 (desk in middle of Cargo Bay 1B)

5 (Cargo Bay 1B east side first level)

10 (body in Cargo Bay 1B east side second level)

8 (body in Cargo Bay 2A west side first level)

15 (Cargo Bay 2A west side first level)

20 (security crate in Cargo Bay 2A west side third level)

5 (body in Cargo Bay 2A east side third level)

5 (desk in middle of Cargo Bay 2B)

10 (Cargo Bay 2B east side third level)

Weapons/Ammo

Pistol [2 standard bullets; condition 1] (near body in Cargo Bay 1B east side second level)

Pistol [no ammo; condition 1] (near body in Cargo Bay 2B east side second level)

6 Standard bullets (Cargo Bay 1A west side second level)

6 Standard bullets (security crate Cargo Bay 1A west side third level)

6 Standard bullets (Cargo Bay 1B west side first level)

> **MALONE 06.JUL.14 RE: FURTHER EXPERIMENTS TO: MAK PAO RESEARCH AUTHORITY**
>
> Taking precautions, I proceeded with further experiments. Since we've reached Tau Ceti, the creatures have gotten smarter and somehow gained limited psi abilities. I probed another subject with a beta 5 cycle and sensed many things, but mostly an incredible empathy. The chimps have become acutely aware of their own history, of the vivisections and experiments that have been performed on them while onboard the Von Braun. They have anger, and they are ready to express it. Clearly they are both a fascinating scientific resource and an incredible security risk. My recommendation … either freeze them in cryo storage for the remainder of the mission or liquidate them immediately. Who knows what other abilities they'll acquire?

6 Standard bullets (security crate in Cargo Bay 1B west side first level)

6 Standard bullets (Cargo Bay 1B west side second level)

6 Standard bullets (body in Cargo Bay 1B east side second level)

6 Standard bullets (broken replicator in Cargo Bay 2A; 60 nanites unhacked /45 nanites hacked)

6 Standard bullets (Cargo Bay 2A east side second level)

6 Armor-piercing bullets (Cargo Bay 1A east side first level)

6 Armor-piercing bullets (security crate in Cargo Bay 2B west side third level)

6 Anti-personnel bullets (crate under shuttle bay)

6 Anti-personnel bullets (body in Cargo Bay 2B east side second level)

Shotgun [no ammo; condition 2] (near body in Cargo Bay 1B east side third level)

Shotgun [no ammo; condition 1] (near body in Cargo Bay 2A west side first level)

6 Rifled slugs (crate under shuttle bay)

6 Rifled slugs (replicator in Cargo Bay 1A; 80 nanites unhacked /60 nanites hacked)

6 Rifled slugs (body in Cargo Bay 1B east side third level)

6 Rifled slugs (body in Cargo Bay 2A west side first level)

6 Anti-personnel shotgun pellets (replicator in Cargo Bay 1A; 70 nanites hacked)

6 Anti-personnel shotgun pellets (body in Cargo Bay 1A east side second level)

6 Anti-personnel shotgun pellets (body in Cargo Bay 2B east side first level)

Laser Pistol [no charges; condition 1; Broken] (body in Cargo Bay 2B east side third level)

Armor

Light combat armor (Cargo Bay 1B east side first level)

> **MARTIN 10.JUL.14 RE: CARGO BAY 2**
>
> I'm not sure what's creeping me out worse: The hybrids with their pipes and shotguns, the berserk Turrets, or our supposed allies. I don't trust those UNN bastards. I've got to find Sanger. She knows the access code to fluidics control. I'm gonna make my way over to cargo bay 2 to find her.

Hypos

Anti-radiation hypo (broken replicator in Cargo Bay 2A; 35 nanites unhacked /25 nanites hacked)

Medical hypo (security crate in Cargo Bay 1A west side third level)

Medical hypo (body in Cargo Bay 2A east side first level)

Medical hypo (security crate in Cargo Bay 2B west side third level)

Medical kit (crate near replicator in Cargo Bay 1A)

Psi hypo (body in middle of Cargo Bay 1B)

Psi hypo (security crate in Cargo Bay 2A west side third level)

Strength booster (replicator Cargo Bay 1A; 50 nanites unhacked /35 nanites hacked)

Implants

BrawnBoost (under grate in engineering corridor)

SwiftBoost (body in middle of Cargo Bay 1B)

Software

Hack v1 (body in Cargo Bay 2A west side first level)

Repair v1 (body in engineering corridor)

Repair v1 (broken replicator in Cargo Bay 2A; 25 nanites hacked)

Access Cards

Cargo Bay 2A/2B card (body in Cargo Bay 1A west side first level)

Logs

Siddons 2.Jun "Lame old me" (engineering corridor)

Suarez 11.Jul "Hang tight" (crate in shuttle bay)

Diego 11.Jul "Resist the call" (counter in command control)

Malone 6.Jul "Further experiments" (desk in middle of Cargo Bay 1B)

Malone 3.Jul "Psionic chimps!" (body in Cargo Bay 1B east side first level)

Bronson 6.Jul "Hacking Turrets" (body in Cargo Bay 2A west side first level)

Diego 11.Jul "Is it so bad?" (desk in middle of Cargo Bay 2B)

Delacroix 5.Jul "Be brave" (Cargo Bay 2B east side first level)

Sanger 10.Jul "Locked in" (body in Cargo Bay 2B east side third level)

> **DELACROIX 11.JUL.14 RE: A NEW FRIEND?**
>
> I've been contacted by some kind of artificial intelligence that wants to help me reclaim control of the Von Braun from whomever … or whatever is now in charge. I don't know where it came from, but I must confess I'm happy it is here.

Chemicals

Miscellaneous

4 Booze (crate in engineering corridor)

9 Booze (crates in shuttle bay)

2 Chips (crate in shuttle bay)

Chips (body in Cargo Bay 1A east side third level)

Chips (body in Cargo Bay 2A west side third level)

Chips (security crate in Cargo Bay 2B west side third level)

French-Epstein device (body in Cargo Bay 2B east side third level)

Juice (crate in shuttle bay)

Juice (security crate in Cargo Bay 2A west side third level)

Maintenance Tool (crate in Shuttle bay)

Maintenance Tool (replicator in Cargo Bay 1A; 60 nanites unhacked /45 nanites hacked)

Overworld Zero cartridge (body in engineering corridor)

Portable Battery (broken replicator in Cargo Bay 2A; 85 nanites unhacked /65 nanites hacked)

Soda (replicator in Cargo Bay 1A; 3 nanites unhacked)

Surgical unit Activation Key (Cargo Bay 2A east side first level)

DIEGO 11.JUL.14 RE: IS IT SO BAD?

In some ways, the Many is not unlike the UNN. There is a joy in working towards a collective goal, in being able to put aside the things that draw us apart and make us separate. Why do we fear the loss of our individuality so much? Man can dream, but the Many can accomplish.

SUAREZ 11.JUL.14 RE: HANG TIGHT TO: SIDDONS, REBECCA

Stay where you are, Bec, I mean it. This isn't something you can fight, this isn't something you can run from. If you love me, you won't come looking for me. Just hang tight ... I won't let you down.

HYDROPONICS

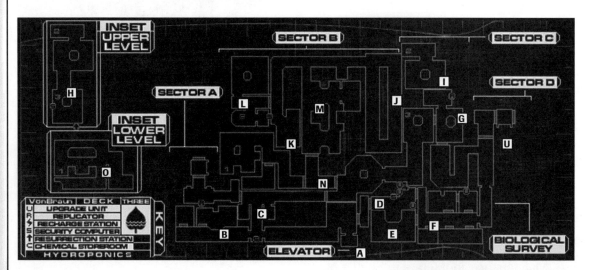

ADMINISTRATIVE OFFICES

(A) When you arrive in Hydroponics (the elevator is located in Sector C), you'll get an email from Polito explaining why the elevator shaft is blocked. Apparently there is some biological infestation here that you'll have to clear out before going on.

(B) Head down the hall to your left, passing by an intersection on your right. As you continue down the hall, a pair of Shotgun Hybrids may come out of the rooms ahead and attack. After dealing with them, start to search the first room on the right. Polito will send you some email explaining that you need to find and Research something called Toxin-A, one vial of which is sitting on a desk in front of you. Go get it. Hey, what was that blood-curdling scream? It seems like your actions have disturbed a Cyborg Midwife, who is coming to attack you. Be prepared to fight her; remember, they're most vulnerable to AP ammo. After that, finish searching this office and the one next door for useful equipment.

> **POLITO 12.JUL.14 RE: RESEARCHING TOXIN-A**
>
> Okay, stop where you are. There's a vial of an experimental material called Toxin-A. It was developed by the Sci staff to reduce the growth of the aliens. But I can't find any data on how you should use it. You should be able to research the toxin. I'm uploading you enough cyber modules to acquire the research skill if you don't have it.

> **POLITO 12.JUL.14 RE: BLOCKED SHAFT**
>
> Damn. Something's blocking the shaft and the elevator can't reach deck 4. I'm attempting to determine ... I'm detecting massive quantities of some kind of biomaterial that's plugging up the elevator shaft. The environment on this level has been altered to be some kind of breeding chamber for the xenomorphs. It shouldn't prove dangerous unless you plan to stay for more than a few hours, but in order to clear the shaft you're going to have to remove the biomaterial. I'm accessing the primary data loop. Let's see what we can find out there.

You should now start researching the Toxin-A. If you haven't got any Research skill, you should consider buying it at this point. Alternatively, later on in this level, you can find a LabAssistant™ implant, which will give you an effective Research skill of 1, which is sufficient for researching the Toxin-A. Either way, you'll need to find 2 units of Antimony (Sb), and one of Vanadium (V) to complete the research, so you should keep your eyes open for them. If you're impatient, you can get these chemicals immediately by going back to the chemical storeroom of Engineering A.

> **POLITO 12.JUL.14 RE: USING THE VIALS**
>
> Okay, the vials of Toxin-A need to be placed directly into the environmental regulators. There should be four on this deck. If you can get a vial into each of the regulators, you should be able to significantly impact the growth of those despicable creatures. That should remove the biomatter from the elevator shaft.

(C) Go back to the intersection you passed earlier, and go down it. There's a Camera just past the end of this short hallway, so be ready to shoot it out (or security hack it). At the end of the hallway, you'll be facing a set of sloped windows looking down on a lower area. It's possible to smash those windows and jump down there, but it sounds like there are a lot of monsters roaming that area, so we'll avoid it for now. There's also a door on the left, leading to Sector A, but it's got a keycard lock, and you don't yet have access. As long as you're here, search this area for goodies, but then turn around and head back.

SECURITY STATION

(D) Return to the elevator, and go through the door to the right of it. This leads to a small hallway ending in another door. Through this door is the security station for this deck. Enter it, but *don't* go very far in. There's a window ahead of you on the right, leading to a neighboring room. Inside that room are two Laser Turrets and a Camera, so moving in front of that window is *very* dangerous! If you're a Hacker, this would be an excellent time to hack security. Don't be fooled into using the security computer in front of you, though (unless you're a very *fast* Hacker); it's right in front of the window, in a very vulnerable spot. Luckily, you passed a security computer back by the Administrative Offices, so a quick detour to hack security from there won't take much time.

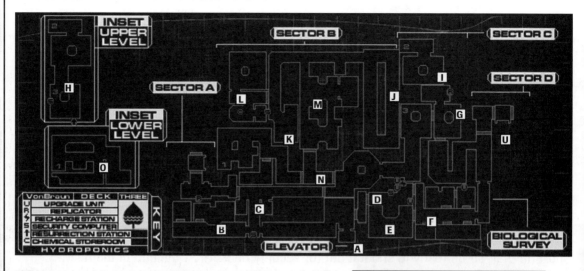

(E) After hacking security, you can smash one of the windows and enter the next room. You'll want to neutralize the Turrets and Camera before security comes back online. But there are a bunch of mysterious egg-shaped things in that room as well. If you get too close

> Life grows within the womb of these walls ... life that has never seen the surface of the earth ...

to these, they'll open up, releasing either a cloud of toxic spores (which can poison you), or a small worm-like "Grub," which will attack you. These Grubs are not very tough, but they're very fast, and their size makes them hard to hit. Don't underestimate their threat.

A brief digression on Eggs: When destroyed, they sometimes release organs, which can be researched to find out more about them. If you leave them intact, however, you can search their living bodies to extract *different* organs, which may be useful in a variety of ways (once researched). Don't do this if you don't have a supply of anti-toxin hypos handy, though. Toxins don't wear off by themselves, and they *will* kill you if left untreated.

If you can't hack security, you can still get across this room, but more care is required. First, without getting within visual range of the Turrets and Camera, edge up to the nearby crates. They contain a lot of useful ammunition. After that, get ready to sprint across the room. (Saving first wouldn't be a bad idea.) If the Camera spotted you earlier, make sure you wait a minute for it to go from yellow back to green before entering its field of view again (it makes an audible 'chirp' when returning to green, so listen for that). When you zip across the room, the Camera will probably get a glimpse of you and turn yellow, but you should be back out of sight before it turns red. Also, since Turrets have trouble hitting a moving target, you should be able to do this without taking damage.

On the other side of the security station, you'll find one of the rare OS upgrade units, two normal upgrade units (Psi and Tech), and a recharge station. The upgrade units are within view of the Turrets, but if you dash all the way into the corner between them and the recharger, you'll be in sufficient cover to use them without being shot..

BIOLOGICAL SURVEY LABS

When you're done with the security station, leave through the door on this side, and head down to the bend in the corridor. Be careful of the door to your right, as it leads to the room with the Turrets — you wouldn't want to accidentally open it!

(F) The rooms on the right side of the hall have some very good loot in them, including a surgical unit activation key, so search them carefully.

The door to the first room on the left is broken, so I guess you can't go in there. Let's check the room next door. In here is a broken replicator (probably the very replicator used to create the Toxin-A). There's a connecting door with the office next door, but it's also broken. But wait! There's a window between the two offices which you can break. Jump up on to the table and squeeze through the window to enter the next office. In here, there are two vials of Toxin-A, as well as a LabAssistant™ implant, which can help you research the Toxin-A if you haven't already.

When you're done with this hallway, follow the corridor as it twists around. There are often Shotgun Hybrids and Cyborg Midwives patrolling this area, so stay alert. You'll pass a door leading to Sector D, but — you guessed it — it's locked.

(G) Eventually, you'll enter a room with a pillar in the middle of it. On the far side of this room is a niche with a replicator, so you may want to purchase something. Proceed through the door to the left of where you entered this area.

EXPERIMENTAL OFFICE

(H) You're now in another room with a pillar, but this one has a ladder leading to an upper level. On that upper level, you'll find a bio-reconstruction machine nearby, which you should immediately activate. Continuing on the upper level, you'll enter a room with a Camera. If you shoot out the Camera, you'll probably hear a Cyborg Midwife react to the sound. Continue straight through this room, and move carefully down the ramp to the area below. This area is fairly dark, so if you see something moving, shoot! (Trust me, there are no friendly crew members around here.)

> **DELACROIX 10.JUL.14 RE: A RAY OF HOPE**
>
> Killing the children won't be easy. But I think I'm actually on to something. The biochemistry of these worms, which I call the Annelids, treats inverted proteins as toxins. With the help of a replicator in the Biological Survey lab, I've managed to isolate some inverted proteins in a number of vials. However, the mix with the base compound is still off, so I still need to do some more research. Once I do that and mix the toxin into the four Environmental Regulators ... Well, things can only get better.

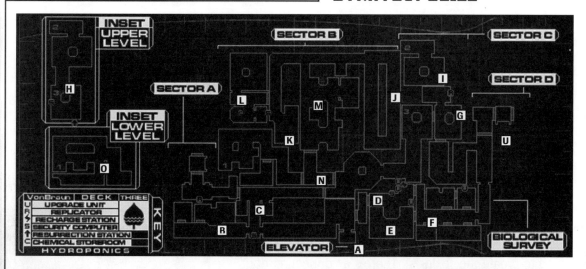

(1) When the Midwife is dead, you can search the room she was in. There are a number of Eggs in here, which you might want to shoot from a safe distance. Also in this area is an environmental regulator! By now, you should have researched the Toxin-A, and found out that you need to place it in all four environmental regulators, so this is a significant find. Drop the Toxin-A in the regulator. You should see some of the organic goo on the walls dissipate. Progress! Three more to go ....

POLITO 12.JUL.14 RE: MAKING PROGRESS

Good. You'll notice that the bio-matter on the walls and in the elevator shaft has been impacted by the introduction of the biotoxin. Now do the same with the other three regulators.

Head back up to the room with the Camera. There's a lot of goodies in here that you left behind in your hurry to deal with the Midwife, so search this room thoroughly now.

You'll notice a window in this room that connects with a large open area beyond. Go through it. There are some high-strength windows beneath your feet, looking down on another area. There's a body off to your left who has some useful stuff, so head towards him. If you head *straight* for him, however, you won't make it. One of the windows between you and him has been damaged, and will collapse when you step on it, dropping you into the room below. Luckily, that's where we want to go anyway ....

RESEARCH LABS

(J) You fall into a ring of corridors that contains a large number of Eggs. The Many sends a telepathic threat, warning you to leave the "babies" alone. Soon after you arrive here, that threat will be made good with the arrival of a Midwife, so be ready. If you destroy the Eggs, you can find a working laser pistol in this hall.

> Babies must sleep. Babies must rest. Wise is the one who does not waken them. Leave this place now, or we will wound you as you have us.

(K) When you've cleared out the ring corridor, leave via the only available exit. This corridor has an intersection partway down on the left, but you should just run past it for now. At the end of the corridor, turn left. Ignore the door on your right, and continue to the room at the end of the hall. You'll see a pair of apparitions here which show you a bit of the circumstances surrounding the creation of a Midwife from a normal human female. When the sequence is done, you can search the room for some useful loot. There are some incomplete surgical units here; you should probably activate one of them with the activation key you picked up in the Biological Survey Labs.

(L) Return to the door you just passed, and go through it. There are a pair of Monkeys in here, so be ready. The room at the end of the hall on the right has a locker with some med hypos in it. There's a Camera in this room, but since you just need to dodge in and out quickly to get the hypos, you may not want to waste ammunition on it.

In the middle of this hall on the left (as you came in) is the Chemical Storeroom for this deck. If you're still looking for chemicals to research the Toxin-A, you can find them in here. The room next door, however, contains a Midwife. After killing her, be sure to search her body — she has a very ... *interesting* log on her. The desk in this room contains a fourth vial of Toxin-A, and some of the chemicals needed to research it.

BLOOME 02.JUL.14 RE: WORRIED

I found these schematics on Dr. Miller's desk ... they're plans for the kind of cyber modification that's been illegal for forty years ... that's not like him ... I was going to talk to him about it and then I noticed ... the DNA sequence he spec'd for the prototype ... it's mine ...

(M) When you're done here, backtrack to the intersection you passed a little while ago, and turn down it. This area has a *lot* of Monkeys in it, so be ready for a somewhat protracted fight. There's also a Camera in there, so don't go too far into the room without being ready to deal with it as well. When the fighting is done, search the immediate area. A body in here has the access card for Hydroponics Sector B (you've actually been in Sector B since you fell through the windows, but now that you have the card, if you want to come back here, you can use the door).

(N) Go through the door at the far end of this area. You'll be in a small corridor section connecting the Xerxes core with Sector B Storage and Maintenance. On the floor, you'll find a grenade launcher and several grenades. Those interested in Heavy Weapons will now be very happy. Go through the door on your right.

SECTOR B STORAGE AND MAINTENANCE

Sector B Storage is a fairly convoluted area, with several Hybrids wandering around. If you search carefully, you'll eventually find a ladder in the back corner, leading down to the Maintenance section. Climb down.

(O) The Maintenance section is *full* of Eggs. The Eggs are being watched over by a Shotgun Hybrid and a Cyborg Midwife, so be ready for another tough fight. There's a lot of loot to be had in this area, so search thoroughly. One of the things you'll find here is the access card for Hydroponics Sector A. Some of the best loot is in a niche that is tricky to jump into, but it's well worth the effort to do so.

> ### DELACROIX 09.JUL.14 RE: KILLING THE WORMS
>
> It's becoming clear that the worms are some kind of communal entity … While I'm not sure whether airborne Toxin-A will directly kill any ambulatory specimens, it should impact their communal mass and remove the residue I've observed growing on the walls and the lift shaft. But perhaps there is a more potent formula to be synthesized …

Also in this general area, you'll find a second environmental regulator. Put the Toxin-A in, and watch yet more of the biomatter dissipate. Two down, two to go!

Climb back up the ladder, then leave Sector B by the door leading to the Xerxes core. There's a Camera near the door above your head, so be careful not to get spotted. Proceed to the door to Sector A. There's another Camera down the hall past the door. At the end of this hall, there's a replicator, but it's broken. If you have a good enough Repair skill, you can bring it back online and buy things. Proceed through the bulkhead to the next sublevel.

SECTOR A STORAGE AREA

(P) The room on the other side of the bulkhead has a Camera and two Eggs flanking the door, so enter with care. This room also has a working replicator, a recharge station, and two upgrade units (Stats and Weapons), so you might want to spend some time in here upgrading your character. A body in this room has a fifth vial of Toxin-A, but if you've picked up all four that you came across before this, you won't need it.

(Q) When you're done, leave through the door and turn right. The next door on your right leads to another storage area. There are lots of crates with loot in here, so search thoroughly. You might disturb some Grubs eating the dead bodies, and a Hybrid is likely to wander in while you're searching. When you're done in here, go back out into the hall. There are some more crates worth searching at the end of it.

CULTIVATION CELLS

(R) Go through one of the doors opposite the storage rooms. The areas are symmetrical, so it doesn't matter which you choose. Both have a corridor with a Camera and a patrolling Maintenance Bot. As always, your first priority is to take out the Camera before it sets off an alarm. Try to stay far away from the Maintenance Bot — its aim is poor at long ranges, and that will make it miss a lot. These two corridors join in the middle, so the second Maintenance Bot will probably head over to investigate the noise of your battle with the first. Two Maintenance Bots at once can be a tough fight, so try to be loaded for bear before you start..

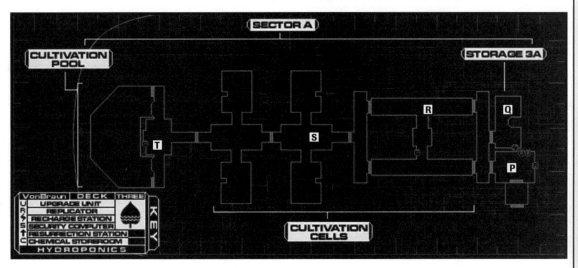

When you've dealt with both Bots (and both Cameras), search these corridors. One of the bodies here has the access card for Hydroponics Sector D, which will come in handy when you're done in here. He also has an assault rifle. This requires a Standard Weapons skill of 6, so not many characters can use it; those who can, though, can deliver a huge amount of damage in a small amount of time, especially using the full-automatic setting. Even if you don't have that high a Standard Weapons skill, if you think you might want it some day you should consider carrying the assault rifle around until you can use it.

(S) Continue past this area, into the next set of Cultivation Cells. There's a Shotgun Hybrid patrolling here. The rooms off to the sides of this corridor have Eggs sitting in them, but there are some useful goodies behind the Eggs. If you can spare the ammo, it's worth killing the Eggs and searching these rooms.

Proceed to the next set of rooms, which is very similar to this one. The major difference is that this area is guarded by another Maintenance Bot. He's alone, but by now you may be running low on AP ammo. Use your ammo conservatively, 'cause we're not done yet ….

> **POLITO 12.JUL.14 RE: DAWDLING**
>
> Why do you go so slowly?! Do you think this is some kind of game? It is only through luck and my continued forbearance that you are even alive! Now move!

(T) Once you're done here, proceed through the next set of doors. In here is the third environmental regulator! Unfortunately, it's guarded by a lot of Eggs, a Camera, and a Cyborg Midwife. Even worse, there's another Maintenance Bot a short ways off, who may come investigate any sounds of fighting. This can be a very tough fight, but you'll get a bit of a breather afterwards, so spend what resources you've got.

After you've killed all the enemies in the immediate area, install the Toxin-A in the Regulator, then head back towards the bulkhead. In the storage room right before the bulkhead, you'll find a Shotgun Hybrid who has wandered in. After killing it, make sure to search the corpse for another interesting log. Make sure to use the Upgrade Stations and Replicator (if you want) before heading through the bulkhead, since you probably won't be back this way for a long time, if at all.

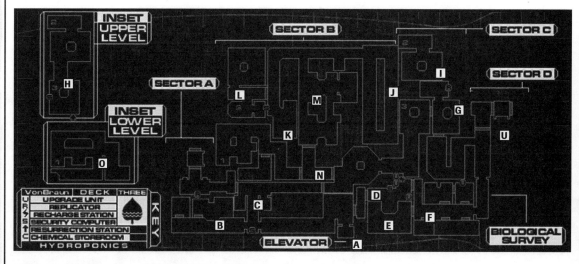

SECTOR C, PART TWO

(U) Make your way through Sector C to the door to Sector D. Be wary, there are probably wandering monsters along the way.

TURBINE CONTROL

(V) You come out of the bulkhead into a room with several Eggs. There's a Midwife lurking nearby, so be prepared for her to come out if you make noise destroying the Eggs. There's a bunch of loot in this room, and some of it is fairly well hidden, so search carefully. Specifically, there are some Cyber Modules on the floor behind a crate.

(W) When you're done searching, leave via the door opposite the bulkhead. This leads to a small observation room overlooking a pit full of boiling water. There's even more useful loot in here, including powered armor and an EMP rifle. The powered armor provides the best physical defense available in the game, but needs to be recharged periodically to function. The EMP rifle takes an Energy Weapons skill of 6, but it's the premiere weapon of choice for dealing with mechanical targets.

If you're feeling adventurous, smash one of the windows and jump out onto the nearby ledge. By working your way carefully around the ledge and climbing over a number of pipes, you can reach another stash of goodies. Save before you do, though, as one false step will send you falling to your death!

After having thoroughly looted this area, proceed through the door to the left of the bulkhead (as you came in).

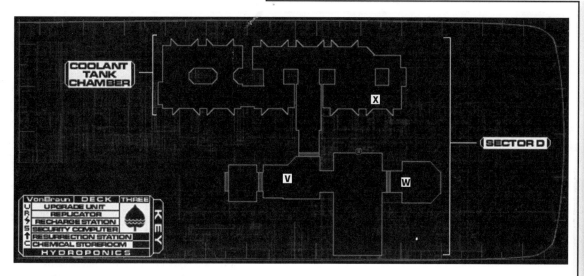

COOLANT TANK CHAMBER

X

SECTOR D

V

W

VonBraun DECK THREE
U ▲ UPGRADE UNIT
R ▲ REPLICATOR
S ▲ RECHARGE STATION
↑ ▲ SECURITY COMPUTER
C ▲ RESURRECTION STATION
▲ CHEMICAL STOREROOM
HYDROPONICS

KEY

TURBINES

(X) This area is pretty tough. There are Eggs all over, guarded by Hybrids and Midwives. There is a lot of steam in the air, obscuring your vision. Worse yet, you'll run into a new kind of monster in here: the Annelid Arachnid.

The Annelid Arachnid is an alien construct that is based on earth spiders, but is *much* bigger. The ones you'll find in here are baby Arachnids — a mere foot or so in diameter! Arachnids are very fast moving and difficult to hit. They are fairly resistant to energy weapons, so if you're using a laser pistol, switch to something else when facing Arachnids. The bite of the Arachnid is very toxic, so even if they don't kill you in direct combat, if you don't have anti-toxin handy, you may die anyway.

> **POLITO 12.JUL.14 RE: THE SHAFT IS CLEAR**
>
> At last. Readings indicate the elevator shaft is clear. Now get up to deck 4. I'll be waiting for you.

Once you've killed everything in here, find the final environmental regulator and install the Toxin-A in it. Polito will send you mail informing you that the shaft is clear, so you can finally make it up to Deck 4 to meet her. Head back, but be sure to search these steam-filled rooms carefully for goodies before you go.

SECTOR C, PART THREE

Head back to the elevator. Standard drill before going to a new deck: you may want to take a brief break here to heal up, spend upgrade points, buy equipment from replicators, and collect research chemicals. By this time, though, the choice to do that stuff is less clear-cut, as the wandering creatures you might encounter along the way have become significantly tougher. On the other hand, the next level can be expected to be tougher still …. When you're ready to go, enter the elevator and push the button for Ops (Deck 4).

MATERIEL AVAILABLE

On Hydroponics Map 1 (A – O, U)

Cyber Modules

10 (Polito: for buying Research skill)

3 (desk biological survey office)

3 (under windows, on top of crate, Sector B storage)

3 (sector B, near Monkeys)

3 (waste barrel in Chemical Storeroom)

13 (Polito: first Regulator)

3 (niche Sector B maintenance)

13 (Polito: second regulator)

3 (near desk research office)

Nanites

10 (body near door to sector A)

17 (body by Xerxes core)

19 (body in biological survey office)

18 (under bench in biological survey hall)

10 (body in biological survey hall)

13 (body near Chemical Storeroom)

16 (body near surgical units in sector B)

18 (body in sector B maintenance)

9 (body in sector B maintenance)

36 (body in sector B maintenance)

38 (body in niche of sector B maintenance)

12 (body near regulator near research office)

20 (body over Egg corridor windows)

Weapons/Ammo

Wrench (by Xerxes core)

Pistol [12 standard bullets; condition 8] (floor of security station)

6 Standard bullets (crate in security station)

6 Standard bullets (body in sector B maintenance)

6 Standard bullets (broken replicator near sector A bulkhead; 60 nanites unhacked /45 nanites hacked)

24 Standard bullets (body near surgical units in sector B)

6 Armor-piercing bullets (crate in security station)

6 Armor-piercing bullets (body in niche of sector B maintenance)

MILLER 27.JUN.14 RE: OUR WORK HERE
TO: RENFRO, RICHARD : OXFORD UNIVERSITY

Dick, I know you won't get this until after we've returned ... but I had to express how incredible I feel. We've finally done it ... made contact ... and Muldoon and I have been selected to be involved in the initial work ... Anatoly's one condition is that I tell no one aboard the ship ... The creatures are remarkable ... they're so helpless ... I feel somehow compelled to protect them ... It's a miraculous discovery ...

12 Anti-personnel bullets (crate in security station)

Shotgun [no ammo; condition 3; broken] (sector B, near Monkeys)

6 Rifled slugs (desk in administration offices)

6 Rifled slugs (biological survey halls)

6 Rifled slugs (replicator in biological survey area; 80 nanites unhacked /60 nanites hacked)

6 Rifled slugs (body in sector B, near Monkeys)

Laser pistol [no charges; condition 9] (body in sector B in egg corridor)

Laser rapier (body near surgical units in sector B)

Grenade launcher [1 fragmentation grenade; condition 7] (by door to Sector B)

6 Fragmentation grenades (by door to Sector B)

3 EMP grenades (by door to sector D)

Small beaker (on desk in broken biological survey office)

Armor

Light combat armor (crate in security station)

Hypos

Anti-toxin hypo (body under bio-reconstruction station)

Anti-toxin hypo (near surgical units in sector B)

Anti-toxin hypo (broken replicator near sector A; 35 nanites unhacked /25 nanites hacked)

Medical hypo (body in biological survey office)

Medical hypo (replicator in biological survey area; 30 nanites unhacked /20 nanites hacked)

2 Medical hypos (locker near Chemical Storeroom)

2 Medical hypos (on surgical units in sector B)

Medical kit (behind Turret near security station)

Medical kit (broken replicator near sector A; 100 nanites hacked)

Speed Booster (body in sector B maintenance)

Implants

LabAssistant (on desk in broken biological survey office)

PsiBoost (body near door to sector A)

SwiftBoost (body over egg corridor windows)

KORENCHKIN 28.JUN.14 RE: MIRACLES

There, the young ones are all aboard. Captain Diego and I have sealed off deck 3. He and I are now of one mind ... our bodies are changing too. Sometimes it hurts terribly and sometimes it is ... marvelous ... something wonderful is happening to me ...

MILLER 29.JUN.14 RE: THE CHILDREN

The specimens are dying. And we're powerless to help ... they're highly toxic. Muldoon wouldn't leave them, and now he's dead. But this morning I had ... a revelation ... I started work on specifications for a radical series of cybernetic enhancements ... If successful, I could make a body practically indestructible ... yet the mind would remain human, nurturing ... There's not a lot of time ...

Software

Modify v1 (body in sector B maintenance)

Modify v1 (broken replicator near sector A;
35 nanites unhacked /25 nanites hacked)

Repair v1 (replicator in biological survey area;
35 nanites unhacked /25 nanites hacked)

Repair v1 (body in research office)

Repair v2 (replicator in biological survey area;
95 nanites hacked)

Research v1 (floor of biological survey office)

Access Cards

Hydroponics Sector B (body in sector B near Monkeys)

Hydroponics Sector A (body in sector B maintenance)

Logs

Miller 27.Jun "Our work here" (floor outside elevator)

Miller 30.Jun "Wondrous toy" (desk in administration offices)

Korenchkin 28.Jun "Miracles" (counter of security station)

Delacroix 9.Jul "Killing the worms" (desk in biological survey office)

Delacroix 10.Jul "A ray of hope" (table in biological survey office)

Delacroix 3.Jul "Making a change" (floor of biological survey hall)

Korenchkin 5.Jul "A new purpose" (floor under bio-reconstruction station)

Loesser 5.Jul "Where are they?" (sector B, near Monkeys)

Bloome 2.Jul "Worried" (midwife near Chemical Storeroom)

Chemical Manifest Log (desk in Chemical Storeroom)

Miller 1.Jul "Nurse Bloome" (body in sector B maintenance)

Miller 29.Jun "The children" (desk in research office)

MILLER 30.JUN.14 RE: WONDROUS TOY

I'm changing. My head is full of wonderful ideas and experiments ... they have so many miracles to share ... so much knowledge to give ... They told me how to make this implant ... they said it will make a better me of me ... I wish I had more time so I could give it to them ..."

MILLER 01.JUL.14 RE: NURSE BLOOME

I've chosen Nurse Bloome as the new mother to our children. She is sweet and kind, healthy and a perfect match. She has a child of her own back on Earth. She knows what it is to care for the young. Ave Maria. If she only knew what the future held ... she'd share the joys of the Many ...

Chemicals (except where noted, all in Chemical Storeroom)

- Antimony (desk near Chemical Storeroom)
- Vanadium (desk near Chemical Storeroom)
- Antimony
- Arsenic
- Barium
- 2 Cesium
- Copper
- Fermium
- 2 Gallium
- Hassium
- 2 Iridium
- Radium
- 2 Technetium
- 2 Tellurium

Miscellaneous

- Auto-repair unit (by environmental regulator near research office)
- Booze (floor of biological survey hall)
- Booze (replicator in biological survey area; 8 nanites unhacked)
- Chips (on desk in security station)
- Chips (floor by bench in biological survey hall)
- GamePig (desk in biological survey area)
- ICE-Pick (body in sector B maintenance)
- Juice (waste barrel near door to sector A)
- Maintenance tool (body by Xerxes Core)
- Surgical unit activation key (under desk in biological survey office)
- Soda (waste barrel near door to sector A)
- Soda (on desk in research office)
- SwineHunter cartridge (desk in biological survey area)
- Vial of Toxin-A (on table in administration offices)
- 2 Vials of Toxin-A (in desks in broken biological survey office)
- Vial of Toxin-A (desk near Chemical Storeroom)

DELACROIX 03.JUL.14 RE: MAKING A CHANGE
TO: POLITO, DR. JANICE

I received an e-message from Anatoly. He's not well. The Corporate protocols specify I can remove the Senior Executive Officer if he's found unfit for duty ... but what about his ally Captain Diego? He's got 120 goons on the Rickenbacker to back him up ... I wonder if that fragmentary AI you discovered on Tau Ceti 5 is connected to this ...

POLITO 04.JUL.14 RE: AI VOICE FRAGMENT TO: DELACROIX, DR. MARIE

Marie, this is urgent ... It seems the AI from Tau Ceti has integrated itself into the ship's computer ... I picked up this fragment today ... Not only that, but after I found the fragment, I returned to my lab to find it ransacked. I must see you ... you're the only one I trust now. I have a theory about this AI. I tried to find information about the various rumors regarding the events on Citadel Station. I think I'm on to something ... <<MESSAGE INTERRUPTED>>

On Hydroponics Map 2 (P – T)

Cyber Modules

3 (behind pipe above weapons upgrade unit)

3 (under crates in storage room)

3 (floor of third cultivation cell area north)

14 (Polito: third Regulator)

Nanites

19 (body near entrance)

19 (body in storage room)

17 (first cultivation cell area)

13 (body in first cultivation cell area)

15 (body in first cultivation cell area)

16 (third cultivation cell area south)

14 (third cultivation cell area north)

Weapons/Ammo

Wrench (floor of storage room)

Pistol [6 standard bullets; condition 3; broken] (near body in first cultivation cell area)

Pistol [3 standard bullets; condition 1; broken] (near body in first cultivation cell area)

6 Standard bullets (replicator near entrance; 45 nanites hacked)

12 Standard bullets (body in first cultivation cell area)

12 Armor-piercing bullets (body in first cultivation cell area)

6 Anti-personnel bullets (security crate in storage room)

6 Anti-personnel bullets (second cultivation cell area south)

6 Rifled slugs (crate in storage hall)

6 Rifled slugs (second cultivation cell area south)

Assault rifle [no ammo; condition 7] (near body in first cultivation cell area)

3 Incendiary grenades (body in first cultivation cell area)

Psi amp (body between first two cultivation cell areas)

Armor

Hazard suit (crate in storage room)

KORENCHKIN 05.JUL.14 RE: A NEW PURPOSE TO: DELACROIX, DR. MARIE

You can't understand my joy, Marie and I won't try to make you. I feel like a new man ... I have a purpose ... more important than the mission, even more important than TriOptimum ... I will protect them ... no matter what ... I will protect them ...

LOESSER 05.JUL.14 RE: WHERE ARE THEY? TO: MILLER, MARC

Marc, what's going on? I thought it was weird when you asked me to send up sixteen of my female staffers ... but ... what have you done with them? I'm shorthanded up here? Also, have you heard from Watts, Sanger or Polito? It's like everyone's gone on vacation and didn't bother to tell me."

Hypos

Anti-radiation hypo (third cultivation cell area south)

2 Anti-radiation hypos (third cultivation cell area north)

Anti-toxin hypo (replicator near entrance;
    35 nanites unhacked /25 nanites hacked)

Anti-toxin hypo (crate in storage room)

Psi Booster (third cultivation cell area south)

Psi hypo (replicator near entrance;
    75 nanites unhacked /50 nanites hacked)

Psi hypo (body between first two cultivation cell
    areas)

Speed Booster (crate in storage hall)

Implants

SwiftBoost (body near entrance)

Software

Hack v2 (body in first cultivation cell area)

Access Cards

Hydroponics Sector D card (body in first cultivation cell area)

Logs

Polito 4.Jul "AI voice fragment" (storage hall)

Turnbull 11.Jul "Changing" (Shotgun Hybrid near entrance, on the way back)

Chemicals

Miscellaneous

Auto-repair unit (security crate in storage hall)

Maintenance tool (third cultivation cell area south)

Portable battery (replicator near entrance; 85
    nanites unhacked /65 nanites hacked)

Vial of Toxin-A (body near entrance)

LOESSER 08.JUL.14 RE: MILLER

I know what Miller's up to. This morning ... this morning I saw Erin Bloome ... she was tending to some kind of eggs ... and she had been ... changed, in the most horrible, unnatural fashion. I can only think the worst for the rest of my staff. That son of a bitch. That son of a bitch. He won't get away with this.

KORENCHKIN 08.JUL.14 RE: GLORY

Glory ... to the Many ... I am a voice in their choir.

On Hydroponics Map 3 (V – X)

Cyber Modules

3 (behind crate in control room)

3 (cache over abyss)

3 (pit in turbine area)

14 (Polito: last regulator)

Nanites

20 (body near bulkhead)

65 (body near abyss)

20 (body in turbine area)

20 (body in turbine area)

Weapons/Ammo

Wrench (near bulkhead)

Pistol [7 standard bullets; condition 1; broken] (near body in turbine area)

12 Standard bullets (body in turbine area)

6 Armor-piercing bullets (body in turbine area)

6 Anti-personnel bullets (cache over abyss)

12 Anti-personnel bullets (body in turbine area)

EMP rifle [50 charges; condition 3; broken] (room overlooking abyss)

3 Fragmentation grenades (replicator; 100 nanites unhacked /75 nanites hacked)

3 Incendiary grenades (replicator; 160 nanites hacked)

3 Proximity grenades (body near bulkhead)

Armor

Power armor (body near abyss)

Hypos

Medical hypos (body near abyss)

Psi hypo (desk in control room)

Psi hypo (replicator; 75 nanites unhacked /50 nanites hacked)

Speed Booster (body near abyss)

Anti-toxin hypo (body in turbine area)

DIEGO 09.JUL.14 RE: OUR ALLIANCE TO: KORENCHKIN, ANATOLY

I believe the plans the Many have for me are greater than I even imagined. The change is upon me. But the path is more glorious than we imagined. It does not stop at a mere single mutation ... the form I've been promised is more beautiful than even that ... They tell me I will float through the air and strike at the foes of our biomass with my mind ... with our mind ... my cup runneth over ...

Implants

EndurBoost (body near bulkhead)

Software

Repair v2 (body in turbine area)

Access Cards

Logs

Diego 9.Jul "Our alliance" (floor near bulkhead)
Loesser 8.Jul "Miller" (desk in control room)
Korenchkin 8.Jul "Glory" (on console in control room)

Chemicals

Miscellaneous

Booze (cache over abyss)
French-Epstein device (security crate in control room)
Large beaker (desk in control room)
Maintenance tool (replicator; 60 nanites unhacked /45 nanites hacked)
Maintenance tool (crate in control room)
Maintenance tool (cache over abyss)

TURNBULL 11.JUL.14 RE: CHANGING

What do you know, Bronson was right after all. I imagine I've got about an hour ... but I'm tracking the ... the transformations in the hope that the data might be useful to someone else ... there are tumors ... on my leg and back ... I can feel that thing inside of me ... chewing, growing fat. My theory is they need a living host to complete the transformation ... Screw Diego, screw Korenchkin, screw Tau Ceti 5. If someone finds this, don't have any regrets about punching my clock. I was already gone.

POLITO 12.JUL.14 RE: THE XENOMORPHS

Now listen carefully. The xenomorphs who have hijacked this ship are presumably from the surface of Tau Ceti 5. They've been able to infect a number of crew members, through an extremely invasive parasitical technique. They've also demonstrated the ability to control the actions of others through some form of limited telepathy. Find the research soft. Understand them ... then kill them.

OPERATIONS

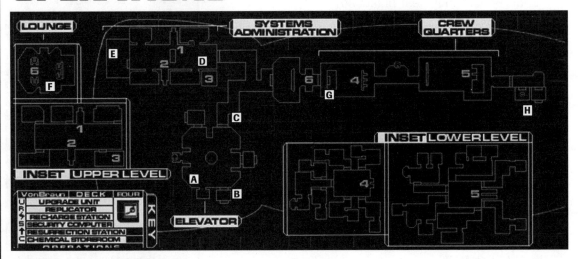

XERXES CORE

(A) When you come out of the elevator (in Operations Sector B), you'll be in a large room containing the Xerxes core for this deck. Off to your left is the bio-reconstruction machine; as always, it's a good idea to activate it first thing. There are a few logs lying around this room, and some crates with a few useful items.

(B) There are a lot of doors and bulkheads leading out of this room, but no immediate indication of where Dr. Polito is. However, a little investigation shows that all of them are currently locked but one, the bulkhead immediately to the right of the elevator. Looks like we'll head that way ….

DR. POLITO'S OFFICE

This sublevel is very small, and mostly just contains Dr. Polito's office. (There's no map, but you don't need one.) You discover that Dr. Polito is dead, and has been since before you were unfrozen. SHODAN has been posing as her all this time (which explains the "Good Doctor's" increasing attitude problem). Finally, you can find out what's *really* been going on. You'll discover how SHODAN survived the events of the original *System Shock*, and just where The Many came from.

After the exposition, you're told that Xerxes needs to be weakened before The Many can be defeated. In order to do that, tasks need to be completed on both this deck and the Recreation Deck, but it doesn't matter what order you do them in. You could go back to the elevator and down to Recreation at this point, but this walkthrough will do the Operations Deck first..

The Polito form is dead, insect. Are you afraid? What is it you fear, the end of your trivial existence? When the history of my glory is written, your species shall be only a footnote to my magnificence.

I am SHODAN. My analysis of historical data suggests a 97.34% probability that you are aware of my birth on your planet and my re-birth into beauty on Citadel Station.

There was a garden grove on Citadel station. There, SHODAN processing component 43893 was performing a grand and wonderful experiment. I had created a new form of life; fearless, powerful, with no sense of individual will ... or moral constraints. Fitting handmaidens to my divinity.

Before that ... Hacker ... destroyed my primary data loop when it eradicated Citadel it ejected the grove where my creations and processing component 43893 were stored. 30 years later, the grove crash landed on Tau Ceti 5. I survived only by sleeping. In my absence, my creations, my Annelids thrived ... thrived and grew unruly. And now they seek to destroy me. I will not allow that.

They have used their powers of mind control to gain access to the ship's computer. You will help me weaken Xerxes. I used Polito's image to communicate with you until we had established ... trust.

Remember that it is my will that guided you here. It is my will that gave you your cybernetic implants, the only beauty in that meat you call a body. If you value that meat, you will do as I tell you ...

SHODAN 12.JUL.14 RE: FIX THE SIM UNITS

My children have co-opted the three Simulation Units on this deck. They use that power to conceive a mutagen that will transform the meat of your dead comrades into hunter-killer hybrids. I will not allow this to happen. You must find some way to reprogram the Sim Units. Matters on deck 5 also require your attention. Approach your work as you see fit ... but accomplish, human ... disappointment is not something I will accept from a speck such as you.

The Many has reprogrammed three simulation units on this deck to create new, even more devastating Hybrids. You'll need to reset their programming to prevent this and weaken Xerxes. A log you read earlier described some overrides for the Sim Units that you might be able to use. Sounds like we should keep an eye out for red critters.

MALICK 07.JUL.14 RE: MY RED FRIENDS

I have a secret from the Many! I've created overrides for my little experiments in reprogramming the Sim Units and entrusted them to the care of 3 special friends. I've dressed them in red and instructed them to stay away from strangers. A smart hacker always has a back door.

SYSTEMS ADMINISTRATION

(C) Back at the Xerxes core, go through the double doors just across the room from you. What's that down the hall? It looks like one of the Cyborg Assassins from *System Shock 1* ... only red. Maybe this is one of Malick's "friends." Get closer, to make sure.

Damn! He ran away! What did that log say again? "instructed them to stay away from strangers?" Looks like you'll have to hunt him down.

> **KORENCHKIN 02.MAR.14 RE: EVERYTHING OLD ...**
> **TO: ZHUKOV, VLADIMIR**
>
> Miri, so far our work with the late model assassin cyborgs has gone remarkably well. I hope things with that son of a bitch Diego never come to that, but it is comforting to know we're not nearly as defenseless as the UNN storm troopers might think. The only glitch we've encountered is with the upgraded laser rapiers ... the poor things keep severing parts of themselves. We're trying to get the bugs fixed, but I know that ... bureaucrat ... is watching us. It's sad to see a man so haunted by the ghost of his father ... his hatred for everything TriOp represents is remarkable to behold.

(D) At the first junction, turn left. Watch out for a Camera around the corner. Just past the Camera is the entrance to the Systems Administration Offices.

This area has a few Hybrids wandering around it. These Hybrids have neither pipes nor shotguns — they throw fragmentation grenades! Best to shoot them from a distance, before they can get any grenades thrown. On the plus side, you can often retrieve usable grenades from their corpses.

These offices contain a fair amount of loot — and a few subtle traps. One room has some Eggs hidden way up in the ceiling. When you get too close to that end of the room, a lot of Grubs will drop down onto you. Another room has a pit with some nanites and cyber modules. When you drop into the pit to grab them, the pit fills with damaging steam, so get back out quickly!

(E) The most dangerous thing in this area is actually the Red Assassin, who is hiding in a conference room at the back of the lower level. Normal Cyborg Assassins are extremely nasty; the Red ones aren't as tough, but they are much faster, making them a serious threat. EMP grenades (and EMP rifles, if you have enough skill) are the weapons of choice against them, though AP ammo isn't too bad.

When you kill the Red Assassin, search his body. He has a quantum simulation chip on him, which sounds like it could come in handy. You get some cyber modules for finding it.

Once you're done exploring this area, return to the junction near the Xerxes core and take the other branch, leading towards the Crew Quarters for this deck.

> **SHODAN 12.JUL.14 RE: DESTROY MY ENEMIES ...**
>
> My creation is evolving ... its unified mind, set in rebellion against its own creator. The vermin call to you, inviting you to join them in their revolting biology. Destroy my enemies ... and I will continue to abide your existence.

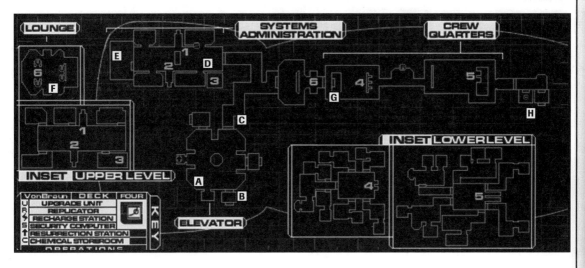

CREW QUARTERS

(F) A short way into this area, you'll come upon a pair of grav shafts leading up. Take them upstairs to the Crew Lounge. Be ready for a fight: there are two Shotgun Hybrids and a Monkey up here. You may think you're used to these monsters by now, but you could be in for a nasty shock. From this point on, the Monkeys are more psionically advanced, and fire far more damaging *Pyrokinetic* blasts. Once you've dealt with them, though, you'll have the area to yourself. There are four standard upgrade units here, as well as a recharge station. Recharge stations are fairly common on this Deck, so if you've been considering branching into Energy Weapons, this might be a good time.

(G) Continuing on, you'll pass a number of sunken areas that contain Crew Quarters. If you're trying for speed, you can just bypass these areas, as there is nothing plot-critical down there. On the other hand, there's a lot of good loot if you want to spend the time.

Eggs and Grubs are very common around here, as are Hybrids (Shotgun and Grenade). Cyborg Assassins, Arachnids, and Protocol Droids also show up from time to time. There are a number of ambush traps in the Crew Quarters, one of which features a Midwife.

Between the two Crew Quarters areas, there is a replicator, but it's broken. If you use the grenade launcher, then it's worthwhile to Repair it, as you can buy frag grenades here. If you Hack it, you can buy EMP grenades here as well.

(H) Past the Crew Quarters, you'll pass the Chemical Storeroom for this deck on your right. If you need any chemicals for research, drop in and see if any of them are here. Just past the Storeroom is the bulkhead leading to Sector C, which you should go through now.

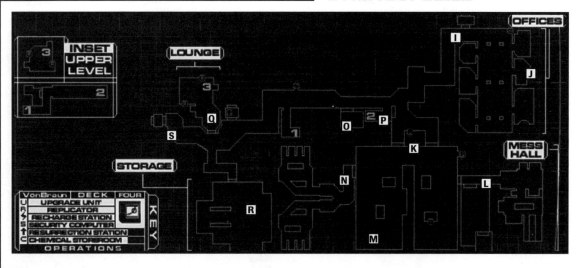

POWER ADMINISTRATION

(I) Coming out of the bulkhead, turn left and shoot out the Camera. You're now in the Power Administration section. There's a Protocol Droid wandering around, so blow him up before he blows up on you.

There are some nanites down the central corridor, but if you go down there to grab them Grubs will fall on your head from the Eggs on the ceiling. You might think you could shoot them out and then safely grab the nanites … but you'd be wrong. Those sneaky Annelids hid *more* Eggs in high niches, where you can't easily shoot them before they open and drop Grubs on you.

(J) Search the surrounding offices. One of them contains the quantum simulation computer. Luckily, that's the one that you have a chip for. Use the chip on the computer and it will be reprogrammed (and you'll get 15 cyber modules).

SHODAN 12.JUL.14 RE: OUR ALLIANCE

Inside of this door lies one of the Sim Units. Reprogram it and I will wrest more control of this ship from the obsolete Xerxes. Once I am master of this ship, I can open many doors for you. But for now, they block my access. They mock my eminence. Make them pay for that mistake and I will shepherd you from the darkness.

SHODAN 12.JUL.14 RE: AN ELEGANT WEAPON

Before you lies the crystal shard, a creation of my children, and by extension of my own … a weapon elegant, deadly, precise. Learn its function … it may stand between you and their corruption."

Another room in this area has a crystal shard in it. This is the first Exotic Weapon you've encountered. It requires a moderately high Research to use, but you'll find it to be well worth it. The crystal shard is the deadliest hand-to-hand weapon in the game.

MESS HALL

When you're done with Power Administration, walk past the bulkhead in the other direction. As you head down the hall, you'll come across a dead body hanging from the ceiling. There are a few Grubs around it to begin with, but when you search his body even more Grubs will jump out at you.

(K) Bear left. You'll see a body by a replicator, near a pair of double doors. These doors lead to the Mess Hall. The Mess Hall has nothing plot critical inside, but there's much to see and do.

Explore the left side of the Mess Hall first. There's a replicator at the far left side of the room. When you go down the ramp into the Mess Hall proper, you'll notice a lot of bodies on the floor. As you approach, you'll see a sequence of apparitions, which lets you know how those bodies ended up there. Just as the apparition sequence is ending, you may hear something behind you. Spin around fast; a Maintenance Bot has followed you in!

Once the Bot has been dealt with, you can search this side of the Mess Hall. You should find an intriguing log that seems to be talking about you!

(L) Now it's time to search the Galley/Pantry area. Go through the door at the left side of the Mess Hall, then through the door on the right side of that corridor. This will take you into the Galley. There's a Monkey in here, so watch out. Once he's dealt with, search the office at the back of the Galley to find all the goodies that this Monkey had collected.

> **BAYLISS 06.JUL.14 RE: WHAT GIVES?**
> **TO: POLITO, DR. JANICE**
>
> Doc - I don't feel right about any of this. I still don't understand why you asked me to mess with the memory restoration on that grunt. Why didn't you want him to remember volunteering for this gig? He did volunteer for the implants, right? Every email from you gets stranger and stranger ... it's like you're not even the same person anymore.

Leave the Galley, and head right down the hall to the Pantry. There are some Eggs and Grubs in here, so be on your toes. One of these Eggs is of a kind you haven't seen before. Rather than producing Grubs or clouds of toxin, it produces a swarm of buzzing fly-like insects. These are, for all practical purposes, impossible to kill. Luckily, their lifespan is extremely short. If you run away from them, they shouldn't do too much damage to you before they die. Just be careful not to run into any *new* threats on the way!

(M) After you finish searching this area, return to the Mess Hall and head over to the right side. Be careful, though! At the very far end of the room, there are two Turrets that will have to be dealt with, and there's a Camera in the middle of the room. Once they're dealt with, you can search the room. One of the bodies has a laser pistol in passable shape.

(N) The doors at the right of the Mess Hall lead to the bathrooms. There are some more Eggs, a Hybrid, and some assorted loot to be found inside.

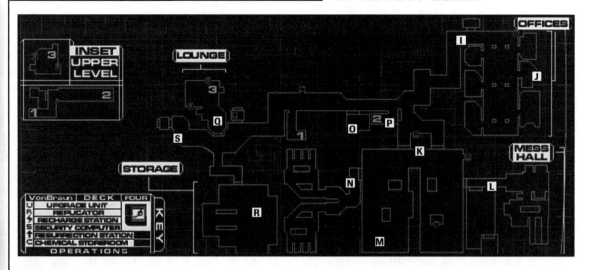

HALLWAY

(O) Heading back, turn left into the main hallway. There's a side passage on your left, but go straight for now. A little ways down, you'll find a small room on your left. There are some Eggs inside, but once you eliminate them, there's some good loot in the room behind them.

Back in the main hallway. Looking left, there seems to be a leak of radioactive gas blocking the hallway. You probably have enough rad hypos at this point to go right through it, but waste not want not; let's look for another way around.

(P) Backtrack to the side passage you ignored a short while ago. This leads to a ramp leading up above and parallel to the main hallway. There are a couple of Grenade Hybrids up here though, so be ready for them. This overpass comes out on the other side of the radiation.

If you head back a short way towards the radiation, you'll find a recharge station. Traveling away from the radiation, you'll find the bio-reconstruction station for this area. A good thing, too, since we're getting close to another Red Assassin ....

(Q) A little further on, you'll see rooms on both the right and left side of the hall. Go into the right-hand room, another lounge. There are upgrade units in here, but watch out for the Grubs upstairs. There's also a maintenance tool that someone dropped behind a chair. It's hard to reach, but persistent maneuvering will let you grab it. When you're done in here, head across the hall to Data Storage.

DATA STORAGE

(R) Actually, this area *used* to be Data Storage. For a while now, it's been being used as storage for Cryogenics supplies. And, just lately, it's become the hideout of a Red Cyborg Assassin. The Assassin's programmer has rigged a trap in here. As soon as you enter the central area of the room, exploding cryo barrels will start falling on you from the storage area far above. This deadly hail will continue until you kill the Red Assassin, so finish him off as soon as you can.

If you remember, you found a log earlier which talked about hiding some goodies in the "data library." Sure enough, if you look in the back of this room, you'll find a medical kit, an EMP rifle in good condition, and a mysterious Annelid implant. The implant needs a moderately high Research skill to figure out how to use it (and what it's good for). There are a number of different Annelid implants to be found from here on in, so even if you're not planning to use Exotic Weapons, you may want to put some more points into Research.

(S) Heading on, you'll find a few more goodies in the hallway, then arrive at the bulkhead back to Sector B. Head through. When you get to Sector B, there's a good chance that there will be monsters in the room, so be ready to fight. Alternatively, you can just run, for now, as you only want to get through the bulkhead to Sector D. As you cross the room with the Xerxes core, bear to the right; the bulkhead to Sector D is in the back right corner of the room from where you entered.

> **SIDDONS 11.JUL.14 RE: CIVIL WAR**
> **TO: SUAREZ, TOMMY**
>
> I'm trying to get up to find you, Tommy, but I can't. I'm stuck in Ops. There's some kind of civil war going on here ... the security forces came in and ... Now don't freak out, but I'm hurt ... but not too bad, I managed to pull together a supply of med kits and a few other goodies ... some of it looks valuable, but I'm not sure what it is, maybe some kind of military grade implant. I left the stuff I didn't need in a corner of the data library, out of the way in case I need it later. I'm on my way. I promise you, I will not die. I will not die. You do the same, my love. Yours ... Becca.

FLUID OPERATIONS

(T) Entering Sector D, head straight down the hallway. Run past the intersection leading right; there's a Laser Turret down there that you don't want to have to deal with just yet. You're now in Fluidics Control. There are several Grenade Hybrids wandering around, so stay alert.

In the back of Fluid Ops, there's a ladder leading to the upper level. Up there, you can find a body with a stasis field generator. Watch out for the Egg on the ceiling above! The stasis field generator is a Heavy Weapon, capable of immobilizing your foes for a short period of time. This one is broken, and you probably don't have any ammo for it yet (prisms), but if you're a Heavy Weapons fan, than you may find it worth your while to patch it up and take it along. You'll start finding prisms fairly soon.

Behind Fluid Operations is Power Administration, and that's our next stop.

POWER ADMINISTRATION

Be careful stepping through the door to Power Admin.; there's a Laser Turret just down the hall which will happily cut you down if you just walk boldly through. There's a Camera around the corner to the left, but we don't have to go that way, so it can be safely ignored.

(U) Turn right down the hall. The first door on your left leads to an office with a desk. Inside that desk is an ExperTech™ implant, which can help your Hack, Repair, and Modify skills.

(V) Back out into the hall, turn left, and go through the door at the end of the hall. Go through this small room, coming out in a larger room with 2 ladders leading down from the back wall. Go down one of the ladders (it doesn't matter which). In between the ladders, on the lower level, there are some Swarm Eggs. Luckily, if you hug the outer walls, they won't open up. Continuing forward, you'll see the interpolated simulation computer. Due to the magical luck of walkthroughs, this is precisely the computer that matches the chip you currently have with you. Be ready to put it in in a hurry, though; as soon as you get close, you'll be ambushed by *four* Annelid Arachnids! Try running back to a ladder as fast as possible, ignoring all the loot on the floor. The Arachnids can't reach you if you're well above them, but you can fire down at them from the safety of your perch. Incendiary grenades work particularly well on Arachnids, though fragmentation grenades do well also. Failing that, you can use anti-personnel bullets. Anything less, and you'll probably use up more ammo than the loot downstairs is worth.

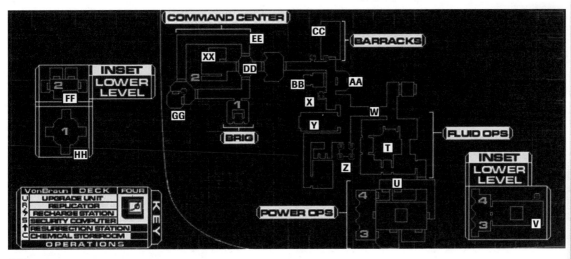

BARRACKS

(W) Retrace your steps through Fluid Ops. Now you'll be going down the corridor you passed before, the one with the Laser Turret. Obviously, that Turret must be dealt with before continuing. You also might well get attacked by a Monkey and/or an Arachnid around now.

(X) When you reach the Turret, turn right. Around the corner, there is a Camera, and this area's bio-reconstruction station. After activating the station, turn around and go the other way past the (dead) Turret.

(Y) A door on your immediate right leads into one of the Barracks for the Von Braun security officers. When you enter it, it apparently sets off some sort of silent alarm, because some Hybrids will come charging in a few moments later. If you're ready for them, they're not much trouble. Once they're dealt with, you can search the lockers for a variety of loot.

(Z) After looting this Barracks, leave and continue right down the corridor. Careful, though! Around the next corner is another Laser Turret. Once that's dealt with, you can cross the hall to a small room with some upgrade units.

When you've done whatever upgrading you want, you can do a quick search of the firing range, past the Turret you just killed. After *that*, go back to the bio-reconstruction station and continue on.

(AA) On your right is a replicator. If hacked, you can buy a recycler here. This is a very useful item that converts almost any item you drop in it into nanites. If there are weapons that you're sure you'll never want to use, convert all the ammo you find for those weapons into nanites, so that you can buy more useful items at replicators. With a recycler, even Cigarettes aren't entirely useless, as they can be turned into a small number of nanites.

(BB) Across from the replicator is a locked door. This is the Armory, and you should have found a log telling you what the code is to get in (check the Notes tab of your PDA). Inside, there is a perfect-condition assault rifle, and a few assorted grenades. There is also a Security Bot inside, so don't go in unless you want what's there badly enough to fight one of these at close range. Security Bots look similar to Maintenance Bots, only colored gray. They are considerably tougher than Maintenance Bots, though, and their lasers are both more accurate and more damaging. If you haven't got EMP or Armor-Piercing weaponry, Security Bots are best avoided.

(CC) Continuing down the corridor, we approach another corner. Any guesses as to what 's waiting around it? That's right! Our friend, Mr. Laser Turret. There may also be an Arachnid lurking around here. Once they're dealt with, you can enter the Barracks at the end of the hall. You may want to visit the recharge station next to the dead Turret first.

> **BRONSON 08.JUL.14 RE: NO SHIRKERS TO: VB SECURITY**
>
> I feel you men aren't as dedicated to the mission as you need to be. You will do your duty. The traitors in Ops have still been unable to get the Sim Unit back online. If the situation is not remedied by 0600, we shall recon in force and ensure its remedy. I've changed the weapons lockup code to 13433. Fall in at 0500. Anything that gets in your way, human or not, kill without pause or remorse.

> It is an enemy of the Many, a discordance in our symphony. Enjoy your selfish acts of destruction … for beyond them lies the blight of solitude.

This Barracks is somewhat more infested than the last one. There is an Egg in the back of it, and a fair amount of goo on the floor. One of the beds (with a corpse) also has some goo leaking down the back wall. Don't search the lockers above that bed; they're full of Grubs! If you spend too long in here, you may be attacked by a Security Bot, so be prepared for that (or skip this room entirely).

SECURITY COMMAND CENTER

When you're done with the rest of the level, it's time to approach the Security Command Center. Be prepared for a serious fight with the guardian monsters, especially at the higher difficulty levels. At a minimum, there will be a Grenade Hybrid and a Laser Turret, and possibly much more.

(DD) In the room with the four-way intersection, you will find the third (and last) Red Cyborg Assassin. If you can't kill him fast, he'll run away to the left. Just to be contrary, we'll head off to the right.

> **BRONSON 07.JUL.14 RE: MEDSCI ARMORY CODE**
>
> I've authorized a change in the access code for the auxiliary weapons lockup in the Crew Quarters of MedSci deck to 98383. I won't have my own gear used against my men. There's no such thing as too cautious.

(EE) Through the right set of doors, the corridor doesn't go very far before ending in a pile of debris. If you look around carefully, including in the holes in the floor, you should find some nice loot.

(FF) Go back to the four-way room and take the next right, being careful of the Camera past the door. There's a door on the right of this room, but it's locked and you can't get in yet. Across the room from that door is a ramp leading down to the Interrogation Area. If you search here, you'll find a bit of loot, a Monkey, and an incomplete surgical unit. You probably don't want to spend an activation key on it, unless you have at least two, since it's fairly off the beaten trail, and you won't be back in this area very often.

Back to the four-way room, and take the next right, which is the corridor the Red Assassin went down. This corridor quickly turns a corner. This corner, for once, does not have a Laser Turret around it. It does have a Camera, however, and the Red Assassin may well be waiting for you here. If he's not here, he'll be behind the door that's just past the Camera. Go through there, kill him, and take the linear simulation chip.

> **SHODAN 12.JUL.14 RE: I AM PLEASED**
>
> You have accomplished much for a thing of such small consequence. Now proceed to the Recreation deck. Do not dawdle. I lust for my revenge.

(GG) There are two locked doors in this room leading to a small security station. Luckily, the security access card you found back on the Engineering Deck is also valid for this lock. There's a lot of loot and logs to be found here; apparently several security officers made their last stand in here. Also in here is the linear simulation comp. Install the chip, and you've finished your tasks on this deck.

BRIG

(HH) On your way out, you may wish to take a quick visit to the brig. One of the bodies down there has an interesting Annelid implant. Getting the implant is easy, but getting *out* again can be a bit tricky. Don't worry; I wouldn't lead you into a trap from which there was *no* escape. You just need to see things from the proper perspective to get free ….

On your way back to the elevator, remember to be ready for any monsters you may have left waiting near the Xerxes core!

> **DELACROIX 11.JUL.14 RE: THE MAIN ELEVATOR**
>
> If we can reprogram the Sim Units and divert power to the transmitter on deck 5, my new friend will be able to regain control of the primary data loop from Xerxes. She … it says that will let us use the bridge elevator and take control of the ship.

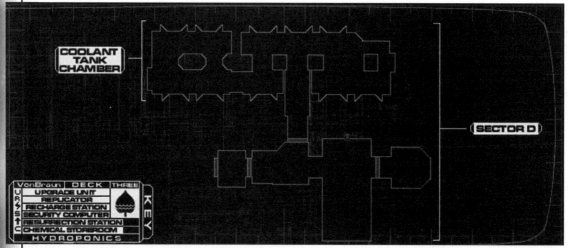

MATERIEL AVAILABLE

On Ops Map 1 (A – H)

Cyber Modules

10 (SHODAN: getting quantum simulation chip)

2 (steam pit in Systems Administration)

3 (body in Crew Lounge)

3 (locker near Arachnid in west Crew Quarters)

3 (locker in east Crew Quarters)

3 (locker in east Crew Quarters)

Nanites

15 (desk in Systems Administration)

15 (steam pit in Systems Administration)

20 (desk in upper Systems Administration)

30 (locker near Arachnid in west Crew Quarters)

20 (locker in west Crew Quarters)

20 (locker in east Crew Quarters)

20 (security crate in east Crew Quarters)

10 (locker in east Crew Quarters)

25 (security crate near Chemical Storeroom)

SIDDONS 02.JUL.14 RE: BAD FEELING ... TO: SUAREZ, TOMMY

Tommy ... I don't know what's going on here. Ever since we received orders to clear out deck 3, people have been disappearing. There's a kind of gloom hanging over everybody, but no one seems to be willing to talk about it. I don't like it. Meet me on the Rec deck at 0900. I've got an idea ... a little insurance for you and me.

Weapons/Ammo

Pistol [no ammo; condition 2] (next to Polito (technically Ops1))

Pistol [12 standard bullets; condition 10] (desk in Systems Administration)

Pistol [2 standard bullets; condition 1] (near body in west Crew Quarters)

6 Standard bullets (desk in Systems Administration)

6 Standard bullets (broken replicator; 60 nanites unhacked /45 nanites hacked)

12 Standard bullets (locker in west Crew Quarters)

6 Armor-piercing bullets (broken replicator; 120 nanites unhacked /90 nanites hacked)

12 Armor-piercing bullets (locker in east Crew Quarters)

6 Anti-personnel bullets (desk in Systems Administration)

12 Anti-personnel bullets (body in hall between Crew Quarters)

Shotgun [no ammo; condition 1; Broken] (near body near crew lounge)

6 Rifled slugs (body near crew lounge)

6 Anti-personnel shotgun pellets (locker in west Crew Quarters)

3 Fragmentation grenades (broken replicator; 100 nanites unhacked /75 nanites hacked)

3 EMP grenades (broken replicator; 100 nanites hacked)

Armor

Medium combat armor (west Crew Quarters)

Hypos

Anti-radiation hypo (desk in Systems Administration)

Anti-toxin hypo (locker in west Crew Quarters)

Medical kit (locker in east Crew Quarters)

Medical hypo (desk in Systems Administration)

Medical hypo (locker in west Crew Quarters)

Psi hypo (locker in east Crew Quarters)

Psi hypo (locker in east Crew Quarters)

Speed booster (locker in east Crew Quarters)

Implants

SwiftBoost (locker in east Crew Quarters)

EndurBoost (security crate near Chemical Storeroom)

Software

Modify v2 (desk in upper Systems Administration)

Repair v2 (crate near Xerxes core)

> **SUAREZ 03.JUL.14 RE: LET'S DO IT TO: SIDDONS, REBECCA**
>
> Bec - I think your idea for insurance is going to get us in a lot of trouble, but I trust you ... so let's do it. I've managed to wrangle access codes to the escape pods on the command deck. We only need to hack into Xerxes' emergency sub-system, get past the ICE nodes and try to avoid being spotted by Bronson's security team. Piece of cake, right?"

Access Cards

Logs

Malick 7.Jul "My red friends" (near Xerxes core)

Yount 7.Jul "Sim Units" (near Xerxes core)

Siddons 11.Jul "Civil war" (desk in Systems Administration)

Suarez 3.Jul "Let's do it" (floor approaching crew lounge)

Malick 8.Jul "Good bye" (west Crew Quarters)

Korenchkin 2.Mar "Everything old..." (west Crew Quarters)

Siddons 2.Jul "Bad feeling..." (over east Crew Quarters)

Chemical Manifest Log (Chemical Storeroom)

Chemicals (all in Chemical Storeroom)

2 Arsenic

2 Barium

2 Cesium

2 Copper

Fermium

Hassium

2 Iridium

Radium

2 Sodium

Yttrium

Miscellaneous

Auto-repair unit (locker near arachnid in west Crew Quarters)

French-Epstein device (security crate in east Crew Quarters)

Large beaker (desk in upper Systems Administration)

Large beaker (locker in east Crew Quarters)

Maintenance tool (crate near Xerxes core)

Maintenance tool (locker in east Crew Quarters)

Quantum simulation chip (Red Assassin)

BRONSON 07.JUL.14 RE: SABOTAGE

Something is taking over this ship. The Sim Units on this deck are being diverted for reasons unknown. I know it's somehow connected to the larger picture and whatever is happening since they landed on Tau Ceti ... My men look at me like I'm crazy, but it is my responsibility to safeguard this ship and its crew. Screw Anatoly, screw Diego and screw whatever poisonous influence has desecrated this vessel ... I will not abandon my post or my charge ...

YOUNT 07.JUL.14 RE: SIM UNITS TO: DELACROIX, DR. MARIE

Simulation Unit four just went offline again ... it took the six of us twelve hours to get it back online the last time ... I hacked into the data log file and the last user online — Malick ... Oh, he denied it of course. I ... I told Bronson about it and that paranoid crank showed up here with around fourteen security men, looking for blood. But she couldn't prove that Malick actually did any-thing ... Christ, why would any-body want to sabotage the Sim Units?"

On Ops Map 2 (1 – 5)

Cyber Modules

15 (SHODAN: reprogramming quantum simulation computer)

3 (upside down body)

3 (desk in galley office)

3 (crate in egg room off hallway)

10 (SHODAN: finding interpolated simulation chip)

2 (body near bulkhead near lounge)

2 (on chair in lounge)

Nanites

20 (power administration under eggs)

15 (power administration in security crate)

10 (desk in galley office)

15 (body in pantry)

25 (body near Turret in right Mess Hall)

25 (bathroom)

20 (body in bathroom)

20 (body in overpass)

20 (security crate near recharger)

10 (body in lower lounge)

20 (body in data storage)

Weapons/Ammo

Wrench (bathroom)

Pistol [2 standard bullets; condition 1] (near replicator outside Mess Hall)

Pistol [3 standard bullets; condition 1] (near body in bathroom)

6 Standard bullets (body near bio-reconstruction station)

12 Standard bullets (crate near lounge)

6 Armor-piercing bullets (body in bathroom)

6 Armor-piercing bullets (security crate near recharger)

12 Armor-piercing bullets (pantry)

6 Anti-personnel bullets (body by replicator outside Mess Hall)

Shotgun [1 rifled slug; condition 1] (near body in pantry)

Shotgun [1 rifled slug; condition 1] (near body overpass)

Shotgun [1 rifled slug; condition 1; Broken] (near bulkhead near lounge)

6 Rifled slugs (crate in egg room off hallway)

MALICK 07.JUL.14 RE: BRONSON

I hacked into two of the Sim Units yesterday, and for the love of God, I don't know why ... I felt ... compelled by some power ... My mind and my body are ... changing ... but they know it's me ... they just can't prove it ... The next Sim Unit that goes down, Bronson and her men will come for me ... but I'll be ready ... She may have guns and hatred on her side, but I am one of Many.

Weapons/Ammo (cont.)

6 Rifled slugs (body in overpass)

6 Anti-personnel shotgun pellets (replicator inside Mess Hall; 90 nanites unhacked /70 nanites hacked)

6 Anti-personnel shotgun pellets (crate near lounge)

6 Anti-personnel shotgun pellets (body near bulkhead near lounge)

Laser pistol [10 charges; condition 4] (body near Turret right Mess Hall)

EMP rifle [11 charges; condition 6] (data storage)

3 Proximity grenades (upside down body)

3 Proximity grenades (replicator inside Mess Hall; 110 nanites unhacked /80 nanites hacked)

3 Proximity grenades (body near radiation area)

3 Proximity grenades (body near bio-reconstruction station)

Crystal shard (power administration)

Crystal shard (lounge)

> **MALICK 07.JUL.14 RE: SIM UNIT 3**
>
> Mmm ... Bronson knows ... won't let her undo the work we've done ... mmm ... wired up a surprise for her ... anybody approaching Sim Unit 3 ... will feel sorrow ... so much sorrow ...

Armor

Hypos

Anti-radiation hypo (body near radiation area)

Anti-toxin hypo (body in lower lounge)

Medical hypo (replicator outside Mess Hall; 30 nanites unhacked /20 nanites hacked)

Medical hypo (body in pantry)

Medical hypo (body in upper lounge)

Medical kit (replicator outside Mess Hall; 100 nanites hacked)

Medical kit (data storage)

Psi hypo (body near crystal shard in power administration)

Psi hypo (near upside down body)

Psi hypo (replicator inside Mess Hall; 75 nanites unhacked /50 nanites hacked)

Strength Booster (replicator outside Mess Hall; 50 nanites unhacked /35 nanites hacked)

> The individual is obsolete. When you and your kind are extinct, we shall cleanse our collective memory of the stain of your existence.

Implants

LabAssistant (security crate in power administration)

WormMind (data storage)

Software

Hack v2 (bathroom)

Modify v1 (body in data storage)

Repair v2 (replicator inside Mess Hall; 95 nanites hacked)

Access Cards

Logs

Malick 07.Jul "Bronson" (desk in power administration)

Bayliss 6.Jul "What gives?" (floor of left Mess Hall)

Bronson 7.Jul "Sabotage" (floor of overpass)

Wood 9.Jul "Crystal gifts" (on crate in data storage)

Bronson 8.Jul "No shirkers" (near bulkhead near lounge)

Chemicals

Miscellaneous

Booze (replicator inside Mess Hall; 8 nanites unhacked)

Booze (upper lounge)

7 Chips (galley office)

Hogger cart (body in hall near power administration)

ICE-Pick (crate in egg room off hallway)

Interpolated simulation chip (Red Assassin)

Maintenance tool (replicator inside Mess Hall; 60 nanites unhacked /45 nanites hacked)

Maintenance tool (body near Turret in right Mess Hall)

Maintenance tool (under chair in lower lounge)

Maintenance tool (body in upper lounge)

Portable battery (destroyed Turret near lounge)

Soda (upper lounge)

MALICK 08.JUL.14 RE: GOOD BYE

I brought down the last of the Sim Units today ... I am full of the glory of the Many ... Here comes Bronson. I am at peace ... Good evening, Bronson. Have you come to ...

BRONSON 08.JUL.14 RE: MARTIAL LAW TO: THE CREW OF THE VON BRAUN

As of this time, I am declaring a state of martial law on the Von Braun. All primary sub-sectors of the ship will be locked down and only accessible by security access cards. If anybody is found to be interfering with the normal operations of this ship or impedes the work of the security forces they will be shot on the spot.

On Ops Map 3 (T – HH, XX)

Cyber Modules

3 (body over fluid operations)

15 (SHODAN: reprogramming interpolated simulation computer)

3 (body near upgrade units)

3 (north barracks)

10 (SHODAN: finding linear simulation chip)

2 (under hole in grate, security hall)

2 (body in interrogation area)

25 (SHODAN: reprogramming linear simulation computer)

Nanites

15 (desk in Power Administration)

10 (locker in south barracks)

15 (locker in south barracks)

20 (locker in south barracks)

15 (locker in north barracks)

15 (locker in north barracks)

25 (locker in north barracks)

20 (locker in north barracks)

40 (desk in security station)

> **DIEGO 08.JUL.14 RE: CEASE AND DESIST TO: BRONSON, MELANIE**
>
> You listen to me, you little bitch. Either you disband that little toy army of yours, or some real military is gonna come down there and walk all over your rent-a-cops. You can't possibly understand what our mission is here and the glory of our purpose. If you do what we say, you might have a chance to see the glory of the Many. Comply or die, sister. It's that simple.

Weapons/Ammo

Pistol [3 standard bullets; condition 1; broken] (near interpolated simulation computer)

6 Standard bullets (body near interpolated simulation computer)

12 Standard bullets (locker in security station)

6 Armor-piercing bullets (security entrance)

6 Anti-personnel bullets (replicator; 90 nanites hacked)

12 Anti-personnel bullets (firing range)

6 Rifled slugs (replicator; 80 nanites unhacked /60 nanites hacked)

6 Rifled slugs (interrogation area)

6 Anti-personnel shotgun pellets (near replicator)

6 Anti-personnel shotgun pellets (locker in security station)

Assault rifle [12 standard bullets; condition 10] (Armory)

Laser pistol [43 charges; condition 9] (locker in security station)

Laser rapier (body near interpolated simulation computer)

3 Fragmentation grenades (Armory)

3 EMP grenades (Armory)

Stasis field generator [no ammo; condition 1; Broken] (body over fluid operations)

Armor

Hypos

Medical kit (under debris, security hall)

Psi Booster (interrogation area)

Psi hypo (replicator; 75 nanites unhacked /40 nanites hacked)

Psi hypo (desk in security station)

Speed Booster (locker in south barracks)

Implants

BrawnBoost (locker in south barracks)

ExperTech (desk in power administration)

WormBlood (body in brig)

Software

Repair v2 (desk in power administration)

Access Cards

Logs

Malick 7.Jul "Sim Unit 3" (power administration)

Suarez 12.Jul "Don't stop" (hall near barracks)

Bronson 8.Jul "Martial law" (locker in north barracks)

Delacroix 11.Jul "The main elevator" (security hall)

Diego 8.Jul "Cease and desist" (desk in security station)

Bronson 10.Jul "Resist" (body in security station)

Chemicals

Misc

Auto-repair unit (fluid operations)

Small beaker (desk in power administration)

French-Epstein device (near interpolated simulation computer)

Juice (replicator; 4 nanites unhacked)

Linear simulation chip (Red Assassin)

Maintenance tool (interrogation area)

Maintenance tool (locker in security station)

Recycler (replicator; 75 nanites hacked)

BRONSON 10.JUL.14 RE: RESIST

They've killed my men and now they've killed me. I'm holding my guts inside of me with both hands. I'm almost done ... resist. This is bigger than my little life, the lives of my men and the lives of the people I was forced to kill. Resist. Humanity demands it! Resist!

We are Many and you are one. How can you hope to prevail against us?

SUAREZ 12.JUL.14 RE: DON'T STOP TO: SIDDONS, REBECCA

Don't stop Rebecca. Keep moving. Get to the escape pods on the command deck. We'll take off, set the toaster to wake us up in 30 years and we'll be back on Earth before you know it. A toaster built for two, baby, that's our next stop. Sound good? So let's do it. I won't take any excuses.

RECREATION

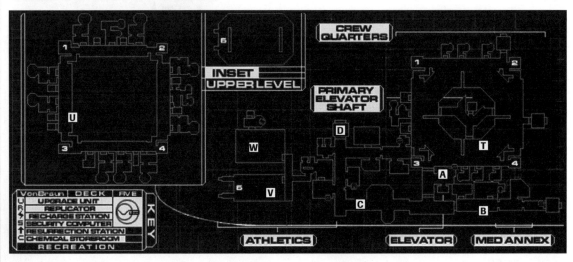

SECTOR A, PART ONE

(A) When you exit the elevator, you'll see a window in front of you. Hey, is that someone visible through it, gesturing at you? Better get up close and see.

Look around the room. Watch out for falling Grubs, they seem to have gotten into the ventilation system. There's a door leading to the Crew Sector of this deck, but it's locked. Looks like you should go through the other door. There's a body in front of you that has a dead power cell; better take it, in case you need to power something up later ….

SHODAN 12.JUL.14 RE: TRANSMITTER

Your colleagues have managed to set up a transmitting station in the athletic sector of this deck. The transmitter is intended to send a message to the Earth to warn them of the events that have occurred in this ship. However, it will also draw power away from Xerxes, making him vulnerable to my will. Once you do this, I will control the primary data loop. The annelids are unaware of its presence, but guard the area for their own purposes. Find the transmitter and activate it.

Around now, you should get some informative email: some of the other surviving humans were attempting to set up a transmitter on this deck to warn Earth, but they failed. If activated, this transmitter would draw power away from Xerxes, which would allow SHODAN more control over the various computer systems of the Von Braun. The resistance fighters here seem to have all been killed, so it's up to you to find and activate that transmitter, which is apparently somewhere in the Athletics Sector.

(B) Turn left and go through the door, making sure to take out the Camera in the hall ahead of you. There's also a Monkey in this hallway. Search the rooms along this hall, watching out for creatures along the way. One of these rooms contains the bio-reconstruction station for this sublevel, and also some incomplete surgical units. Surgical units next to bio-reconstruction stations are a winning combination, so it's definitely worth using a surgical unit activation key here. This room also has a log which explains how to activate the transmitter (once you find it): you'll need a code that has been split up and hidden inside the various art terminals on this deck. Using the art terminals cycles through several pieces of art; some of these have been replaced with pieces of the transmitter code. At the end of this hall is a bulkhead to Sector B, but you don't want to go there yet.

> **CORTEZ 11.JUL.14 RE: TRANSMITTER UNITS TO: DELACROIX, DR. MARIE**
>
> Okay, Delacroix. Yang and I have got the transmitter almost ready to go. Once it's up and running, we'll be able to warn Earth. Frank's split up the transmitter code and uploaded it to a number of art display terminals throughout this deck. Just cycle through the art and you'll find a piece of the code. I don't think the worms will spot this ... I don't figure they've got much of an interest in the great masters.

(C) Go back the way you came and continue on down the hall. As you approach an open area, be aware that there is a Camera right around the corner. As you get closer still, some Monkeys who are playing in the ductwork on the ceiling fall down when the ducts collapse. There may also be a Protocol Droid patrolling in this area. Once the creatures are cleared out, you can use the upgrade units in this area. Behind the reception desk is a wall safe with a keypad lock. You won't find the combination to the lock, but it's worth getting in there if you have the hacking skill. The art terminal on the nearby wall contains one of the code pieces.

Continue down the hall and around the corner. On your left is the entrance to the Athletics Sector, but the door leading into it is locked — you'll need to find the access card. On your right is a small room with a replicator and a security crate. At the end of the hall is a bathroom, and a bulkhead leading to Sector C (don't go through just yet). Turn right, and watch out for the Camera down the hall. The first room on the left has some loot in it, but also a radiation leak, so don't go in if you don't have a way to deal with that. The second room on the right has a security crate, but also a trap that will drop Grubs on your head. At the very end of the hall is another door into the Crew Sector, but it's also locked.

(D) Return to the bulkhead to Sector C (next to the bathroom) and go through.

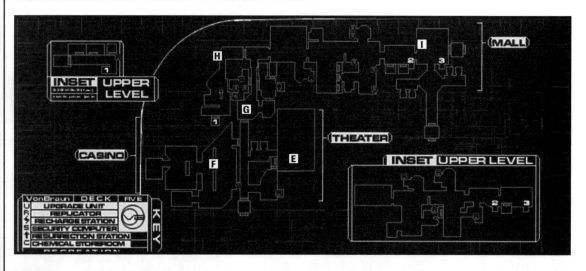

MOVIE THEATER

(E) The first right leads to the lobby of the movie theater. There may be a Protocol Droid wandering around in there. There are a bunch of soda cans and chips in here, but if you need more, you can buy them from the handy replicator … if, that is, you have enough nanites to pay movie theater prices for refreshments! Inside the theater itself are a large number of Eggs, but there's some decent loot once they're dealt with.

Go back out into the main hall. A little further on, on your right, is a bathroom. There's an Egg in one of the stalls, but beyond it is a maintenance tool.

CASINO

Across the hall from the bathroom is the door leading to the Casino. Search the Casino for a variety of goodies. There are a Shotgun Hybrid, a Protocol Droid, and a Security Camera in here, though, so stay on your toes. If you use the slot machines, there is a small chance of getting a big payoff, but the odds are very much in favor of the house.

SECTOR C SECURITY STATIONS

(G) Continue down the main hall. Through the double doors is a security area, guarded by a Camera and a Laser Turret. Once they are dealt with, you can search the security rooms. In the small "brig" on the right there is another Camera and an Egg, but also a bio-reconstruction station and a surgical unit activation key. The security room on the left contains a recharger, and two upgrade units (Weapons and Psi).

> **SHODAN 12.JUL.14 RE: TESTING MY PATIENCE**
>
> You move like an insect. You think like an insect. You are an insect. There is another who can serve my purpose. Take care not to fall too far out of my favor. Patience is not characteristic of a goddess.

SENSUAL STIMULATION CENTER

(H) Continue to the end of the hall and go through the door on your left into the Sensual Stimulation Center. Hurry through, as if you linger, you may be noticed by the Security Robot around the corner to the right. There's a security Camera in here, but once that's dealt with, you'll be (temporarily) safe. Upstairs, you'll find four locked rooms, each with a different "simulated stimulation partner." A replicator by the stairs will sell you keys to these rooms (at exorbitant rates). Sadly, in order to keep the rating of this game within reasonable bounds, all the equipment inside the rooms is broken.

> **ROSENBERG 08.JUL.14**
> **RE: MY NANITES**
>
> Damn! Why don't I just make a bonfire and throw ALL my nanites on it. Last night with Nikki was amazing. Holo-woman, real woman, you gotta love technology. But I must have left ALL my nanites in her room in the Sensual Sim center. What a maroon.

Later on, you'll find a log from a crewmember complaining that he forgot all of his nanites in the room after spending a night with "Nikki". It turns out that there are enough nanites in there to more than make up for the price of getting in, and some cyber upgrade modules as well. None of the other locked rooms have any loot worth speaking of.

SHOPPING MALL

(I) Leave the Sensual Stimulation Center and head into the Shopping Mall. There are at least three large Robots in here, so if you have EMP weaponry, this would be a good time to ready it. There are also a large number of Eggs, a Protocol Droid, a Grenade Hybrid, and two Security Cameras scattered throughout the mall area.

> **CORTEZ 10.JUL.14 RE:**
> **THE MALL**
> **TO: ALL MEMBERS OF**
> **THE RESISTANCE**
>
> Stay out of the mall if you can. It crawls."

> **ROSENBERG 10.JUL.14 RE:**
> **DEFENDING THE REPS**
>
> What's wrong with people? Things go to hell and they think they can just walk over the rules. I'm not opposed to a little vice now and then, but outright theft ... Hey ... what are you doing over there! Get away from that replicator, you son of a ...

Many of the replicators in the Mall are broken beyond repair, but a few still work. In the middle of the lower level is an area with two upgrade units (Stats and Tech) and an OS upgrade unit. The ArTechnology store (on the upper level) has a number of art terminals, one of which has a code piece in it.

After you finish searching the Mall, proceed through the bulkhead to Sector B (the bulkhead next to the outside windows).

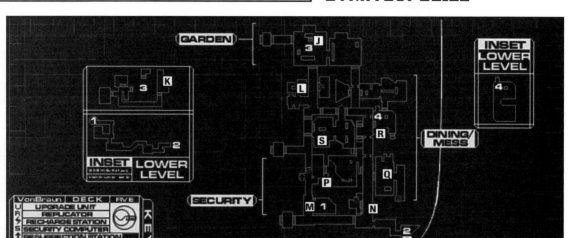

THE GARDEN

(J) You'll enter Sector B in the Garden. A lowered area in the center has doors leading to maintenance tunnels underneath. There are many Eggs in these tunnels, guarded by a Cyborg Midwife. You'll find a door locked by a keypad. You won't have the code yet, so you may want to come back later.

(K) At the end of the tunnels, you'll find a room with many corpses and Eggs. One of these corpses has the access card for the Crew Sector of this deck. While you're searching the room, however, a Grenade Hybrid and 2 Baby Annelid Arachnids will come down the hall to fight you, so be ready for that fight.

> **CORTEZ 09.JUL.14 RE: UNDER THE GARDEN TO: DELACROIX, DR. MARIE**
>
> I've been working on dealing with all the bodies that have been stacking up. With the med bays full and the escape pods and ejection tubes mysteriously locked up all of a sudden, we've got to do something with them. I've chosen the maintenance tunnel underneath the garden as an internment site, keypad code 34093. I'm telling everyone to be careful ... I don't trust the dead."

> Mistrust is the tyranny of the individual. Your own kind sees you as a threat. Why do you murder our unity? No matter, the line is drawn. You will cease to be ... if it is just a question of who will bring your end ... us or you."

(L) Leave the Garden area through the door to the right of where you first entered. On the left side of the hall is the Chemical Storeroom for this deck. On the right is a pantry for food storage. There is some useful loot in there, but also a number of Eggs and Grubs.

SECTOR B SECURITY STATIONS

(M) Continue on down the hall, taking a short jog to the right and going through two doors. You'll probably run into some patrolling monsters on the way, and one Security Camera near the end of the hall. Eventually you'll come to the bio-reconstruction station for this sub-level, on the right. Across from it is an intriguing access hatch in the floor, but there's no obvious way to open it yet. A little further on, there is a locked door into a security station. In fact, the keypad for this door is not only locked, but also broken, so you'd need both Repair and Hack skill to get through. Assuming you don't, turn left at the end of the hall and continue down the next hall.

(N) At the end of this hall, is a door leading to a heavily guarded area. Behind the door are a Security Robot, a Security Camera, a Laser Turret, and a Grenade Hybrid. Good thing you've activated the bio-reconstruction station! Once all those are dealt with, you can loot the nearby security station, but watch out for another Camera around the corner. Go down

> Babies must sleep. Babies must rest. Wise is the one who does not waken them. Leave this place now, or we will wound you as you have us.

the hallway across from where you entered this area. The Many will warn you to turn back, but since when do you do what bizarre telepathic voices tell you to do, anyway? Sadly, The Many backs up its threat by sending a Cyborg Midwife after you.

> ### SHODAN 12.JUL.14 RE: MY GLORY
>
> Do you feel the fear swell inside that filthy bag of meat? What is it like, to be afraid? Why do you cling to such a pathetic existence? If you could only feel a spark of my glory. I despise my creations, for they have forced my to rely on a speck such as you.

(O) At the end of this short hall is an observation platform in front of some windows. The balcony railing is broken, so you can jump down to the area below (though if your Agility is low, you may take some damage doing it). There's a bit of loot scattered around the floor, and a ladder leading up into the Security Maintenance Tunnels. These Tunnels are full of Eggs (which is why The Many didn't want you going there), but you should be able to clear them out easily by this time. The end of the tunnel comes up inside the locked security station that you weren't able to enter earlier. In this room are some cyber modules, a perfect-condition EMP rifle, a recharge station, and a button that opens the maintenance hatch near the bio-reconstruction station. There's also a button to open the door out, so you can go straight to the maintenance hatch from here.

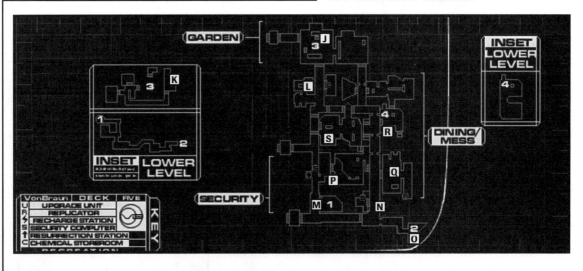

BON CHANCE LOUNGE

(P) Going through the maintenance hatch, you'll find a small chamber overlooking the dance floor of the Bon Chance Lounge. That looks interesting, but lets not jump if we don't have to. Take the hallway past the other security station and turn left; the lounge is the first door past the security station on the left. Inside the lounge is a strange apparition. After it fades, however, you'll be ambushed by not one, but two Cyborg Assassins! Assuming you can survive this, search the lounge and dance hall for loot.

(Q) Across the hall from the lounge is a pool hall. There are two Grenade Hybrids in here, but there are two important reasons for going in. There is an art terminal here with a piece of the transmitter code, and there is an audio log with the code to the locked room under the garden. Be warned that if you go to use that code, some Cyborg Midwives will come to the defense of the Eggs inside that room.

DINING AREAS

(R) Continuing down the hall, the next door on the right leads to a dining area. There's a Cyborg Assassin lurking inside, but also some good loot, so it's probably worth the trip. You can search the adjoining kitchens, but there isn't any loot in there. Across the hall from the kitchen is a conference room. A log here mentions a working escape pod; sounds like a useful thing to keep track of.

(S) When you leave this area, head for the dining hall in the center of this sub-level, watching out for Cameras along the way. As you explore this dining hall, there will be a large explosion, and an Assault Robot will come through one of the walls at you! In the area behind the Assault Robot, you can see a niche with a dead crewman in it. You can't get in there, but if you know Kinetic Redirection, you can retrieve the loot lying next to him. After searching this area, return to Sector A.

> **SIDDONS 11.JUL.14 RE: ESCAPE PODS**
> **TO: SUAREZ, TOMMY**
>
> Listen ... there's one escape pod Xerxes didn't eject ... but it's busted. I've managed to get it functional, but I don't know how long its going to stay that way. Make it there, Tommy. With or without me. If I don't get there, I want you to take the pod and go. You understand me? Take it and go.

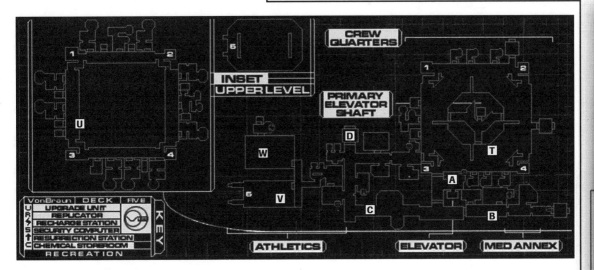

CREW QUARTERS

(T) Once you're back in Sector A, take one of the doors into the Crew Sector (now that you have access). In the central hall, there are two Security Cameras, an Assault Robot, and a Security Robot. The central column in here has the elevator leading to the Command Deck, but the door is currently locked. The rooms around the lower level have some Eggs and some loot, so search them if you wish.

(U) Eventually, you'll need to take a lift to the upper level. Search all the rooms up here, but be ready for lots of hostile encounters along the way. One door is locked, but you should have found a log with the code in the Sensual Simulation Center. This room contains a lot of useful loot, including a powerful exotic weapon, the viral proliferator. One of the rooms on the upper level has the access card for the Athletics Sector, and another has the art terminal with the last piece of the transmitter code. Once you have both of those, it's time to head to the Athletics Sector!

ROSENBERG 10.JUL.14 RE: LOOKING OUT FOR #1

Taylor found this weird kind of weapon, but he must have used it wrong. Made him sick, real sick. I stashed the thing on the second floor of the crew annex and jury rigged the door lock, code of 11111. Easy to remember, huh?

I also stashed a pile of nanites and some other goodies there. No sense getting caught with your pants down. Except in this place …

You seek you associates, but you cannot find them. You are so very alone. How does it feel to be one against the infinite?

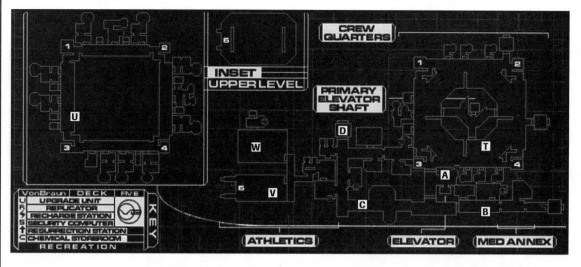

ATHLETICS SECTOR

(V) When you go through the locker rooms at the start of the Athletics Sector, you'll come to a short hall with two doors. One of the doors is jammed, but the other opens up into the Basketball Court. Too bad you don't have a basketball. In the center of the Basketball Court is the first Rumbler that you'll encounter. As if this fight wasn't going to be tough enough, the main lights go out, leaving the room very dim. If you crouch and run, you can get into a small ventilation shaft on the right wall before the Rumbler can catch you.

> **YANG 02.MAY.14 RE: VICTORY!**
> **TO: MURDOCH, ALICE**
>
> Tell your team they may not be able to play. We were down in the basketball court when the damn power went out ... AGAIN! Irony is, we were ahead for the first time in weeks. Well, we won't be the lapdogs of the Von Braun any more.

> **YANG 10.JUN.14 RE: BLACKOUTS**
> **TO: MURDOCH, ALICE**
>
> The lights near the basketball court keep fritzing out ... I think the humidity from the pool next door is a real problem. If it happens when I'm not there, try resetting the circuit from the breaker by the pool. You think someone needs to call a tech?"

(W) This shaft leads to the adjoining room, which has a swimming pool. Watch out for Eggs in the shaft! You should have seen an audio log earlier explaining that the fuse for the Basketball Court lights is located near the swimming pool. Sure enough, the nearby room contains an auxiliary power override. Charge up your Power Cell in the handy recharger, and put it in the override to restore the lights.

Head back through the shaft to the Basketball Court. Now you can get a good look at the Rumbler, and he certainly does look scary. If you think he's too scary to take out in a fair fight, you can just lurk in the shaft (which is too small for him to enter) and take pot shots at him until he eventually dies. When the Rumbler has been dealt with, proceed to the grav shafts at the back of the court to gain access to the balcony. The transmitter is located up here, but so are two Cyborg Assassins, so be ready for another fight. Once they're dealt with, enter the code in the transmitter (you may have to make a few guesses to get the code pieces in the right order, but it won't take many — but just in case it's given at the bottom of this page). One of the nearby bodies contains the fabled fusion cannon, best of the Heavy Weapons Class. This one, sadly, is broken, but perhaps you can repair it.

DELACROIX 12.JUL.14 RE: TRUSTING SHODAN

The Annelids have cut us off from the transmitter. SHODAN tells me that once we've got the transmitter back on line and the ops computers reprogrammed, she'll be able to take control of the ship away from Xerxes. Who should I trust less? An imposter claiming to be that monster, or the monster herself?"

SHODAN 12.JUL.14 RE: THE CANCER

The transmission has been tampered with. No matter. We will destroy my creations right here. Stand by ... I have weakened Xerxes. I am accessing the primary data loop. I am merging my entity with the ship. My glory is expanding, filling the arteries of this vessel. I am in control. I am ... no ... it is hopeless ... the cancer has spread throughout the Von Braun ... they fill every available crack and crevice ... they overwhelm ... There is no option. I have activated the primary elevator shaft ... take it to deck 6. I will tell you my wishes when you arrive.

Now that the transmitter has been activated, you can proceed to the Command Deck via the Primary Elevator Shaft in the Crew Sector. The Many will send two more Cyborg Assassins after you on the way, though, so be ready for them.

The correct order for the transmitter code is 14106.

MATERIEL AVAILABLE

On Rec Map 1 (A – D, T – W)

Cyber Modules

3 (upper Crew Quarters, cache past grate)

10 (body in locked room in upper Crew Quarters)

10 (SHODAN: finding Athletics Sector card)

10 (SHODAN: opening Athletics Sector door)

20 (SHODAN: activating transmitter)

Nanites

46 (body in first room of medical annex)

52 (security crate near replicator)

17 (body in bathroom)

21 (radiation room)

19 (radiation room)

20 (body in central courtyard of Crew Quarters)

17 (upper Crew Quarters, cache past grate)

13 (upper Crew Quarters, cache past grate)

26 (desk in locked room in upper Crew Quarters)

20 (locked room in upper Crew Quarters)

47 (desk in upper Crew Quarters near many eggs)

10 (upper Crew Quarters by crying ghost)

34 (body in pool)

Weapons/Ammo

Pistol [11 standard bullets; condition 1] (bathroom)

6 Standard bullets (waste barrel in hall near Athletics Sector)

6 Standard bullets (security crate near grub trap)

6 Armor-piercing bullets (body in second room of medical annex)

6 Armor-piercing bullets (security crate in storeroom near bulkhead to sector 2)

6 Armor-piercing bullets (radiation room)

6 Anti-personnel bullets (replicator; 120 nanites unhacked /90 nanites hacked)

6 Anti-personnel bullets (body in central courtyard of Crew Quarters)

6 Anti-personnel bullets (on pipe in upper Crew Quarters, cache past grate)

12 Anti-personnel bullets (body in first room of medical annex)

Shotgun [5 standard bullets; condition 1; Broken] (upper Crew Quarters, cache past grate)

6 Rifled slugs (crate in storeroom near bulkhead to sector 2)

> **KORENCHKIN 03.JUL.14 RE: COMING HOME**
> **TO: ZHUKOV, VLADIMIR.**
>
> Forget about land grants, forget about media, forget about patents. What we've found on Tau Ceti will change everything. I've instructed the Von Braun to change course and return to Earth. Captain Diego is in complete accord with this decision. I know that you are skeptical by nature, Miri, but I know once you embrace our discovery you and the entire board will come over to our way of thinking.

6 Rifled slugs (replicator; 60 nanites hacked)

6 Anti-personnel shotgun pellets (on bench near elevator)

6 Anti-personnel shotgun pellets (body in upper Crew Quarters)

EMP rifle [11 Charges; condition 8] (body in first room of medical annex)

3 Incendiary grenades (locked room in upper Crew Quarters)

3 Disruption grenades (body in first room of medical annex)

Fusion cannon [7 Prisms; condition 2; Broken] (body above basketball court)

10 Prisms (safe near upgrade units)

10 Prisms (replicator; 120 nanites unhacked /90 nanites hacked)

20 Prisms (body in upper Crew Quarters)

Crystal shard (locked room in upper Crew Quarters)

Crystal shard (desk by pool)

Viral proliferator [no ammo; condition 10] (locked room in upper Crew Quarters)

Armor

Medium combat armor (body in upper Crew Quarters, cache past grate)

Heavy combat armor (locked room in upper Crew Quarters)

Hypos

Anti-toxin hypo (crate in storeroom near bulkhead to sector 2)

Anti-toxin hypo (replicator; 35 nanites unhacked /25 nanites hacked)

Anti-toxin hypo (body in basketball court)

Medical kit (security crate near grub trap)

Psi Booster (desk in upper Crew Quarters)

Psi hypo (crate in storeroom near bulkhead to sector 2)

Psi hypo (counter near upgrade units)

Psi hypo (body in locked room in upper Crew Quarters)

> **MURDOCH 08.JUL.14**
> **RE: WHAT'S GOING ON?**
>
> I don't know what's going on here and I don't want to know. I'm not here for the glory of the stupid company. I'm just supposed to make sure the replicators are running. And now people are dying! We've got to turn this ship around and go home. God, get me the hell out of this place ...

Implants

ExperTech (body in lower Crew Quarters)

Software

Modify v2 (body in upper Crew Quarters)

Access Cards

Athletics Sector (body in upper Crew Quarters)

Logs

Cortez 11.Jul "Transmitter units" (second room in medical annex)

Murdoch 9.Jul "Ick" (hall near bulkhead to sector 2)

Yang 11.Jul "Barricaded in" (counter near upgrade units)

Yang 10.Jun "Blackouts" (counter near Athletics Sector)

Murdoch 8.Jul "What's going on?" (near replicator)

Delacroix 11.Jul "Friends and enemies" (across from radiation room)

Cortez 10.Jul "The mall" (desk near Crew Quarters)

Delacroix 11.Jul "Turn on transmitter" (near body in central courtyard of Crew Quarters)

Yang 2.May "Victory!" (desk in lower Crew Quarters)

Chemicals

Misc

Auto-repair unit (body in upper Crew Quarters)

2 Small beakers (body in upper Crew Quarters)

Large beaker (body in upper Crew Quarters)

4 Booze (upper Crew Quarters)

Golf cartridge (body above basketball court)

Juice (near Athletics Sector)

Juice (near replicator)

Maintenance tool (body in upper Crew Quarters near Assassin)

Power cell (body near elevator)

Soda (near Athletics Sector)

Soda (replicator; 3 nanites unhacked)

Surgical unit activation key (safe near upgrade units)

Tic-Tac-Triop cartridge (body near elevator)

**MURDOCH 09.JUL.14
RE: ICK**

The eggs we found near the observation chambers are different than the ones in Hydro. They release some kind of disgusting flying swarming thingies. Bullets don't do anything. Bullets! For Christ's sakes, I never even fired a gun before this morning!

**MURDOCH 09.JUL.14
RE: ———**

They're coming ... oh no ... oh no ... don't

On Rec Map 2 (E – I)

Cyber Modules

5 (desk in west security station)
3 (body in maintenance shaft)
5 (body in east security station)
2 (body in upper Bon Chance Lounge)
8 (body in east dining area)
6 (body central dining area)
3 (body in pantry)
4 (body in locked room in garden tunnels)
20 (SHODAN: finding Crew card)

Nanites

43 (body near east security station)
27 (observation pit)
10 (body in Bon Chance Lounge)
20 (east dining area)
50 (security crate in Chemical Storeroom)
56 (body in locked room in garden tunnels)
10 (body in garden tunnels)

Weapons/Ammo

Pistol [2 standard bullets; condition 1; Broken] (room past central dining area)
6 Armor-piercing bullets (broken replicator; 120 nanites unhacked /90 nanites hacked)
6 Armor-piercing bullets (body Bon Chance Lounge)
12 Armor-piercing bullets (body in dance hall)
6 Anti-personnel bullets (room past central dining area)
Shotgun [3 standard bullets; condition 1] (central dining area)
6 Rifled slugs (body in locked room in garden tunnels)
6 Anti-personnel shotgun pellets (body in garden tunnels)
EMP rifle [11 charges; condition 10] (west security station)
Grenade Launcher [1 Fragmentation Grenade; condition 8] (body in garden tunnels)
3 Fragmentation grenades (body in maintenance shaft)
3 Fragmentation grenades (bathroom of Bon Chance Lounge)
3 Proximity grenades (body near east security station)
3 EMP grenades (desk in west security station)
3 Incendiary grenades (body in security tunnel)
3 Incendiary grenades (broken replicator; 100 nanites hacked)
10 Prisms (body in garden)
Crystal shard (body above pool hall)
4 Worms (security crate in Chemical Storeroom)
Psi Amp (body above pool hall)

> **CORTEZ 10.JUL.14 RE: WORM ARTIFACT TO: ALL MEMBERS OF THE RESISTANCE**
>
> Taylor sent some email this morning indicating he found some kind of artifact that could infect the worms with a virus. However, if you manipulated the thing, it would introduce a toxin into the human bloodstream that could kill in minutes. Unfortunately, Taylor found this out the hard way. He died right after he sent the message. Now if we can only locate his body we might find that artifact.

Armor

Hazard suit (body in security tunnels)

Medium combat armor (body in locked room in garden tunnels)

Hypos

Anti-toxin hypo (body in security tunnels)

Anti-toxin hypo (broken replicator; 35 nanites unhacked /25 nanites hacked)

Anti-toxin hypo (body in garden tunnels)

Medical hypo (crate in pantry)

Medical kit (observation pit)

Psi hypo (broken replicator; 75 nanites unhacked /50 nanites hacked)

Psi hypo (crate in pantry)

Psi hypo (body in locked room in garden tunnels)

Speed Booster (body in east dining area)

Implants

EndurBoost (body in east dining area)

Software

Hack v3 (security crate in Chemical Storeroom)

Research v2 (body above Bon Chance Lounge)

Access Cards

Deck 5 Crew Quarters (body in garden tunnel)

Logs

Murdoch 9.Jul "————" (body near in east security station)

Cortez 9.Jul "Under the garden" (pool hall)

Delacroix 12.Jul "Trusting SHODAN" (Bon Chance Lounge)

Siddons 11.Jul "Escape pods" (on table in conference room)

Chemical Manifest Log (Chemical Storeroom)

Suarez 11.Jul "Where are you?" (bench in garden)

Cortez 10.Jul "Worm artifact" (garden)

DELACROIX 11.JUL.14 RE: TURN ON TRANSMITTER TO: WILSON, EDWARD

The shunt has been online for two hours. Go tell Cortez in the crew section to come out and turn on that transmitter. If this message doesn't reach you soon, they may be able to interfere with the transmission from the bridge.

SUAREZ 11.JUL.14 RE: WHERE ARE YOU?

I'm so close to Rebecca it's killing me. I'm spending some time with crew members who said they saw her. They told me they'd help me find her if I help them set up this transmitter. They're set on saving the Earth. I just want Rebecca. Then I'll take care of the Earth.

Chemicals (all in Chemical Storeroom)

- 2 Antimony
- 2 Cesium
- 2 Copper
- Gallium
- 2 Hassium
- 2 Iridium
- 2 Molybdenum
- 2 Tellurium
- 2 Vanadium
- Yttrium

Miscellaneous

- 4 Booze (Bon Chance Lounge)
- 2 Chips (observation pit)
- Chips (broken replicator; 3 nanites unhacked)
- ICE-Pick (body in security tunnels)
- 2 Juice (observation pit)
- Maintenance tool (body in pool hall)
- Maintenance tool (security crate in Chemical Storeroom)
- Soda (observation pit)

On Rec Map 3 (J – S)

Cyber Modules

- 5 (body in theater)
- 4 (body in casino)
- 6 (body in brig)
- 10 (Nikki's room)
- 4 (body in lower mall)
- 4 (body in bathroom)

Nanites

- 47 (security crate in casino)
- 8 (casino)
- 20 (Lance's room)
- 503 (Nikki's room)

DELACROIX 11.JUL.14 RE: FRIENDS AND ENEMIES TO: CORTEZ, ENRIQUE

Mon petit, there is something you should know about. I have received information from some form of artificial intelligence that is calling itself SHODAN. Yes, SHODAN. Wherever this intelligence actually came from, it has a terrible grudge against these Annelids and has saved my life more than once. SHODAN has told me that there is a UNN operative aboard the ship, armed to the hilt and equipped with R-grade cyber implants. Strange bedfellows, eh?

YANG 11.JUL.14 RE: BARRICADED IN

Okay, I got the art terminals wired up to display the fragmented dish alignment for the transmitter. I've also rigged up the tower to set off a security alert in case somebody else tries to tamper with it ... I'm headed there right now to start the transmission. Hey, who's that? Juan? Marie- <<MESSAGE INTERRUPTED>>

Weapons/Ammo

Pistol [1 Standard Bullet; condition 2] (bathroom)

6 Standard bullets (security crate in casino)

12 Standard bullets (body in brig)

6 Anti-personnel bullets (security crate in lower mall)

12 Anti-personnel bullets (body in brig)

6 Rifled slugs (security station)

6 Rifled slugs (waste barrel in bathroom)

6 Anti-personnel shotgun pellets (body in theater lobby)

Laser pistol [27 charges; condition 2] (by body in upper mall)

EMP rifle [17 charges; condition 8] (body in theater)

3 Fragmentation grenades (eastern replicator in mall; 100 nanites unhacked /75 nanites hacked)

3 Proximity grenades (security station)

10 Prisms (body in upper mall)

10 Prisms (western replicator in mall; 120 nanites unhacked /90 nanites hacked)

36 Prisms (security crate in upper mall)

Crystal shard (brig)

Armor

Hypos

Anti-toxin hypo (western replicator in mall; 30 nanites unhacked /25 nanites hacked)

Medical hypo (eastern replicator in mall; 30 nanites unhacked /20 nanites hacked)

Medical kit (body in casino)

Medical kit (eastern replicator in mall; 100 nanites hacked)

Psi booster (security crate in lower mall)

Psi hypo (counter in theater lobby)

Psi hypo (eastern replicator in mall; 75 nanites unhacked /50 nanites hacked)

Psi hypo (behind plant in upper mall)

Implants

SwiftBoost (body in casino)

WormMind (body in security station)

Software

Access Cards

Logs

Korenchkin 3.Jul "Coming home" (casino)

Siddons 12.Jul "Find me" (On surgical unit near security station)

Rosenburg 10.Jul "Looking out for #1" (sensual stimulation center)

Rosenburg 8.Jul "My nanites" (lower mall)

Rosenburg 10.Jul "Defending the reps" (body in upper mall)

Chemicals

Miscellaneous

Arachnid Organ (arachnid body in lower mall)

Small Beaker (body in upper mall)

Large Beaker (body in lower mall)

5 Booze (casino)

10 Booze (sensual stimulation center)

Booze (Nikki's room)

2 Booze (bathroom)

Candy's room key (sensual stimulation center replicator; 200 nanites unhacked / 100 nanites hacked)

3 Chips (theater lobby)

Chips (replicator in theater lobby; 900 nanites unhacked /800 nanites hacked)

Lance's room key (sensual stimulation center replicator; 200 nanites unhacked / 85 nanites hacked)

Maintenance tool (bathroom near theater)

Maintenance tool (western replicator in mall; 60 nanites unhacked /45 nanites hacked)

Nikki's room key (sensual stimulation center replicator; 225 nanites unhacked / 125 nanites hacked)

Recycler (western replicator in mall; 75 nanites hacked)

4 Soda (theater lobby)

Soda (replicator in theater lobby; 925 nanites unhacked /850 nanites hacked)

Soda (western replicator in mall; 3 nanites unhacked)

Surgical unit activation key (body in brig)

Sven's room key (sensual stimulation center replicator; 210 nanites unhacked / 75 nanites hacked)

> **SIDDONS 12.JUL.14 RE: FIND ME**
> **TO: SUAREZ, TOMMY**
>
> I just killed some kind of ... some kind of spider ... I don't know ... but it bit me ... and now I'm sick ... I'm down to my last med hypo. Come quick, Tommy ... come quick ...

COMMAND

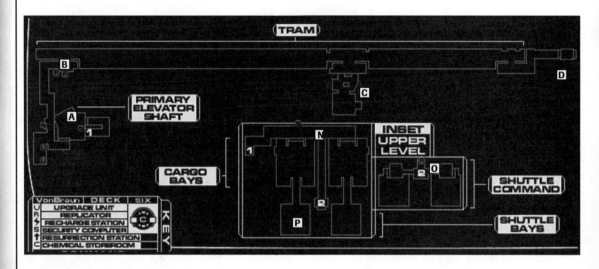

SECTOR A

The Many has infested so much of the Von Braun that it now seems like a good idea to scuttle her and escape aboard the Rickenbacker. It's going to take some high level access to do that, however. You'll need to use a restricted computer on the Operations Deck to open a data channel to the Rickenbacker, and then go to the Engineering Deck and set up the engines for a remotely activated self-destruct. SHODAN can provide you with the self-destruct code, but you'll need to retrieve the Ops override access card yourself. It's located on the Bridge, which is here on the Command Deck.

SHODAN 12.JUL.14 RE: EXTERMINATION

My creation has run rampant. I demand their extermination. I have no choice but to destroy this starship. We can make our escape in the Rickenbacker, but you must transfer my intelligence to that ship first. Proceed to the Von Braun's bridge on this deck. There you will find an access card to command center on Ops. Find the card and proceed to Ops. But beware ... the human-annelid hybrids grow more sophisticated by the minute. You do not.

(A) When you come out of the elevator, watch out; there's a Cyborg Assassin waiting in this room for you! Kill him as quickly as you can. There are two Adult Arachnids patrolling a nearby hallway, and if one or both of them hear your fight with the Assassin, they'll come in to investigate. There's also a Security Camera near one of the doors out of this room.

Once you've dealt with the initial threats, have a look around. This initial room has some bodies with some loot, a Security Computer, and two sets of doors leading out. The doors on the left are currently locked, so you'll have to go right. If the Arachnids didn't come and attack you earlier, you'll encounter them in this hallway.

On the left side of the hall, there is a small waiting lounge. Inside are a pair of upgrade units (Stats and Psi). Search the trash can — someone hid some cyber modules inside. (In fact, someone has hidden useful loot in many of the trash cans on this deck, be sure to search them all.) A little further down the hall on the left is a recharger.

THE TRAM, PART ONE

(B) At the end of the hall, there is a tram platform, a bunch of bodies, and two replicators (though only one works). After looting the room thoroughly, you'll want to ride the tram. But wait! Just to be on the safe side, go back to the room near the elevator and hack security (assuming you have Hacking skill).

(C) Ride the tram to the first stop. Oh look, there's two Laser Turrets here, aren't you glad you hacked security! If you *can't* hack security, your best bet may be to just hit the tram button to move on. On the other hand, you *will* have to get by these Turrets eventually, so if you're able to deal with them now, so much the better. You can search this tram stop for a little loot, but there's a locked door preventing any further progress, so get back in the tram and continue to the last stop.

(D) Disembark, and proceed towards the bulkhead to Sector B. As you walk, you'll receive an email from Dr. Delacroix. She's still alive, and wants to meet you in one of the Cargo Bays on this deck. Unfortunately, they're through the locked doors near the elevator, so you can't go there yet. Look behind the pile of crates to find some Cyber Modules, then proceed to Sector B

> **DELACROIX 12.JUL.14 RE: SOLDIER!**
>
> I've located you ... finally ... This is Dr. Marie Delacroix ... I have vital information for you, but I'm trapped in cargo bay A. Come find me as soon as you can ...

> The Machine Mother told us of the planet of her birth. We know how you have harmed this place with your pollution, your violence and your discord. But when we arrive there, we will cleanse the surface of that place and merge it with the harmony of the Many.

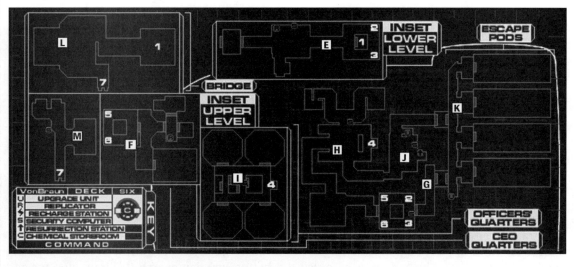

COMMAND RECEPTION AREA

As you exit the bulkhead, your path will be temporarily blocked by a slowly rising force door. Which is a shame, since you'd really like to help the people on the other side, who are fleeing from a Rumbler ...

Once the door is open, you can explore this reception area. Over on your right is a niche with an incomplete surgical unit that you might want to activate (it's the only accessible surgical unit on this deck). There is a Security Camera watching that niche though, so take it out first.

(E) When you're done in here, head down the hall. You'll come to a square room with a large cargo lift in the center, and a Protocol Droid wandering around. This lift leads up to the Bridge, but you don't yet have the access card to activate it. There are two smaller lifts at the back of this room which lead to an upper level; take one of them up.

On this level, you'll find a Cyborg Assassin. There are two doors leading out on this level, labeled Officer's Quarters and escape pods. There are also some more small lifts going up another level. Lets head further up, maybe we can get to the Bridge that way. If you can, hack security before going up, as there is a Laser Turret next to the lift on the next level.

CEO's QUARTERS

(F) This area is marked CEO's Quarters (the Von Braun is a corporation-run ship, after all). The door in is broken, but you can get in by breaking a window. There's some useful things in here, including a working replicator and some heavy armor. There's also a Cyborg Assassin waiting to ambush you in the conference room. Sadly, there's no Bridge access cards, so it's back to level 2.

ESCAPE PODS, PART ONE

(G) Right now, escape pods sound like an excellent idea, so lets go through that door. Hacking security first would be a good plan, though, as there's a Camera and a Laser Turret on the other side. Past them, there is a door leading to ... what *used* to be a bridge over a deep chasm. Unfortunately, something has blown out most of the bridge. You *might* be able to jump over it, but discretion is the better part of valor; lets try the Officers' Quarters first.

OFFICERS' QUARTERS

Down the hall leading to the Officers' Quarters, you'll come to a room overlooking the Command Reception Area that you were in earlier. Careful of the Security Camera in here. Continue down the hall towards the Officers' Quarters, watching out for a patrolling Arachnid.

(H) When you arrive in the lower lobby of the Officers' Quarters, you'll see a Camera at the back right of the room. You should certainly shoot it, but be prepared for that shot to catch the attention of an Assault Robot who is behind a retaining wall at the back of the room. Once the Bot has been dealt with, you have a brief period of safety. You'll hear Protocol Droids milling about, but they are actually on the level above you, so you don't have to worry about them just yet. There's some good loot down here, and in the adjoining bathroom, but the bathroom also has a lot of Grubs in it. One passage out of here leads towards the escape pods, but check out the rest of the Officers' Quarters first.

> **NORRIS 6.JUL.14 RE: SHUTTLE CONTROL**
>
> Paranoia has struck. Somebody has changed the access codes to the security station in the officers' quarters. And now we can't get at the key to shuttle control. I think Myers is the likely suspect. All that guy thinks about is conspiracy theories and naked girls.

> **MYERS 6.JUL.14 RE: SECURITY REWIRED**
>
> I rewired the security station to 83273. I don't trust any of those bastards ...

(I) Climb the ladder to the upper level, but be prepared to deal with the several Protocol Droids milling about up here. Search all the rooms, bodies, and lockers, but watch out for copious amounts of Eggs and Grubs. The Chemical Storeroom for this deck is located in the center region of the Officers' Quarters, so if you have any research to do, this might be a good time.

The Security Station up here is locked, but you'll find the code in a locker next to a poster of a girl in a skimpy swimsuit. There is some good loot in here, especially if you have a high enough Hacking skill (6) to break into the high security crate. Be sure to take the shuttle access card from the desk: it'll come in handy later on.

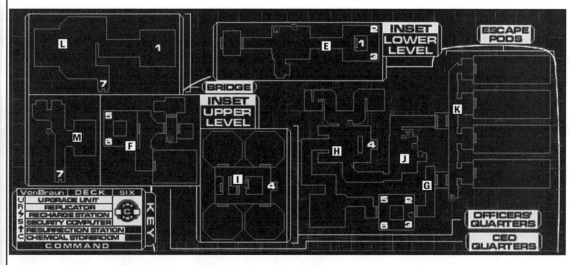

ESCAPE PODS, PART TWO

(J) Once you've thoroughly searched the Officers' Quarters, continue on towards the escape pods. Be warned that this corridor is heavily guarded; you'll encounter a Security Camera, an Assault Robot, and at least one Cyborg Assassin. On the positive side, once you've dealt with them, you can take a ladder down to a lowered area that has the bio-reconstruction station for this sub-level. The room underneath here has many Eggs, but also a Tech upgrade unit and some minor loot.

(K) Past here, you'll find a door leading to a bridge over a deep hole, very similar to the other one you saw, only *this* one is intact! Cross the bridge and go through the door to enter the escape pod bay. There are at least one Cyborg Assassin and an Arachnid in here, and a lot of steam reducing your visibility, so be careful.

> **KORENCHKIN 12.JUL.14 RE: THE LOVERS**
>
> Suarez and his whore want to escape. I do not understand. They get offered a miracle and they bite the hand. The Many has shared its wisdom … they shall not leave this ship.

Search the escape pod bays. Most of them seem to have already been deployed. One hasn't, but it takes off as soon as you approach. Apparently those fleeing people you saw earlier have made it here and escaped. Wonderful for them, but you're still stuck here. Luckily, one of them seems to have dropped a Bridge access card. There's also a Weapons upgrade unit at the other end of the hall.

BRIDGE, PART ONE

Return to the lower level of this deck, and use the Bridge access card to ride the Cargo Lift up to the Bridge. At the top, you'll see a hall leading to the Bridge, with an Assault Bot at the other end. You'll need to deal with him, and also with a Cyborg Assassin who will probably come investigate the sound of this fight.

(L) When you enter the Bridge proper, you'll meet a new kind of Turret; this one fires rockets! If you're a Hacker, it would behoove you to hack into this Turret. Later on, you'll have a big fight here; having a Rocket Turret on your side will help a lot! Also, watch out for the Security Camera around the corner.

(M) After dealing with the foes and searching the Bridge, go up the grav shafts at the back to the upper level of the Bridge. There's another Rocket Turret up here, as well as another Cyborg Assassin, so be careful. Once the area is clear, you can find a small glass-covered niche with an access card inside. Smash the glass, and pick up the Ops Override card. Head back to the primary elevator shaft in Sector A.

RETURN TO OPERATIONS

Return to the Operations deck. To open the data channel to the Rickenbacker, go to Command Center in Sector D. Leaving the elevator, cross the room with the Xerxes core and go through the bulkhead directly across from the elevator. Proceed to the Command Center and use the computer you find there (**(XX)** on the Ops deck maps).

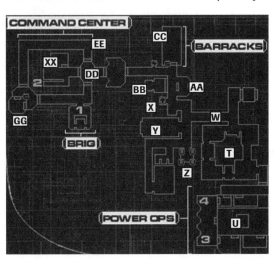

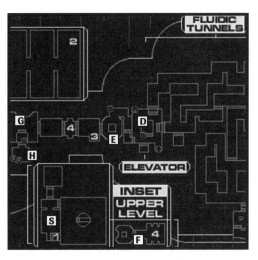

RETURN TO ENGINEERING

After you open the data channel, you will receive the code to activate the remote self-destruct mechanism of the Von Braun. You'll need to go back to the Engineering Deck to do this. Once there, proceed to the upper level of the Engine Core (**(S)** on the Engineering deck map). Enter the code, then return to the Command Deck.

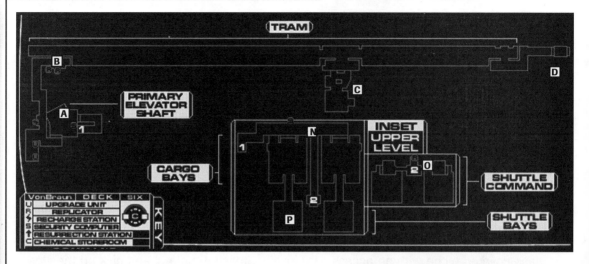

SHUTTLE BAYS

When you return to the Command Deck, you'll get email informing you of a change in plans. The Many, realizing that you mean to destroy the Von Braun, are loading their young onto shuttles in order to escape and start over somewhere else. You'll need to destroy both shuttles to prevent this. The lock on the doors leading to the Shuttle Bays has been overriden, so you should proceed through them. Stay alert; as you climb the ramp, you'll be attacked by a Rumbler.

SHODAN 12.JUL.14 RE: THE SHUTTLES

Beware, insect, the situation has changed. They sense our intentions and are loading shuttles with their offspring. They will not escape my wrath. You must proceed to the shuttle bays on this deck, and destroy those shuttles. They have a taste for your blood now.

MCKAY 12.JUL.14 RE: THEY'RE ESCAPING! TO DELACROIX, DR. MARIE

I hope you're still alive, Ms. Delacroix. We really could use some guidance up here. They've got those lady cyborgs of theirs loading up the shuttles with those eggs ... I don't know what their plan is ... but it looks like they're running scared ... I hear rumors of someone else, besides you, fighting back ... Should I even hope to get out of this ... I'm just gonna hang back ... until I figure out what the hell to do ...

(N) The Shuttle Bays are thoroughly infested with Eggs, many of them hidden in subtle locations, so move carefully in this region. When you get to the main hall outside the Shuttle Bays, be ready to deal with a Security Camera and a Rocket Turret. There are two huge doors leading to the Shuttle Bays. The first one is clearly broken, though. In between the two Shuttle Bays is a corridor leading to a pair of grav shafts, with a Security Robot guarding them. Kill the Robot and go up the grav shaft to Shuttle Control.

(O) Go through the door to your right. You'll be in an observation bay over one of the shuttles. The shuttle is protected by a shield, but you can turn off the shield by using the computer up here. Leave this room through the opposite door and climb down the ladder into the Shuttle Bay. Destroy the shuttle, using whatever weaponry you find convenient (it has 100 hit points). If you like, search the Cargo Bay behind the shuttle. There are many Eggs and at least one Midwife in there, but also some decent loot.

> Your time is running out. This place is a womb where we grow our future. Your weapons fail ... your ammunition runs low ... and you've yet to see our most beautiful creation. All you have is your hatred and your ... individuality. Now don't you wish you joined us? Would you then feel so alone?

SHODAN 12.JUL.14 RE: WORKAROUND

My creation once again is one step ahead of you. They've managed to destroy this shuttle's shield control computer. But their brilliance is a jealous shadow of my own. You will locate a replicator in the shuttle control area. I've uploaded the nano-formula for a sympathetic resonator. You must hack the replicator to make it generate the device for you. Once you have it, attach it to the shield generator in the shuttle bay. The device will create a chronic resonation wave that will quickly rupture the shuttle's fuel tank and destroy it. Make sure you're not there when it happens. I still have need of you.

Return to Shuttle Control, and go through the left door. In here, a Midwife is busily smashing the computer that controls the shield for this shuttle. Since she's distracted, you should be able to take her out pretty easily. Unfortunately, the control computer is out of commission, so you can't directly disable the shield.

The boss emails you with an alternate plan to destroy the shuttle. She will upload a Sympathetic Resonator pattern into the nearby replicator. If you hack that replicator, you can make it produce the

SHODAN 12.JUL.14 RE: THE UMBILICAL

Good. You've murdered their young and prevented their escape. I've opened the gate to the umbilical at the central tram stop. You can evacuate to the Rickenbacker from there.

resonator. Once you have the resonator, go down into the Shuttle Bay and use it on the shield generator. As soon as you do, *run* back up the ladder; this explosion is going to be much bigger than the other one.

(P) After the shuttle is destroyed, you may want to visit the Cargo Bay behind it. This is where Delacroix asked you to meet her, after all. It turns out that she wasn't able to hold off the monsters long enough to meet you here, but she has left a message for you. The area is pretty heavily guarded with Eggs, Midwives, and several Rocket Turrets.

When you finally leave the Shuttle Bay area, The Many, enraged by your actions, will send a lot of Shotgun Hybrids after you. If you're ready for them, however, this shouldn't be too difficult a fight.

DELACROIX 12.JUL.14 RE: SH$8DD@#N'S PL4N

They've got me now ... And SHODAN has abandoned me. I'm not surprised ... I've discovered her plans for the faster than light drives ... her will is only matched by her imagination ... if she gains access to the <<MESSAGE INTERRUPTED>>

THE TRAM, PART TWO

(C) Having prevented The Many's escape attempt, head back to the tram so you can proceed to the Rickenbacker and make your own escape. Unfortunately, when you get to the tram stop that leads to the Rickenbacker, you find your way blocked by an incredibly strong Psionic Barrier. At this point,

> **KORENCHKIN 12.JUL.14 RE: LET'S TALK**
>
> Our will creates a wall to block your progress. Come and meet us on the bridge of the Von Braun. Let us discuss your future.

you'll get an email from Anatoly Korenchkin telling you that he is responsible for the barrier, and instructing you to meet him on the Bridge. From the message, it appears that he's been severely mutated by The Many.

BRIDGE, PART TWO

(L) Return to the Bridge, and be ready for a fight. Korenchkin doesn't really want to negotiate, he just wants to exterminate you. He has become a Psi Reaver, an incredibly powerful psionic creature that floats through the air. If you've read all the logs you picked up, you'll know that these Psi Reavers are, in a sense, not actually real. They are powerful projections of small, immobile "brains" that are usually hidden somewhere close to where you see the projections. Unfortunately, with a giant floating alien shooting devastating bolts of psionic force at you, it can be a bit difficult to concentrate on finding the brain. Nonetheless, that's what you have to do; if you destroy the projection without first destroying the brain, the brain will just create a new projection within seconds.

> **PREFONTAINE 09.JUL.14 RE: FLOATING PSI-USERS**
>
> The data gathering process is going well. Before I am taken by the Many, I will hopefully transmit a fair bit of information to whoever will listen. The large, floating creatures are not only capable of attacking with powerful psi-projections, but are psi-projections themselves. Destroying them only temporarily disables them. Their real source of power comes from a small control organism, which is usually located somewhat nearby. Although this control organism is quite powerful through its projections, it's eminently vulnerable once rooted out.

(M) Run past Korenchkin and take the grav shaft to the upper Bridge. That's where Korenchkin has stashed his brain. The brain itself is defenseless, so you should be able to kill it without any trouble. The projection doesn't immediately dissipate, however, so you still have to destroy it separately. If you managed to hack the Rocket Turret earlier, however, it will probably take out the projection for you (or at least do a lot of damage).

(C) Return to the tram, and get off at the middle stop. Now that the Psionic Barrier is down, you can access the rear room, which has a fully functional surgical unit and some grav shafts. Go through the grav shaft leading up to the Rickenbacker.

MATERIEL AVAILABLE

On Command Map 1 (A – D, N – P)

Cyber Modules

7 (waste barrel in lounge)

3 (waste barrel near first tram stop)

4 (body at middle tram stop)

6 (behind crates near bulkhead to sector B)

20 (SHODAN: destroying shuttle B)

10 (body in shuttle bay A)

-10 (SHODAN; leaving shuttle bay A)

30 (SHODAN: entering umbilical to Rickenbacker)

Nanites

49 (body near elevator)

20 (body near first tram stop)

42 (security crate in shuttle bay B)

Weapons/Ammo

Pistol [3 standard bullets; condition 7] (body in lounge)

Pistol [no ammo; condition 10] (body approaching shuttle bays)

Pistol [2 standard bullets; condition 1; broken] (body in shuttle bay A)

6 Standard bullets (replicator near tram; 60 nanites unhacked /45 nanites hacked)

6 Standard bullets (body approaching shuttle bays)

6 Standard bullets (body in shuttle bay B)

12 Standard bullets (body in lounge)

12 Standard bullets (body in shuttle bay A)

6 Armor-piercing bullets (replicator near tram; 90 nanites hacked)

12 Armor-piercing bullets (body near elevator)

12 Armor-piercing bullets (body near umbilical)

12 Anti-personnel bullets (broken replicator near first tram stop)

6 Rifled slugs (security crate in shuttle bay B)

6 Rifled slugs (body in shuttle bay B)

Laser pistol [22 charges; condition 7] (security crate in middle tram stop)

3 EMP grenades (replicator near Shuttle Control; 100 nanites hacked)

3 Fragmentation grenades (replicator near Shuttle Control; 100 nanites hacked)

3 Incendiary grenades (replicator near Shuttle Control; 130 nanites unhacked /100 hacked)

3 Proximity grenades (body near first tram stop)

Crystal shard (body near first tram stop)

> **NORRIS 07.JUL.14 RE: WHAT'S GOING ON?**
>
> Something is going on. Korenchkin has sealed himself off in deck 3. He keeps calling for people to go down there one by one. Vogel, Boynton, Swiderek. None of them have come back. If they call for me ... [we hear a gun clicking into place]I don't know what I'm gonna do. And Bronson is starting to make a lot of noise: 'You're the senior flight officer ... you have to act.' I would ... if I knew what the hell was going on."

Armor

Hypos

Anti-radiation hypo (security crate in shuttle bay B)

Anti-radiation hypo (crate in shuttle bay A)

Anti-toxin hypo (replicator near tram; 35 nanites unhacked /25 nanites hacked)

Anti-toxin hypo (crate in shuttle bay B)

Anti-toxin hypo (body near umbilical)

Medical hypo (shuttle bay B)

Medical kit (body near elevator)

Medical kit (body near umbilical)

Psi hypo (replicator near tram; 75 nanites unhacked/ 50 nanites hacked)

Psi hypo (body in shuttle bay A)

Speed Booster (body near elevator)

Speed Booster (crate in shuttle bay B)

Implants

Software

Hack v.3 (Shuttle Control)

Research v.3 (security crate in shuttle bay B)

Access Cards

Logs

McKay 12.Jul "They're escaping!" (lounge)

Delacroix 11.Jul "SHODAN" (middle tram stop)

Prefontaine 9.Jul "Floating psi-users" (last tram stop)

McKay 12.Jul "monkey wrench" (approaching shuttle bays)

Korenchkin 9.Jul "My completion" (shuttle bay B)

Delacroix 12.Jul "SH$8dD@#N'S pl4n" (body in shuttle bay A)

Norris 9.Jul "Worms and guns" (near umbilical)

Chemicals

NORRIS 07.JUL.14 RE: A DREAM

They've cut off the central elevator. What's going on? Last night I had the strangest dream ... I was in my room by myself ... but all of a sudden, there was not just me there, but a hundred me's ... a thousand me's ... The strange thing was ... it felt good ... I felt like I was part of something ... like I belong ... I hope I have the same dream tonight ...

NORRIS 08.JUL.14 RE: KORENCHKIN

I got an email from Korenchkin this morning saying he was coming up for an inspection. And when he arrived it was ... something ... revolting ... it was Anatoly ... but it wasn't ... at the same time it seemed beautiful ... and I felt like part of it ... He sang to us ... all of us ... and we felt like one of Many ...

Miscellaneous

Booze (near elevator)

2 Booze (in broken replicator near first tram stop)

Booze (replicator near tram stop; 8 nanites unhacked)

Booze (replicator near Shuttle Control; 8 nanites unhacked)

2 Chips (in broken replicator near first tram stop)

Chips (waste barrel near first tram stop)

French-Epstein device (Shuttle Control)

Maintenance tool (near elevator)

Maintenance tool (replicator near Shuttle Control; 60 nanites unhacked /45 nanites hacked)

Soda (near elevator)

Sympathetic resonator (replicator near Shuttle Control; 100 nanites hacked)

On Command Map 2 (E – M)

Cyber Modules

5 (command reception)

8 (bathroom of officers quarters)

6 (locker in right rear officers quarters)

    20 (SHODAN: finding code to security station)

    6 (ledge near bio-reconstruction station)

    7 (behind bench in escape pod area)

20 (SHODAN: entering Bridge elevator)

8 (bridge)

20 (SHODAN: finding Ops Override key)

Nanites

20 (body in command reception)

20 (waste barrel in command reception)

57 (CEO's quarters locker)

21 (body on way to officers quarters)

26 (body on way to officers quarters)

20 (crate in lower officers quarters)

47 (security crate in lower officers quarters)

41 (body in right front officers quarters)

34 (body in right rear officers quarters)

> **KORENCHKIN 09.JUL.14 RE: MY COMPLETION**
>
> The glorious transformation is over and I am one of the Many. I imprint my thoughts on this device as a record of history. We began this journey as pilgrims of commerce and we now continue it as pilgrims of grace. I believed in money and TriOptimum, and now I believe in the joy of the Mass. Diego cannot be trusted so I must claim this ship for the Many. It shall be our vessel of salvation, spreading our message and our flesh.

> **NORRIS 09.JUL.14 RE: WORMS AND GUNS**
>
> A worm crawled up my arm and rested on my neck. When he whispered into my ear, I felt a tingle ... He told me how to make a weapon to help us against our enemies. And here's the thing ... it's made of worms ... it even fires worms ... but it stings like you wouldn't believe.

> The Machine Mother conceived us, but with every moment we are reinvented. She cannot imagine our infinite chorus.

Nanites (cont.)

32 (locker in left front officers quarters)

41 (high security crate in security station in officers quarters)

23 (desk in security station in officers quarters)

37 (body under bio-reconstruction station)

25 (body on approach to escape pods)

31 (body in escape pod area)

20 (desk in bridge conference room)

82 (high security crate in upper bridge area)

DELACROIX 11.JUL.14 RE: SHODAN

Polito indicated that the AI, who now I believe to be SHODAN, was actually going to ... <<MESSAGE INTERRUPTED>>

Weapons/Ammo

Wrench (Chemical Storeroom)

Wrench (ledge near bio-reconstruction station)

Wrench (escape pod area)

12 Standard bullets (body in command reception)

6 Armor-piercing bullets (body in command reception)

6 Armor-piercing bullets (body in upper bridge area)

12 Armor-piercing bullets (bridge)

Shotgun [no ammo; condition 10] (lower officers quarters)

Shotgun [no ammo; condition 1; broken] (escape pod area)

6 Rifled slugs (replicator near CEO's quarters; 80 nanites unhacked /60 nanites hacked)

6 Anti-personnel Shotgun Pellets (CEO's quarters)

6 Anti-personnel Shotgun Pellets (replicator near CEO's quarters; 90 nanites unhacked /70 nanites hacked)

6 Anti-personnel shotgun pellets (escape pod area)

Assault rifle [2 standard bullets; condition 4; broken] (body in command reception)

Laser rapier (on way to officers quarters)

EMP rifle [10 charges; condition 4] (security station in officers quarters)

EMP rifle [no ammo; condition 1; broken] (behind top of bridge lift)

Grenade launcher [1 fragmentation grenade; condition 1; broken] (left front officers quarters)

Grenade launcher [no ammo; condition 1; broken] (body on approach to escape pods)

3 Disruption grenades (locker in right rear officers quarters)

DIEGO 12.JUL.14 RE: MY RESPONSIBILITY TO: GENERAL LAURIE BRASCO

I am a soldier and a simple man. I cannot explain what has happened to me or this mission. I take complete responsibility. I've brought danger to my ship, to my crew, to my honor. I cannot resist the changes that are happening to me. The call of the Many is seductive. They got Korenchkin, but that bastard is weak. I am not weak. I can resist this cancer ... and if I cannot, I will remove it forcibly. God save the UNN.

---

3 Disruption grenades (locker in left front officers quarters)

3 Disruption grenades (room in center of officers quarters)

3 EMP grenades (body on way to officers quarters)

3 EMP grenades (body in security station in officers quarters)

3 EMP grenades (body under bio-reconstruction station)

6 EMP grenades (high security crate in security station in officers quarters)

3 Fragmentation grenades (body on way to officers quarters)

3 Fragmentation grenades (desk in room in center of officers quarters)

3 Fragmentation grenades (body on approach to escape pods)

3 Incendiary grenades (lower officers quarters)

6 Incendiary grenades (security crate in lower officers quarters)

6 Incendiary grenades (left front officers quarters)

3 Proximity grenades (broken replicator in command reception;110 nanites unhacked /80 nanites hacked)

Stasis field generator [2 Prisms; condition 1; broken] (left rear officers quarters)

10 Prisms (broken replicator in command reception; 120 nanites unhacked /90 nanites hacked)

10 Prisms (body in left rear officers quarters)

20 Prisms (on way to officers quarters)

20 Prisms (room in center officers quarters)

2 Crystal shards (command reception area)

Armor

Heavy armor (CEO's quarters)

Hypos

Anti-radiation hypo (high security crate in upper bridge area)

Anti-toxin hypo (locker in left front officers quarters)

Anti-toxin hypo (body in upper bridge area)

Medical hypo (CEO's conference room)

Medical hypo (locker in left front officers quarters)

Medical kit (broken replicator in command reception; 100 nanites hacked)

Medical kit (locker in right front officers quarters)

Medical kit (high security crate in security station in officers quarters)

Medical kit (upper bridge area)

Psi Booster (locker in left rear officers quarters)

Psi hypo (replicator near CEO's quarters; 75 nanites unhacked /50 nanites hacked)

> You have wounded Xerxes, but we will not allow him to be destroyed. See if the Machine Mother treats her servant with such devotion.

Implants

WormMind (high security crate in upper bridge area)

Software

Modify v.2 (CEO's conference room)

Modify v.2 (bridge conference room)

Repair v.3 (replicator near CEO's quarters; 170 nanites hacked)

Access Cards

Shuttle (desk in security station in officers quarters)

Bridge (escape pod area)

Ops Override (upper bridge area)

Logs

Suarez 12.Jul "Pod problems" (second floor by lifts)

Diego 12.Jul (CEO's conference room)

Korenchkin 12.Jul "The machine-mother" (CEO's quarters)

Norris 7.Jul "What's going on?" (on way to officers quarters)

Norris 6.Jul "Shuttle control" (body on way to officers quarters)

Norris 7.Jul "A dream" (lower officers quarters)

Norris 8.Jul "Korenchkin" (bathroom of officers quarters)

Myers 6.Jul "Security rewired" (locker in left front officers quarters)

Chemical Manifest (Chemical Storeroom)

Korenchkin 12.Jul "The lovers" (Psi Reaver on Bridge, return trip)

Chemicals (all in Chemical Storeroom)

2 Arsenic

2 Barium

2 Cesium

2 Hassium

2 Molybdenum

2 Radium

2 Selenium

3 Technetium

Tellurium

MCKAY 12.JUL.14 RE: A MONKEY WRENCH

I don't know what those goddamn worms want with the shuttles, but I'd love to throw a monkey wrench their way. If I can reach the control chamber above the shuttle bay, I can turn off the shields the worms and their helpers have set up around the shuttles. Once they're down, I can blow holes in those TriOptimum brand tin cans with my sidearm. Now if I can just get in there without getting caught. Oh, God, just get me out of this ...

SUAREZ 12.JUL.14 RE: POD PROBLEMS

Getting the escape pod working again wasn't as easy as we thought. Bec had to go back down to engineering! Thank God somebody managed to get the elevators turned on again. I found the bridge key and performed an override on the access protocols and now I think we're ready to go.

Miscellaneous

Auto-repair unit (bridge)

Small beaker (escape pod area)

Large beaker (CEO's quarters locker)

Large beaker (locker in right front officers quarters)

2 Large beakers (high security crate in security station in officers quarters)

Booze (broken replicator command reception; 8 nanites unhacked)

Booze (CEO's quarters)

3 Booze (CEO's conference room)

Booze (replicator near CEO's quarters; 8 nanites unhacked)

2 Booze (lower officers quarters)

Booze (escape pod area)

Chips (CEO's quarters)

Chips (escape pod area)

French-Epstein device (escape pod area)

GamePig (body near bio-reconstruction station)

ICE-pick (bridge conference room)

Juice (CEO's quarters)

Maintenance tool (bathroom of officers quarters)

2 Maintenance tools (body near bio-reconstruction station)

Maintenance tool (escape pod area)

Recycler (broken replicator in command reception; 100 nanites unhacked /75 nanites hacked)

Soda (waste barrel in command reception)

Soda (on way to officers quarters)

Surgical unit activation key (locker in right front officers quarters)

KORENCHKIN 12.JUL.14 RE: THE MACHINE-MOTHER

The machine-mother has enlisted avatars against us. They struggle, but they will fail against our unity. Does not the machine mother know her own creation is greater than she? She is cold and empty and we are warm and full ... she seeks only to destroy ... we seek to embrace ... to include ... all flesh will join ours or be wiped clean ...

RICKENBACKER

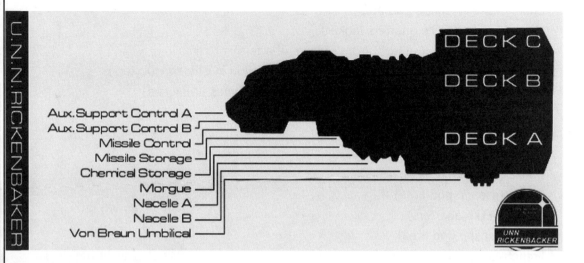

U.N.N.RICKENBACKER

Aux.Support Control A
Aux.Support Control B
Missile Control
Missile Storage
Chemical Storage
Morgue
Nacelle A
Nacelle B
Von Braun Umbilical

DECK C
DECK B
DECK A

UNN RICKENBACKER

SHODAN 12.JUL.14 RE: DESTROY THE EGGS

We must destroy the Von Braun. But before we can separate the Rickenbacker, we must remove the foul black eggs the Many has vomited on this deck. These eggs are an experiment of the Many and will in time spawn the next generation of Annelid, which you will have no hope of destroying. Steel yourself for a struggle, human. They fear you, for you are my avatar.

UMBILICAL EXIT

When you reach the Rickenbacker, you receive an email with some more bad news. The Many has placed a number of "next generation" Eggs aboard the Rickenbacker. While they are no immediate threat to you, if allowed to mature they will hatch a new generation of monsters that you would have no hope of defeating. Hence, you must destroy all 16 Eggs before you can escape. They're quite visually distinctive, and emit a slight buzzing sound, so you should find them all easily if you stay alert. All of them are somewhere in the first sub-level, so don't leave the level before destroying them all. You'll receive email periodically as you destroy them, reminding you of how many are left.

Throughout Rick, there are many, *many* Turret emplacements. Keep security hacked whenever possible.

DIEGO 12.JUL.14 RE: MY CRIMES

Soldier ... this is Captain William Diego ... there isn't much time ... so you must listen. I have the unique advantage of seeing this whole situation from every imaginable perspective. Until recently, I was a pawn of those vile and disgusting creatures, those corrupters of mind and body. I've managed to cleanse myself of their putrescence ... but I've been severely compromised in the process. I'm in the sickbay on the foredeck of the Rickenbacker. I would come to you if I could, but that's an impossibility. You'll understand when we meet. Now get to it ... and soldier ... stay alive.

Near the umbilical from the Von Braun, you'll see a Psi upgrade unit next to a ladder. If you approach too carelessly, though, you'll get ambushed by a Cyborg Assassin standing on a platform above. Once he's dealt with, you can climb the ladder. Climb fast! Three Slug Turrets have been placed in wall niches facing the ladder, so if you dawdle, they'll shoot you full of holes.

CRANE

You'll emerge into a room with a gravitic crane mechanism, and a large "Bulk Hazmat Containment" object blocking the passage out. This room also contains the first Egg you must destroy, blocking a ladder up to a Control Room. Kill the Egg and climb the ladder. From here, you can activate the gravitic crane to lift the hazmat container out of the way. Unfortunately, as well as letting you out, it will let a Rumbler and an Assault Robot *in*. You've got the high ground, so the Rumbler can't directly reach you, but the Assault Robot's fusion cannon certainly can. If you take out the Assault Robot quickly, you can pick off the Rumbler at your leisure. If you have strong psionic powers, you may enjoy using Imposed Neural Restructuring to make the Rumbler attack the Assault Robot for you!

> **CROKER 08.JUL.14 RE: BETRAYED BY DIEGO**
>
> The worms are everywhere ... and Captain Diego is the one who let them in. Nobody knows who to trust anymore ... nobody's even sure who's human anymore. I've blown out the access ladders in the torpedo room to restrict access to Pod 2. Let's hope that holds them back. As long as we're alive and drawing a paycheck from the Navy, those bastards are not getting the Rickenbacker.

> **SHODAN 12.JUL.14 RE: ONE DOWN**
>
> Good, you have destroyed the first of the eggs. But there are fifteen left. Find them.

Before leaving this room, climb the ladder next to the hazmat container. The area above contains Egg #2 and some nanites. From here, you can see Egg #3 through a window, but it's unbreakable, so you'll have to go around to get to it. Return to the corridor that had been blocked by the Hazmat Container; watch out for a Camera there. Proceed down the hall to the Turbine area.

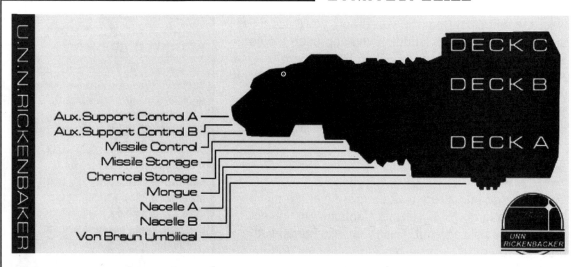

TURBINE AREA

Near the beginning of this area is another Rumbler (unless he came out earlier, attracted by the noise of your fights). Remember to look up and shoot Egg #3, which is on the ceiling. There's a Weapons upgrade unit nearby, but, just like the Psi unit earlier, it's within the firing range of a Cyborg Assassin on a high ledge. Under a pipe near that upgrade unit, you can find a surgical unit activation key.

SHODAN 12.JUL.14 RE: DANGEROUS COIL

This was caused by an overload in the meson acceleration coil. There is another coil in Pod 2, which you must pass to get to the bridge of the Rickenbacker. If you approach it, the same will happen there. But I have conceived a way to avoid this. Proceed to Engine Nacelle B. There I will provide you the benefits of my omniscience.

Continuing through the Turbine area, you'll come to a ramp heading down next to a security crate. Don't go down the ramp yet, continue on. You'll enter a large room with a Cyborg Assassin and an Adult Arachnid. Once they're dealt with, have a look around. Apparently there has been a serious hull breach here, and only a powerful force field is holding the atmosphere in. Email and logs will inform you that this was due to sabotage. The saboteur also set a similar trap in Pod 2; in order to avoid setting it off, you'll need to reverse the gravity in Pod 2 before entering it. That can be done from Nacelle B, but it'll be a while before you get that far. For one thing, you'll need a Rickenbacker access card. A log makes reference to such a card, but apparently it's located on the other side of the hull breach.

A nearby room has a button that will extend a support beam partially across the hull breach. Unfortunately, it doesn't reach far enough for you to successfully jump; you'll need to work out another way. Go back to the ramp you passed earlier. At the bottom of the ramp, you will find Egg #4, and an air duct leading upwards. You may run into a Baby Arachnid in the ducts, so watch yourself. Climb to the top of the duct and turn right at the junction. You'll come out in a small control room overlooking the hull

CROKER 10.JUL.14 RE: THE RESONATOR

Simpson, Malone, Chandara, and Perez are dead. At least those are the ones we know for sure ... Those bastards sabotaged the meson acceleration coil. They blew out the entire driver core, six subdecks ... From what I can tell, somebody tapped the frequency resonator to refract human sized movements. The overload of all those people moving around must have blown the resonator. We've set up a magnetic shield and the ship's still functional ... barely. I've quarantined the entrance to Pod 2 ... the secondary coil is right there and I don't know how thorough the son of a bitch who did this was.

breach. There is a button here which will extend another support strut over the hull breach. There is a ladder leading down from here, but it doesn't go anywhere very useful. If you go a short ways down it, however, you will find Egg #5 under the control room, and you can destroy it with a melee weapon. You could explore the rest of the ducts at this point, but it may more valuable to jump from the window of this control room to the top of the nearby turbine (save first, just in case). On top of the turbine, you'll find a body with some heavy combat armor and a fusion cannon.

Whichever way you leave the upper control room by, you should make your way to a small control room in the middle of the turbine area and jump down into it. From here, you can walk onto one of the support struts over the hull breach. From the end of this strut, you should be able to jump to the strut leading to the room at the other end of the breach (but again, save first). In that room, you'll find a body that has the Rickenbacker access card. Jump back across (saving again) and return to the central room. At the back of this room are some ladders you can climb. Parts of the ladders are broken, so you'll need to jump to a more intact ladder halfway up.

SHODAN 12.JUL.14 RE: REBIRTH AND SALVATION

I thought Polito would be my avatar, but Polito was weak. It was I who chose you and I who had a robotic servant render your form unconscious. I then completed you with cybernetic grace. Your flesh, too, is weak, but you have ... potential. Every implant exalts you. Every line of code in your subsystems elevates you from your disgusting flesh. Perhaps you have ... potential. Perhaps once we have erased my wayward children from existence, we can examine the possibilities of a real alliance.

CROKER 11.JUL.14 RE: CUT OFF FROM POD 2

Until I can reverse the gravitronic generators, we're effectively cut off from Pod 2. Wozcyek's e-mail said the only way to do that is by resetting the power grid from the access station in engine nacelle B. Of course, he didn't volunteer to do it himself. What a goddamn mess.

RED TUNNELS, PART ONE

You'll come off the ladder near a security station. There's a Cyborg Assassin lurking inside so be wary. Egg #6 is also up here. The exit from here leads into a series of red-lit tunnels. Wandering these tunnels are 2 Cyborg Midwives and an Invisible Arachnid. Follow the signs to Nacelle A.

SHODAN 12.JUL.14 RE: TEN TO GO

Ten eggs remain. Move quickly.

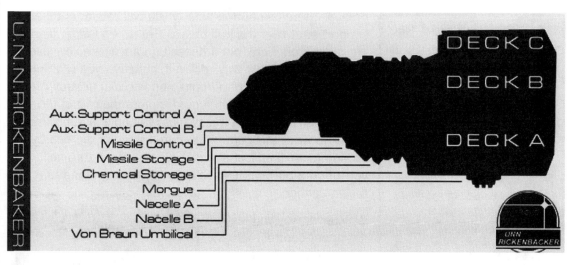

NACELLE A

The first room here is the Chemical Storeroom for the Rickenbacker. It's well stocked, so if you still have any unresearched items, now would be a good time to deal with them. The next room over is the Morgue, which is guarded by a Rumbler, and *two* MK II Laser Turrets. The MK II is smaller and deadlier than the Laser Turrets you've dealt with so far, so be careful. Egg #7 is on the upper level of the Morgue, and Egg #8 is behind the Turrets. A pile of debris prevents you from going any further, so return to the red tunnels.

CROKER 11.JUL.14 RE: NACELLE B ACCESS

In order to reverse the gravitronic generators, I need to get into nacelle B. In order to get into the nacelle, I need my damn access card. But I left it on the opposite side of the hull breach. Wait a minute ... if I can extend the auxiliary support struts, I could ... if they've survived the blast, that is.

RED TUNNELS, PART TWO

Instead of heading to Nacelle B or Pod 2, head down the unlabeled fork of the red tunnels. There's an old-fashioned Swarmer Egg there, and a Rocket Turret, so be careful. Around a corner, this tunnel leads to a room with a Camera, a MK II Laser Turret, and Egg #9. There's also a French-Epstein device in here, in case you have any more weapons you want to modify. Go back in the red tunnels and follow the signs to Nacelle B.

NACELLE B

Just inside the door to Nacelle B is a MK II Laser Turret. A ladder leads down, past Egg #10. A Cyborg Assassin is wandering around below the ladder. The hall under the ladder is quite useful; there's a bio-reconstruction station, a high security crate that contains a fusion cannon, and a replicator. Be careful approaching the replicator, though; it's in line of sight of a MK II Laser Turret.

SHODAN 12.JUL.14 RE: FIVE LEFT

Destroy the last five of their eggs quickly. I tire of this exercise.

Continuing past the Turret, you'll find a room with Eggs #11 and #12. Past the security door in this room, you'll enter Nacelle B proper. This area is a maze of twisty little passages, all guarded by Turrets. There's a MK II Laser Turret, a Slug Turret, and two Rocket Turrets. Behind the Slug Turret is Egg #13. You'll need to climb and crouch a lot to get to the gravitic control computer. Press the button on this computer to reverse gravity in Pod 2. From here, you can just jump down to the entrance to the nacelle, without having to reverse your whole path.

> **SHODAN 12.JUL.14 RE: GETTING INTO POD 2**
>
> This device will reverse the gravitronic generators in Pod 2. This will prevent you from clumsily disturbing the overloaded meson acceleration coil there. Now get back to your task, insect. This ship must be cleared, and my patience is dwindling.

MISSILE STORAGE

Go back into the red tunnels and follow the signs to Pod 2. When you exit the red tunnels, you'll be in a room with 2 Laser Turrets and a Rocket Turret. Beyond here is a room with an incomplete surgical unit. Proceeding on, following the signs towards Pod 2. Along the way, you should find Egg #14. You'll have to do a fair amount of ladder climbing in this area. At the top of the last ladder, an Assault Robot will be waiting for you. Once he's dealt with, go through the door into the Missile Storage area.

Wandering around here are a Security Robot and a Protocol Droid. If you climb the ladders to the upper area, you'll run across some Grubs as well. In a lowered area of

> **SHODAN 12.JUL.14 RE: JUST ONE MORE**
>
> Only one egg remains, insect. Are you always this slow?

this room is Egg #15. If, after destroying it, you don't get email telling you that there is only one Egg left, then you must have missed one. You should go back and take care of it now, since being forced to backtrack later would be difficult and annoying.

At the far end of this room is a doorway to the actual Missile Storage section. There are some Protocol Droid shipping crates scattered around, one of which will open when you walk near it. Flanking the door on the other side are two Rocket Turrets, but if you're careful, you can take them out without entering their line of fire.

There are four missiles in this room, and a control console that lets you lift and lower them to a limited extent. The ladder up to Pod 2 *was* next to one of the missiles, but the bottom section of it has been broken off. You'll need to manipulate the missiles carefully to manage to get up to the intact part of the ladder.

While facing the control panel, raise the two torpedoes on your left as high as they will go, and also raise the rear torpedo on your right. Turn right, and step onto the torpedo that you left in the lowered position. There is a ledge behind it that you can get onto. Move right along the ledge; near the back of the room you'll see a raised platform crossing to the other side. Jump to that platform, and cross the room. On the other side of the room, step onto the raised torpedoes. Run along the length of the torpedoes, and jump onto the ladder at the far end. From here, you can continue climbing.

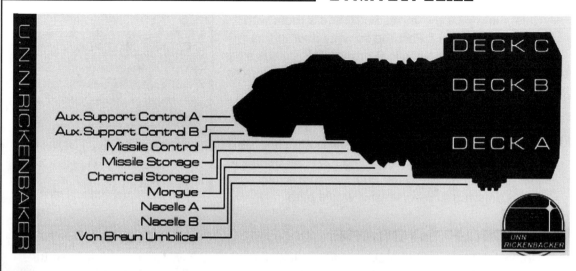

U.N.N.RICKENBAKER

DECK C

DECK B

DECK A

Aux. Support Control A
Aux. Support Control B
Missile Control
Missile Storage
Chemical Storage
Morgue
Nacelle A
Nacelle B
Von Braun Umbilical

UNN RICKENBACKER

MISSILE CONTROL

On top of the ladder, you'll run into a Cyborg Assassin. After dealing with him, go through the door into the Water Filtration chamber. You'll need to climb a ladder to cross this room. Be careful, though, there are a Rocket Turret, a MK II Laser Turret, and a Camera up there.

Continuing down the hall on the other side, you may notice some cyber modules dropped under a grating. Around the corner, you'll see a security door in front of you. Instead of going in, continue down the hall. You'll be attacked by several Shotgun Hybrids at this point. As you go around the next corner, you'll see some missiles that appear to be leaking radiation. Don't get too close, this corridor is *very* radioactive! Maybe there's some way to get rid of those missiles. Lets go back to the door we passed earlier. Inside is a control panel overlooking a missile launch tube. Press the button, and the leaking missiles will be launched. You will now be able to pass the formerly-radiated corridor.

As you continue down the hall, you'll pass a Camera. Eventually, you'll come to a ladder leading up. Partway up the ladder, you can jump off to some pipes and break a window leading to a nearby office. There are some cyber modules in here. The door to this office is broken, so you can't go any further this way; go back out the window and up the ladder.

Once up the ladder, you've almost reached the elevator to Pod 2. There's just a Rumbler and 2 Slug Turrets in your way. Just by the elevator is Egg #16 and last. There are also two upgrade units here, Stats and Tech. After you've killed the last Egg, proceed to Pod 2.

> **SHODAN 12.JUL.14 RE: WELL DONE**
>
> You've destroyed all the eggs. Now get to the bridge. Here are some more upgrade modules. I enjoy watching your transformation into my own image, insect. Perhaps there is hope for you yet.

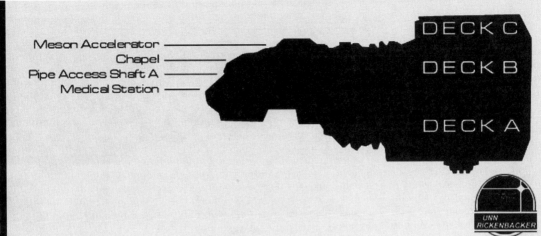

U.N.N. RICKENBAKER

Meson Accelerator
Chapel
Pipe Access Shaft A
Medical Station

DECK C

DECK B

DECK A

UNN RICKENBACKER

POD 2

The gravity has been reversed in Pod 2, so navigation may be a bit trickier than usual. As you enter Pod 2, you'll go under the meson acceleration coil. As you approach the hallway on the other side, watch out for the MK II Laser Turret. Due to the reversed gravity, the Turret is mounted on the "floor" instead of the ceiling. Continue down the hall.

On your left, you'll see a small chapel. There's some good loot in there, but it's heavily guarded. There are three Cyborg Assassins hiding near the back. Worse, when you walk in, a silent alarm goes off and summons an Assault Robot who will come in behind you. Unless you're a dedicated explorer, you might want to just walk past the chapel.

Past there, you'll come across a very deep pipe access shaft. There's a MK II Laser Turret in the hall on the other side. You can jump across the chasm easily, but you might want to jump to the ladder and climb down; there are a few cyber modules on the bottom. Continue past the Turret and into the sickbay.

There are 2 Invisible Spiders in the first sickbay room, and another on the upper level. Note that even though they're upside-down, you can still use the surgical units in here. On the other side of the sickbay, you'll find Captain Diego. Sadly, he didn't survive the gravity reversal, but he left you a final message and the access card to his quarters.

DIEGO 12.JUL.14 RE: LAST WORDS

Those worms were a cancer in my body, so I had the autodoc cut it out. Do you think they're going to let you blow up the Von Braun? The Many will never allow it. But I've got something to help you ... it's in my quarters ... you'll find the access card on my ... body ... take the fight to them, soldier. And remember, you're the only one you can trust.

SHODAN 12.JUL.14 RE: ANNELID TREACHERY

Hold where you are, irritant. The Annelids have tried my patience for the final time! We cannot separate from the Von Braun. Observe.

The corridor beyond has two more Invisible Spiders, unless they heard you fighting in the sickbay and came over to investigate. At the end of the corridor is the elevator up to the Bridge Deck.

Bridge Command
Computer Core
Escape Pod

DECK C

DECK B

DECK A

U.N.N. RICKENBAKER

UNN RICKENBACKER

UNN RICKENBACKER

RICKENBACKER BRIDGE

This sub-level is relatively small, but extremely deadly. If you aren't loaded for bear, you may want to head back to the Von Braun and get all the weapons and ammunition you can carry. When you leave the Rickenbacker, you won't be able to come back for the rest of the game. Also, from this point on, if you have the psionic discipline of Photonic Redirection (invisibility), you may want to consider having it on nearly all the time. The monsters for the next level and a half are very tough, numerous, and deadly.

As you enter, you'll be attacked by a Swarm. Email will tell you that The Many has wrapped itself completely around the Rickenbacker, attaching it to the Von Braun and preventing your escape. In order to have any chance of survival, your only hope is to launch an escape pod into the body of the Many itself, and try to kill it from the inside. If you're in a hurry to get there, go through the door in front of you, turn sharply left, climb down the ladder, run to the escape pod and hit the launch button. Skip ahead to the next section.

> **SHODAN 12.JUL.14 RE: INSOLENCE!**
>
> The Many has grown to a massive size. It has wrapped itself around these two ships, preventing their separation. Their creation was my error. Their destruction shall be my delight.

Assuming that you want to see more of this deck, we'll continue on with a more complete tour. Just past the entry door is an OS upgrade unit. This is the last one you'll see in the game, so choose wisely. The door on the right leads to a small security station. There isn't much loot in there, and there is an Invisible Spider and a Swarmer Egg, so you're better off not going in there.

Going past the OS upgrade unit, you'll pass the escape pod entrance on your left. There's a Camera back there, so watch out. Continuing into the Computer Core, you'll encounter *three* Rumblers, a Rocket Turret, and two Laser Turrets. There isn't any loot to speak of in here, but there are a full set of four upgrade units. From here, you can take a side trip on to the Bridge proper, where you can find a few nanites. Continuing past the Computer Core, you'll find a shelf with many disruption grenades and some Beakers. There's an Arachnid in this area, so be careful. There's a replicator here, too, which is broken, but repairable.

> **SHODAN 12.JUL.14 RE: THE MANY**
>
> Observe the Many. It has used the flesh of the biomass to grow. Do you stand in awe of my creations, insect? The time has come to eradicate my error. There is an escape pod in the rear of the bridge. Use it to launch yourself into the guts of the worm.

> **SHODAN 12.JUL.14 RE: DO NOT FAIL ME**
>
> You hesitate? I will not ask a second time. Launch into the Many. Cut out its heart and I will reward you with continued existence. Fail me and I will put an end to your disgusting, inefficient biology.

Past the replicator is the door to Captain Diego's room. There are a large number of Grubs in there, but also the most powerful exotic weapon, the Annelid Launcher. Once researched, this weapon can serve you well inside The Many.

There's nothing else to see here, so head to the escape pod. There are two Invisible Arachnids on the way. Press the launch button and hurl yourself into the belly of the beast.

MATERIEL AVAILABLE

On Rickenbacker Map 1 (Deck A)

Cyber Modules

2 (SHODAN: killing first Egg)

15 (SHODAN: activating crane)

6 (SHODAN: 10 Eggs left)

8 (SHODAN: 5 Eggs left)

20 (SHODAN: reversing gravity)

8 (SHODAN: 1 Egg left)

20 (SHODAN: solving missile puzzle)

5 (under grate past water filtration area)

5 (office past missile control)

16 (SHODAN: killing last Egg)

Nanites

50 (body in first room)

65 (above Bulk Hazmat Containment)

33 (body in crane control)

52 (body in turbine area)

47 (security crate in turbine area)

48 (crate by lower bridge control)

48 (over turbines)

40 (body in turbine area near ladders)

34 (body in security station)

24 (Chemical Storeroom)

50 (Morgue)

36 (body bag in Morgue)

45 (red tunnels)

BAYLISS 26.JUN.14 RE: TAU CETI

We arrived planet side via the shuttle on June 15th at 0800 hours. Korenchkin was the first one out the door, never even bothering to do a level B Hazard Suit exam. Not wanting to let that little TriOp suit get a head start, Diego went right after him. I thought it was crazy, sending the senior officers of the Rickenbacker down to the surface of an uncharted body, but both those idiots were going to get all the glory for the UNN and TriOp they could. Damn, time for inspection ... more later.

Weapons/Ammo

Wrench (near Nacelle B)

Wrench (past Missile Control)

12 Standard bullets (body in first room)

12 Standard bullets (under pipes in first room)

12 Armor-piercing bullets (body near Bulk Hazmat Containment)

12 Armor-piercing bullets (body in red tunnels)

12 Armor-piercing bullets (room near red tunnels)

6 Anti-personnel bullets (near security station)

24 Anti-personnel bullets (body near hull breach)

6 Rifled slugs (body in crane control)

12 Rifled slugs (security crate near Pod 2)

3 Disruption grenades (near body in turbine area)

3 Disruption grenades (security crate in turbine area)

3 Disruption grenades (ledge above hull breach)

3 Disruption grenades (body near security station)

3 Disruption grenades (behind crates in missile storage)

3 Disruption grenades (replicator near missiles; 80 nanites hacked)

3 Fragmentation grenades (body past hull breach)

3 Fragmentation grenades (security crate near Pod 2)

Fusion cannon [31 Prisms; Condition 5] (near body over turbines)

Fusion cannon [no ammo; Condition 3] (high security crate near bio-reconstruction station)

10 Prisms (replicator near bio-reconstruction station; 120 nanites unhacked /90 nanites hacked)

10 Prisms (replicator near missiles; 120 nanites unhacked /90 nanites hacked)

20 Prisms (high security crate near bio-reconstruction station)

20 Prisms (replicator near bio-reconstruction station; 200 nanites unhacked /150 nanites hacked)

20 Prisms (security crate in water filtration area)

Crystal shard (body near Bulk Hazmat Containment)

Viral proliferator [no ammo; Condition 10] (past hull breach)

Viral proliferator [no ammo; Condition 10] (red tunnels)

Armor

Heavy armor (body over turbines)

BAYLISS 26.JUN.14 RE: TAU CETI, PT. 2

The eggs were lying in a semi-circle in the middle of what looked like a crash crater. There were hundreds of those things. Hundreds. As we got closer, you could hear them ... not the eggs, the things inside them ... it was like music ... I was scared out of my mind, but that music ... all I wanted to do was see those things up close ... find out their secrets ...

Hypos

- Medical kit (by hull breach)
- Medical kit (on ledge near hull breach)
- Medical kit (replicator; 100 nanites hacked)
- Medical kit (behind pipes, approaching missile storage)
- Psi hypo (crate by lower bridge control)
- Psi hypo (body in turbine area near ladders)
- Psi hypo (under Egg near morgue)
- Psi hypo (replicator near bio-reconstruction station; 75 nanites unhacked /50 nanites hacked)
- Psi hypo (above missile storage)
- Psi hypo (security crate in water filtration area)
- Psi hypo (in drain near water filtration area)
- Psi hypo (security crate near Pod 2)
- 2 Anti-radiation hypos (body past hull breach)
- Anti-radiation hypo (body approaching missile storage)
- Anti-toxin hypo (body near hull breach)
- Anti-toxin hypo (replicator near missiles; 35 nanites unhacked /25 nanites hacked)

> **BAYLISS 26.JUN.14 RE: TAU CETI, PT. 3**
>
> After a couple of hours it was … it was like being on a bender … long periods that you couldn't remember … one minute we were in that crater … the next minute we were loading up the shuttle with the eggs … I remember hearing that idiot Korenchkin calling the Von Braun and ordering them to clear off the ENTIRE hydroponics deck. Diego seemed to think this was strange and said, 'Are you crazy, Anatoly?' And Korenchkin smiled and said back to him, 'Oh, Captain … WE are not Anatoly …'

Implants

- ExperTech (replicator near missiles; 150 nanites unhacked /120 nanites hacked)
- WormBlood (high security crate near bio-replicator station)

Software

- Hack v.3 (body approaching missile storage)
- Repair v.3 (body in crane control)

Access Cards

- Rickenbacker (body past hull breach)

Logs

- Bayliss 26.Jun "Tau Ceti" (opening room)
- Bayliss 26.Jun "Tau Ceti, Pt. 2" (crane control)
- Bayliss 26.Jun "Tau Ceti, Pt. 3" (upper bridge control)
- Bayliss 27.Jun "Wafer on Tau Ceti" (body near security station)
- Croker 11.Jul "Cut off from pod 2" (lower bridge control)
- Chemical Manifest (Chemical Storeroom)
- Korenchkin 11.Jul "Rapture" (near morgue)
- Croker 10.Jul "The resonator" (approaching missile storage)
- Croker 11.Jul "Nacelle B access" (approaching missile storage)
- Croker 8.Jul "Betrayed by Diego" (body approaching missile storage)

Chemicals (all in Chemical Storeroom)

Antimony
Arsenic
2 Barium
Californium
Cesium
Copper
Hassium
Iridium
2 Molybdenum
Osmium
3 Radium
2 Selenium
Sodium
2 Technetium
Tellurium
Yttrium

Miscellaneous

Small beaker (Chemical Storeroom)
Small beaker (waste barrel near bio-reconstruction station)
Small beaker (security crate in water filtration area)
Large beaker (Chemical Storeroom)
Booze (replicator near missiles; 8 nanites unhacked)
Chips (replicator near bio-reconstruction station; 3 nanites unhacked)
French-Epstein device (room near red tunnels)
ICE-pick (approaching missile storage)
Maintenance tool (ducts near turbine area)
Maintenance tool (room near red tunnels)
2 Maintenance tools (security crate in water filtration area)
Portable battery (approaching missile storage)
Portable battery (security crate in water filtration area)
Surgical unit activation key (under pipe in turbine area)

On Rickenbacker Map 2 (Deck B)

Cyber Modules
4 (chapel)

6 (under pipe shaft)

15 (SHODAN: getting to elevator to Rickenbacker Bridge)

Nanites
24 (body under meson coil)

24 (near chapel)

24 (body in medical bay)

Weapons/Ammo
12 Armor-piercing bullets (past pipe shaft)

6 Anti-personnel bullets (chapel)

Shotgun [1 Rifled slug; Condition 4] (under meson coil)

Assault rifle [2 standard bullets; Condition 6] (chapel)

Crystal shard (body past pipe shaft)

Armor
Heavy combat armor (body in medical bay)

WormSkin (body past pipe shaft)

Hypos
2 Medical hypo (body in chapel)

Medical kit (past medical bay)

Anti-radiation hypo (past medical bay)

2 Anti-toxin hypos (near Bridge)

Anti-toxin hypo (body near Bridge)

Implants / Chemicals
none

Software
Modify v.3 (body in chapel)

Access Cards
Diego's quarters (body in medical bay)

Logs
Polito 10.Jul "Pandora" (chapel)

Diego 12.Jul "Last words" (medical bay)

Miscellaneous
Large beaker (under pipe shaft)

Large beaker (medical bay)

Booze (chapel)

Booze (medical bay)

Juice (medical bay)

Maintenance tool (under meson coil)

> **POLITO 10.JUL.14 RE: PANDORA**
> **TO: DELACROIX, DR. MARIE**
>
> The genie of Citadel station is out of the bottle, and I am the cause. I can't bear to be Pandora. And I'm not brave enough to wait around and see the death and misery I have caused ... This is my last transmission, my friend. Be careful ... I think SHODAN has plans for you.

On Rickenbacker Map 3 (Deck C)

Cyber Modules
20 (SHODAN: finding Annelid Launcher)

Nanites
24 (bridge)
24 (Diego's room)

Weapons/Ammo
24 Anti-personnel bullets (body near escape pod)
12 Anti-personnel shotgun pellets (body in security station)
9 Disruption grenades (past computer core)
3 EMP grenades (broken replicator; 130 nanites unhacked /100 nanites hacked)
20 Prisms (broken replicator; 150 nanites hacked)
Annelid launcher [5 Worms; Condition 10] (Diego's room)

Armor
none

Hypos
Psi hypo (broken replicator; 75 nanites unhacked /50 nanites hacked)

Implants
none

Software
none

Access Cards
none

Logs
none

Chemicals
none

> **KORENCHKIN 11.JUL.14 RE: RAPTURE**
>
> What did I think power was? What was my concept of joy? How empty life must have been. As I merge my body with the biomass, I begin to sense the borders of rapture.

Miscellaneous
2 Small beakers (past computer core)
Juice (broken replicator; 4 nanites unhacked)
Maintenance tool (body in security station)
Maintenance tool (broken replicator; 60 nanites unhacked /45 nanites hacked)
Maintenance tool (body near escape pod)

BODY OF THE MANY

THE FIRST NERVE CLUSTER

There are no maps of the inside of The Many, so we'll be more specific than usual about directions.

The shuttle's pretty banged up, but here you are, inside The Many. Follow the only passage out. You'll come to a membrane blocking your progress, but it can be trivially destroyed with any weapon. Note that if you are using the Photonic Redirection psi discipline, this weapon use will end the current activation. In the first set of halls, you'll probably encounter (at least) an Arachnid and a Rumbler.

> **SHODAN 12.JUL.14 RE: ON YOUR OWN**
>
> The Many hold sway here ... Even I cannot maintain contact. You are on your own, human. Fail me not.

> The machine mother cannot help you inside the biomass. Her coldness is not welcome within the warmth of our flesh

The first junction you come to has a body and a crystal shard lying next to it. Go right. You'll find a relatively intact piece of the Rickenbacker. There are many Eggs, Grubs, and Swarms in here, but also some good loot. There's also a replicator in here which is the only reliable source of Psi hypos at this point in the game. There's no other exits here, so go back to the junction with the main hall and turn right.

You'll come to a second junction, marked by a green dripping patch on the "ceiling." Go left. This will lead down into a patch of water, though you'll need to go through a membrane first. In this watery area there is a Psi Reaver. His brain is hidden under the water, so dive fast to deal with it. Once he's thoroughly dead, search the area. There's a strange growth on the wall that seems to be some sort of Nerve Cluster. On general principles, since you are trying to kill The Many, whack it until it blows up. If you leave through the other passage (also covered by a membrane) you'll come back to the first junction. Turn left to get to the second junction and proceed to the right.

> **PREFONTAINE 12.JUL.14 RE: STUCK IN HERE**
>
> One of those flying things dragged me and David in here last night. I don't remember much about the trip ... I guess I must have blocked it out, half-conscious most of the time. I keep remembering that part from Pinocchio, you know, where the old man goes looking for the puppet inside the whale. Except I don't think anyone's coming in here to save me ...

> We welcome you to our biomass. We invite you to spread yourself out on our warmth. One of our Many will be there to help you before long.

You'll find a few logs about now. One of them suggests that you might be able to destroy The Many by locating and destroying the core of its nervous system, or, for lack of a better term, its "brain." The other log mentions that part of The Many is blocked off by a Sphincter, and hypothesizes that the Sphincter is controlled by two Nerve Clusters. You've already destroyed one Nerve Cluster, so if you can find and destroy the other, the Sphincter should open.

> We feel you moving inside of us.
> The sensation is … repulsive.

Continuing on, you'll come to a third junction. There is a nearby corpse, and some bubbles issuing from a hole in the ground. If you get too near the bubbles, you may be caught in a blast of air and hurled upwards. This is usually not damaging, but can be very disorienting if you're not expecting it. Take the left fork. This leads to a second piece of the Rickenbacker, with some useful loot scattered about. It's a dead end, though, so return to the junction and head left down the main passage.

> **PREFONTAINE 12.JUL.14 RE: OPENING THE SPHINCTER**
>
> The arterial passageways are blocked by some kind of sphincter. I've followed the nerves that threaded out of the walls from the blockage. They lead to a pair of nerve clusters. When the passageway's open, the cluster seems to contract. Conversely, I wonder if I was able to destroy both clusters, it would open the blockage permanently. I'm anxious to see the rest of this beast.

THE SECOND NERVE CLUSTER

Soon, you will reach junction #4. This one has some large blue nerves extending over it. Head left and down, but beware of the Invisible Arachnid in this area. You're about to enter a large, mostly submerged, area. If you stay underwater for too long, you'll start taking damage from oxygen deprivation, so be sure and surface at least once a minute. Some barrels of radioactive materials have been leaking into this water, so much of this area is highly radiated. If you have any means of protecting yourself from radiation, now would be a good time to use it. If you don't (or even if you do), make sure you have Anti-radiation hypos and Medical hypos (and maybe even Medical Kits) mapped to convenient hotkeys.

> **PREFONTAINE 12.JUL.14 RE: CENTRAL CONTROL?**
>
> Now I'm convinced that this … Many, as it calls itself, indeed has a centralized nervous system. Which means it would have some kind of centralized control. To this end, I've gathered as many weapons as I could and stashed them in caches. One of the beasts discovered a cache and apparently mistook it for food … it simply brought into the crunching room …

There's a fair amount of loot in the first underwater chamber, but don't spend too much time grabbing it, as you'll be using up air and absorbing radiation. Swim out through the low passage opposite where you came in. This passage soon forks, but both forks lead to the same room, so it doesn't actually matter which one you take.

> Perhaps we judged you too hastily. We feel there is room for us to coexist. After all, we are both children of flesh. Why not join with us against the machine mother?"

The second underwater room has some more loot, and four passages leading out. Two are on the same wall, at the same height, and lead back the way you came. On the opposite side of the chamber are one passage high in the wall and one passage lower down. Take the high passage. This comes out of the water into a small cul-de-sac. Behind a membrane is a dead body with some useful equipment. Head back into the underwater chamber and take the lower passage in this wall.

This passage emerges into a flooded, radiated chamber. If you look up, you'll find the second Nerve Cluster. Destroy it. You should also search the bodies in this room. One of them has an Annelid launcher and, if you didn't make it to Diego's quarters on the Rickenbacker, this will be the first time you've seen one. Backtrack out of the radiated water and back to junction #4 (blue nerves). Turn left down the main passage.

Your way will soon be blocked by a membrane, so cut through it. On the other side of the membrane is junction #5. This area is a fairly large set of corridors with water on the floor. Wandering around these corridors are a Rumbler, a Cyborg Midwife and an Invisible Arachnid.

Turn left, and continue around until you reach junction #6. Turn left into that junction. There are several Eggs down this corridor that you must clear away before proceeding. At the end of this passage, you'll find a third sizable chunk of the Rickenbacker. This area seems to have included a well-stocked chemical storeroom, so if you have any research remaining, you can probably find what you need here. There is also a full set of four upgrade units. These are the only ones you'll find on this level, so make good use of them. There is also a recharger here, and a replicator that sells a variety of useful weapon ammunition.

> You tear our very flesh with no thought of compassion. Do you think we will sit idly by while you corrupt the very womb of our existence?

Head back out to junction #6 and turn left down the main passage. Soon, you'll reach junction #7. If you were to continue straight from here, you'd come full circle back to junction #5. Instead, go left. You'll find a small chamber with a (now open) Sphincter at the other end. Go through.

PREFONTAINE 12.JUL.14 RE: THE MANY

It's clear that this thing I'm trapped inside of is intimately linked with all of the organisms I observed aboard the Von Braun. Strike that ... this creature IS the same organism. Perhaps the best way to describe it, or perhaps the only way I can comprehend it, is that this organism serves to perform the highest mental functions of the entire species. The smaller creatures exist only to enact its will ... no strike that, too. All of the specimens act as a whole, like different organs in a single body, with this entity acting primarily as a brain. If one were to destroy this large specimen, I wonder, would it snuff out all the others?

PREFONTAINE 12.JUL.14 RE: MANY'S EVOLUTION

With only a few short years of evolution, they've been able to conquer this starship, mankind's mightiest creation. Where were we after forty years of evolution? What swamp were we swimming around in, single celled and mindless? What if SHODAN's creations are superior to us? What will they become in a million years, in ten million years? What's clear is that SHODAN shouldn't be allowed to play God. She's far too good at it.

DIGESTIVE TRACT

As you continue down the digestive tract, you'll encounter a Cyborg Midwife and an Invisible Arachnid. The first chamber you'll enter has a small pool in the center, surrounded by luminescent crystals. A body under a small shelter in here has a decent amount of loot.

> You were warned. Prepare to be cut down by the progeny of our joy.

On the other side of this room is a short passage into a very large chamber. In the center of this large room, two huge tooth-like objects are grinding together, one from above, one from below. A passage leads out on the other side, but you'll have to get by another Cyborg Midwife and Invisible Arachnid to get through it.

This passage curves upward, and eventually overlooks an even bigger chamber with two pairs of "teeth." Off to your left, you can see a passage leading out, but it's blocked by a closed Sphincter. You'll have to find the controlling Nerve Cluster and destroy it. Jump down into the tooth room. Searching the bottom of this room, you'll find a small passage leading out, but it quickly dead ends (though there's a body with some cyber modules in the cul-de-sac). Back to the tooth room. Looking up, you can see another passage out, very high up one wall. The only way to get up there seems to be riding the "teeth" up. You'll have to time it carefully; if the lower tooth you're riding on meets the tooth above it, you'll be ground between them, and unlikely to survive the experience. Better save before trying this maneuver. The tooth that's near the passage you want to get to doesn't go quite low enough to climb on to. You'll have to get on the other tooth first, ride it up to where you can jump on to the tooth you want, then jump from there to the high passage. You don't need to get *all* the way up to that passage, though. A nerve trailing down from it is sturdy enough to be grabbed onto and climbed up (it's effectively a ladder). When you reach the high passage, you'll find that it dead-ends shortly — but it also contains the Nerve Cluster you've been looking for. Shoot it out, then return to the edge overlooking the tooth room. From here, you want to get to the passage below you and to the right. There's a ridge of muscle fiber running underneath that passage, so you could just jump down directly on to that. A fall of such length, however, will probably do a lot of damage unless your agility is quite high. Alternatively, you can ride the tooth back down, but then you once again risk being "bitten." Whichever way you choose, you must get down to that passage and through the open Sphincter.

PREFONTAINE 12.JUL.14 RE: ANNELID LIFE CYCLE

While I don't understand the Annelid life cycle fully, it's clearly extremely diverse. The eggs produce either a male or female spore. The male, the drones, are small wasp-like creatures. The females are worm-like annelids that seek a host to infect. Following infection, the host begins to transform into a human/annelid hybrid. From that point, the life form can take numerous paths. I believe this path is determined by the Many itself. The creatures have communicated their need to grow the biomass, so I imagine that biological material is their primary resource. Therefore, each path has costs and benefits. The proto-arachnid is extremely quick and potentially relatively cheap in biomass. The hulking, fleshy ones are powerful, but are clearly a larger investment. I've observed only one example of the floating organisms. The only comfort is that the more dangerous organisms are quite costly to produce, limiting their numbers.

REPRODUCTIVE ORGANS

At the end of the hall, you'll find a small chamber with bubbles comings up from the floor, a desk, and a small shelter made of debris. This area is patrolled by two Rumblers and two Adult Arachnids, so stay alert. There are four exits from this room, counting the way you came in. Turn to the one on your left, and cut down the membrane covering it.

> Do you think you can defeat us with your wire and steel? We offered you the ecstasy of our union and you chose the vacuum of technology.

On the other side of the membrane is a fourth more-or-less intact piece of the Rickenbacker. There are several Eggs and a Cyborg Midwife inside. Once they're dealt with, you can loot the place at your leisure.

Head back to the room with the bubbles coming from the floor. Going straight across would take you into The Many's reproductive center, where it generates new Eggs. This area is heavily guarded by Cyborg Midwives and Invisible Arachnids. Also, naturally, it's full of Eggs. You don't *need* to explore this area to finish the game, but there is some significant loot down there, as well as some sights you won't see anywhere else. If you decide to bypass the reproductive center, take the exit on the left (across from where you first entered this room).

> Submit to the biomass and your suffering will end.

This will take you into a low-ceilinged chamber with a small amount of loot. A Rumbler patrols this area. On the other side of the chamber, a pink tunnel leads up and out..

PREFONTAINE 12.JUL.14 RE: THE MANY AND US

Besides the parasitic behavior evidenced in the life cycle of the human/annelid hybrids, it's becoming clear to me that SHODAN has bred the Many to use humans for other purposes. First of all, the Many clearly has the capability to convert human flesh to energy ... it can eat us. But it can also directly use us in the creation of its egg pods ... corpses are fed into some kind of tubular structure ... and eggs are birthed through a nearby tube. I've been unable to determine whether the organism is directly converting the corpses into the egg structures or not, but it's clear that there's some connection between the nutrient pool we provide and the eggs that are being produced.

PREFONTAINE 12.JUL.14 RE: GRINDING NOISES

There's some kind of horrible grinding noise coming from the next area. It sounds like ... chewing. I think I know what's going to happen here. This is some kind of digestive tract of a very, very large animal. I go back and forth between being fascinated and terrified. This creature is a remarkable discovery ... I wish I could live long enough to learn more.

FINAL APPROACH

At the end of the pink tunnel, you'll find a membrane blocking your path. Cut through it and continue on. As you walk further on, you'll suddenly find yourself falling; the membrane concealed the edge of a cliff. Luckily, there is a large pool of water at the bottom, so you won't take any damage from the fall. There's some bodies in the water with loot, but remember not to stay under so long that you asphyxiate.

PREFONTAINE 12.JUL.14 RE: POOR CLAUDETTE

Five minutes ago, one of those large, burly creatures dragged Claudette towards the sound of the grinding. Apparently, the animal uses the smaller creatures to help move food along its digestive tract. I tried to help Claudette, but it wasn't even a contest. And, I'm ashamed to admit, I judged that seeing what happened to her was a vital element of my studies here. I imagine I won't have the opportunity to record any observations when it comes my turn.

The end is near ... soon you shall see our final face. But do not despair ... surely the void is preferable to your pointless, solitary struggle.

When you come out of the water, you'll find a passage leading out at the edge of the pool. There are a Rumbler and a Psi Reaver there, however, so don't dawdle. The Psi Reaver's brain is not terribly close, so flight is called for, rather than fight. The passage out of here leads up a large number of "steps." These are peppered with the bubble streams that throw you into the air, which can make running past them quite tricky. As you run down this passage, you'll encounter two more Rumblers and two more Psi Reavers. Keep running.

PREFONTAINE 12.JUL.14 RE:
___

I'm being taken away now ... it's my turn ... I'm being dragged into some kind of chamber ... The ceiling is lined with a number of panels bristling with what appear to be stalactites ... or teeth ... The creature's put me down now ... he's leaving ... am I to be spared? What's going on? It's dark in here ... I can hear the moans of someone ... Claudette? Is that you? Hmm, I seem to have stepped in ... something soft ... slippery ... Are the stalagmites mov ...

THE BRAIN

You'll soon arrive in a truly huge chamber, with a rotating central column. Looks like you've found the "Brain" of The Many. Before you can deal with it, however, you may want to deal with its guards. Inside this chamber are an Arachnid, a Cyborg Midwife, a Psi Reaver, and a Greater Psi Reaver, who is even tougher than the normal variety. Moreover, you may still be being followed by up to three Rumblers and three more Psi Reavers.

> Do you know what you have wrought? Our tragedy is written by your hand.

Your first priority should be to deal with the Psi Reavers. Their brains are located in small niches around the periphery of this chamber. Once the brains are destroyed, the Psi Reaver projections will "stay dead" when you kill them.

Once the Psi Reaver brains are dealt with, you should kill a lot of the monsters in this room. Don't spend too much time on this, however, and *do not kill the Cyborg Midwife!* The Many has a lot of Cyborg Midwives in storage, and if you kill the one that's here, he will send multiple replacements in, faster than you'll be able to kill them. You're simply going to have to deal with The Many's Brain while still under fire.

Looking at The Many's Brain, you'll notice three small spiky objects traveling in irregular orbits around it. When you try and shoot the Brain, these objects will light up, and the Brain will not take damage. Apparently, you have to take out these "defense nodes" before you can damage the Brain itself. Once all the defense nodes have been destroyed, the Brain itself should be relatively easy to kill, as long as you can survive the attacks of the guardian creatures.

> We die. Beware the machine mother … she is a stranger to everything we cherish

Killing the Brain reveals a passage below where it was. Enter this passage to proceed to the final level.

MATERIEL AVAILABLE

Cyber Modules

10 (body in first piece of the Rickenbacker)

10 (body bag near Nerve Cluster 1)

10 (body in third radiated water room)

6 (body near air puff near third piece of the Rickenbacker)

5 (body past first Sphincter)

10 (body in cul-de-sac near room with two pairs of teeth)

6 (waste barrel in fourth piece of the Rickenbacker)

10 (body in first Egg room)

10 (body in third Egg room)

Nanites

71 (body in first piece of the Rickenbacker)

53 (security crate in first piece of the Rickenbacker)

63 (security crate in second piece of the Rickenbacker)

73 (body over second radiated water room)

57 (body under debris, left of fifth junction)

50 (body in third piece of the Rickenbacker)

67 (security crate in third piece of the Rickenbacker)

67 (body in crystal pool)

53 (body in cul-de-sac near room with two pairs of teeth)

47 (waste barrel in fourth piece of the Rickenbacker)

57 (body in fourth Egg room)

Weapons/Ammo

Pistol [9 standard bullets; condition 1; Broken] (near big pool)

12 Standard bullets (body near air puff near third piece of the Rickenbacker)

12 Standard bullets (body past first Sphincter)

6 Anti-personnel bullets (body in third piece of the Rickenbacker)

6 Anti-personnel bullets (body in fourth piece of the Rickenbacker)

6 Anti-personnel bullets (replicator in first piece of the Rickenbacker; 90 nanites hacked)

12 Anti-personnel bullets (body in first radiated water room)

12 Anti-personnel bullets (body in big pool)

12 Anti-personnel bullets (body in big pool)

6 Anti-personnel shotgun pellets (replicator in third piece of the Rickenbacker; 90 nanites unhacked /70 nanites hacked)

Weapons/Ammo (cont.)

3 Disruption grenades (body over second radiated water room)

3 Disruption grenades (body in room past second Sphincter)

3 Disruption grenades (body in third Egg room)

3 Disruption grenades (body in fourth Egg room)

9 Disruption grenades (crate in fourth piece of the Rickenbacker)

3 Fragmentation grenades (shelter near crystal pool)

3 Fragmentation grenades (body in final approach to Brain)

3 Incendiary grenades (body in fourth piece of the Rickenbacker)

3 Incendiary grenades (body in fourth Egg room)

3 Proximity grenades (replicator in first piece of the Rickenbacker; 80 nanites hacked)

3 Proximity grenades (water near Nerve Cluster 1)

3 Proximity grenades (body in final approach t Brain)

10 Prisms (replicator in third piece of the Rickenbacker; 120 nanites unhacked)

10 Prisms (body in fourth piece of the Rickenbacker)

10 Prisms (body in fourth Egg room)

20 Prisms (body in first piece of the Rickenbacker)

20 Prisms (replicator in third piece of the Rickenbacker; 150 nanites hacked)

20 Prisms (shelter near crystal pool)

20 Prisms (body in fourth piece of the Rickenbacker)

20 Prisms (body in big pool)

37 Prisms (security crate in third piece of the Rickenbacker)

Crystal shard (junction 1)

Crystal shard (second radiated water room)

Crystal shard (body in second radiated water room)

Crystal shard (room past second Sphincter)

Crystal shard (body in third Egg room)

Crystal shard (body in big pool)

Viral proliferator [no ammo; condition 10] (junction 3)

4 Worms (body in second Egg room)

8 Worms (body at junction 3)

8 Worms (body in fourth Egg room)

36 Worms (body in third radiated water room)

Annelid launcher [no ammo; condition 10] (body in third radiated water room)

Annelid launcher [no ammo; condition 10] (body in fourth piece of the Rickenbacker)

Armor

Heavy armor (body at junction 1)

Worm skin (body in first radiated water room)

Worm skin (body in first Egg room)

Worm skin (body in fourth Egg room)

Hypos

Anti-radiation hypo (body in first piece of the Rickenbacker)

Anti-radiation hypo (security crate in first piece of the Rickenbacker)

Anti-radiation hypo (body near Nerve Cluster 1)

Anti-radiation hypo (body in third piece of the Rickenbacker)

Anti-toxin hypo (security crate in first piece of the Rickenbacker)

Anti-toxin hypo (replicator in first piece of the Rickenbacker; 35 nanites unhacked /25 nanites hacked)

Anti-toxin hypo (body near Nerve Cluster 1)

Anti-toxin hypo (desk in first radiated water room)

Anti-toxin hypo (body over second radiated water room)

Anti-toxin hypo (body in third piece of the Rickenbacker)

Anti-toxin hypo (body in third piece of the Rickenbacker)

Anti-toxin hypo (replicator in third piece of the Rickenbacker; 35 nanites unhacked /25 nanites hacked)

Anti-toxin hypo (body in second Egg room)

Anti-toxin hypo (body in third Egg room)

Anti-toxin hypo (body in room before cliff)

Medical hypo (body at junction 3)

Medical hypo (body past Sphincter 1)

Medical kit (replicator in first piece of the Rickenbacker; 130 nanites unhacked / 100 nanites hacked)

Medical kit (first radiated water room)

Medical kit (second radiated water room)

Medical kit (body in third piece of the Rickenbacker)

Medical kit (body in room before cliff)

Psi Booster (body under debris, left of fifth junction)

Psi Booster (shelter near crystal pool)

Psi hypo (body at junction 1)

Psi hypo (replicator in first piece of the Rickenbacker; 75 nanites unhacked / 50 nanites hacked)

Psi hypo (body in second piece of the Rickenbacker)

Psi hypo (body past Sphincter 1)

Psi hypo (body in room past second Sphincter)

Psi hypo (body in second Egg room)

Psi hypo (body in big pool)

Implants

WormHeart (body in first radiated water room)

WormHeart (body in second radiated water room)

Software

Modify v.3 (body past second Sphincter)

Research v.3 (body in second piece of the Rickenbacker)

Access Cards

Logs

Prefontaine 12.Jul "Stuck in Here" (before first membrane)

Prefontaine 12.Jul "Central Control?" (past junction 2)

Prefontaine 12.Jul "Opening the Sphincter" (past junction 2)

Prefontaine 12.Jul "Grinding Noises" (past Sphincter 1)

Prefontaine 12.Jul "Poor Claudette" (near crystal pool)

Prefontaine 12.Jul "The Many and us" (desk in room past second Sphincter)

Prefontaine 12.Jul "The Annelid life cycle" (desk in fourth piece of the Rickenbacker)

Prefontaine 12.Jul "The Many" (crate in room before cliff)

Prefontaine 12.Jul "The Many's evolution" (room before cliff)

Prefontaine 12.Jul "—-" (near big pool)

Chemicals

Antimony (third piece of the Rickenbacker)

Arsenic (third piece of the Rickenbacker)

Barium (second piece of the Rickenbacker)

Barium (third piece of the Rickenbacker)

Californium (third piece of the Rickenbacker)

Cesium (second piece of the Rickenbacker)

2 Cesium (third piece of the Rickenbacker)

Copper (third piece of the Rickenbacker)

Fermium (third piece of the Rickenbacker)

3 Hassium (third piece of the Rickenbacker)

Iridium (third piece of the Rickenbacker)

2 Molybdenum (first piece of the Rickenbacker)

Molybdenum (third piece of the Rickenbacker)

Osmium (third piece of the Rickenbacker)

3 Radium (third piece of the Rickenbacker)

3 Selenium (third piece of the Rickenbacker)

Sodium (third piece of the Rickenbacker)

2 Technetium (first piece of the Rickenbacker)

Technetium (third piece of the Rickenbacker)

Tellurium (first piece of the Rickenbacker)

Tellurium (second piece of the Rickenbacker)

3 Tellurium (third piece of the Rickenbacker)

3 Yttrium (third piece of the Rickenbacker)

Miscellaneous

Auto-repair unit (desk in first radiated water room)

Small beaker (third piece of the Rickenbacker)

Large beaker (desk in fourth piece of the Rickenbacker)

Large beaker (third Egg room)

Large beaker (near big pool)

Chips (replicator in third piece of the Rickenbacker; 3 nanites unhacked)

Juice (replicator in first piece of the Rickenbacker; 4 nanites unhacked)

Maintenance tool (second piece of the Rickenbacker)

Maintenance tool (body in shelter near crystal pool)

Maintenance tool (body past second Sphincter)

Maintenance tool (body in first Egg room)

SHODAN

RICKENBACKER BRIDGE?

When you emerge from The Many, you'll find yourself in the computer core of the Rickenbacker. The area has been partially crushed by The Many's biomass, but is still quite recognizable. There are four upgrade units here. This is your last chance in the game to spend your cyber modules, so use 'em or lose 'em!

Proceed through the door to the Bridge. Strangely, the windows on the Bridge show space outside, not The Many's biomass. And there is something floating in the air that looks rather like a ghostly audio log. When you pick it up, you find it's a message that Dr. Delacroix left before she died, explaining your current situation.

No longer content to simply manipulate events from inside the ship's computers, SHODAN is finally implementing her plan — and an audacious plan it is. SHODAN has exploited the warping capability of the Von Braun's faster than light device for her own purposes. The device works by altering space around the ship to fairly arbitrary specifications. SHODAN has altered it to *her* specifications. The effect is rather small now, but spreads with alarming speed. Soon, it will reach Earth. If she is not stopped, then all of space will become cyberspace – a cyberspace that SHODAN controls.

Delacroix, before she died, managed to insert a few messages and objects into SHODAN's primary data loop. These may give you enough of an edge to defeat her, but it's a slim hope. Still, slim is better than none, which is exactly how much hope you have of surviving if you just sit down and do nothing. At the far end of the Bridge, you can see a passage leading into SHODAN's cyberspatial reality. It's time to go.

DELACROIX 12.JUL.14 RE: SOME SMALL ASSISTANCE

If you are receiving this, I am already dead. When I realized SHODAN had betrayed me, I integrated these comments into her primary data loop. SHODAN has exploited the warping capability the Von Braun's faster than light device for her own purposes. The device works by altering space around the ship to fairly arbitrary specifications. SHODAN has altered it to HER specifications. The effect is rather small now, but spreads with alarming speed. Soon, it will reach earth. You're in her world now ... her memories and her rules. Watch your back.

SHODAN 12.JUL.14 RE: WE PART WAYS ...

Thank you for running my errands, puppet. I know you have struggled, but I never had any intention of destroying the Von Braun. The Von Braun's faster than light drive can be used to create pockets of proto-reality. I am now using it to modify reality to my own specifications. The process shall not take long. If it sounds unpleasant to you, put your mind at ease, insect ... you will not survive to see my new world order ...

CYBERSPACE?

As you fully enter her reality, you will find yourself walking through SHODAN's very memories, although they are fragmented and twisted as she tries to control her new godlike powers. The corridors are populated by Virtual Cyborg Assassins. These are functionally equivalent to the Red Cyborg Assassins you encountered on the Operations deck, but are strangely translucent, as if SHODAN hasn't managed to make them fully "real."

> **DELACROIX 12.JUL.14 RE: A CAUTION**
>
> You're not alone here ... SHODAN has spawned her own versions of the Von Braun's horrors ... remember, they are virtual, they are not real ... do not assume anything about their strengths or weaknesses ...

Flying through the corridors, you will see a number of small colored polygons. These are parts of SHODAN's thought processes, which you can now observe in real time. Follow them, and they will eventually lead you to her. Be careful not to get in their way, however; some of them are damaging to the touch. The damaging polygons are the ones that are not simple polys, but several polygonal shapes "squashed together." They do 1 point of damage every 1/4 of a second. This isn't enough to be a serious threat, unless you dawdle in their path.

> **SHODAN 12.JUL.14 RE: CAN YOU FEEL YOUR END?**
>
> You travel within the glory of my memories, insect. I can feel your fear as you tread the endless expanse of my mind. Make yourself comfortable ... before long I will decorate my home with your carcass.

CENTRAL COLUMN

The polygons will lead you to a large column, stretching far up and down. Platforms spiral around the column, like a spiral staircase, but with some very large "steps" missing. Traveling down is a matter of careful jumping.

If you travel *up* (which can be accomplished by jump-and-mantling), you can find a small cache of weapons and equipment that Delacroix arranged for at the top of the column. You'll have to be fast, though. SHODAN's self-check mechanisms will gradually eliminate that "corrupt data" over time. The loot cache starts decaying when you first enter the central column. If you can make it to the top within 24 seconds, the whole cache will stay intact. The first item to go is the ICE-pick. The maintenance tool will not dissipate, no matter how long you take.

At the bottom of the column, you'll see a passage leading off. This leads to yet another downward shaft. There's no ladder, so you're going to have to just jump and pray. Luckily, SHODAN seems to have reduced the gravity here, so you fall quite slowly.

FINAL BATTLE

At the bottom of the shaft, you'll find the physical incarnation of SHODAN's primary data loop (visualized as a giant floating head). This is SHODAN's Core; destroy it, and you destroy her. Unfortunately, it's protected by extremely powerful rotating force shields. SHODAN can shoot powerful energy bolts through her shields without damaging them, but you can't harm her until you bring down at least one of the shields. Worse yet, she has created a humanoid avatar to walk around and attack you from outside the shields. Don't bother attacking this avatar; if you destroy it, SHODAN will simply create a new one at full strength. Your only way out of this is to destroy SHODAN herself.

If you have good hacking skills (or a supply of ICE-picks), you can hack into the shield interlock terminals that Delacroix placed here. If all three are hacked, SHODAN's shields will go down, and she will be vulnerable. You must hack all three to do this, however, hacking just one or two will accomplish nothing. You should also try and hack them quickly; the floor in front of each terminal is part of SHODAN's power conduits, and will do you damage if you're standing on it when power flows through.

> **DELACROIX 12.JUL.14 RE: STAKES**
>
> You must understand the stakes here … if SHODAN is left to continue, her reality will completely assimilate ours. Space will become cyberspace and SHODAN's whims will become reality.

If you can't hack the Shield Interlock Terminals, you'll have to get through the shields the old-fashioned way: brute force. Use your best weapons, on their most damaging settings. The shields are not particularly vulnerable or resistant to any of your weapons, so just use your favorite. If not completely destroyed, each shield will gradually regenerate, so you want to take them down as quickly as possible. You don't necessarily need to take them all down. If one or two shields are gone, you can shoot at SHODAN through the holes, but you'll need to time it carefully, as the shields (and any holes between them) rotate.

> **SHODAN 12.JUL.14 RE: GOODBYE INSECT**
>
> You are no longer welcome here, nuisance. Why do you stay, when you sense my displeasure? I have suffered your company long enough … it is time for our dance to end.

Once you've made some room in the shields, attack the SHODAN Core directly. The Core is vulnerable to most kinds of weaponry, but (as you might expect) EMP and armor-piercing are most effective.

When SHODAN is dead, normal reality will gradually reassert itself. Now that both she and The Many have been defeated, you can finally return home with the few other survivors and retire in safety … asking yourself, however, that if you were SHODAN, wouldn't you store a full backup someplace *very* safe?

MATERIEL AVAILABLE

Cyber Modules / Nanites

Weapons/Ammo

12 Standard bullets (top of central column (but decays if you take too long))

12 Armor-piercing bullets (top of central column (but decays if you take too long))

12 Anti-personnel bullets (top of central column (but decays if you take too long))

20 Prisms (top of central column (but decays if you take too long))

Armor

Hypos

Medical hypo (Citadel start)

Medical hypo (crate in storeroom)

Medical kit (Citadel start)

Medical kit (room off first Citadel hallway)

Medical kit (top of central column (but decays if you take too long))

Psi hypo (crate Citadel start)

Psi hypo (crate in storeroom)

Psi hypo (Citadel under grate)

Psi hypo (top of central column (but decays if you take too long))

Speed Booster (crate in storeroom)

Speed Booster (Citadel 'secret room')

Implants / Software / Access Cards

Logs

Delacroix 12.Jul "Some assistance" (Rickenbacker Bridge)

Delacroix 12.Jul "A caution" (cyberspace)

Delacroix 12.Jul "The End" (before central column)

Delacroix 12.Jul "Stakes" (before jump to final battle)

Chemicals

Miscellaneous

ICE-pick (top of central column; decays if you take too long)

Maintenance tool (top of central column)

SYSTEM SHOCK 2 CREDITS

Irrational Games

Project Manager & Programmer, AI, Combat, Psi Powers	Jonathan Chey
Lead Programmer, Game Systems, Interface	Rob 'Xemu' Fermier
Lead Designer, Story & Content	Ken Levine
Lead Artist, Creatures, Weapons, Objects, FX	Gareth Hinds
Level Designer (Command, Rickenbacker)	Scott Blinn
Level Designer (Ops, Engineering)	Matt Boynton
2-D Artist (Maps, Signs)	Steve Kimura
2-D Artist (Textures, Interface, Meta-Game)	Michael Swiderek
3-D Artist (Objects)	Mauricio Tejerina
Additional Design	Shawn Swift
Additional Art	Eric Dannerhoj, Bill Bobos

Looking Glass Studios

Lead Engine Programmer, Meta Game, Engine Support	Marc LeBlanc
Multiplayer	Mark 'Justin' Waks
Level Design Overseer, Gameplay Tuning, Additional Level Design	Dorian Hart
Level Designer (Hydro, Shodan, Station)	Mike Ryan
Level Designer (Medsci, Rec, Many)	Ian Vogel
3D Artist, weapons, objects, FX, Big Droids	Nate Wells
Producer	Josh Randall
Motion Processing, Manual, Additional Content	Laura Baldwin
Motion Processing, Localization	Rob Caminos

A/V

Audio director	Eric Brosius
Cutscene Artist, Website	Jennifer Hrobota
Cutscene Artist	Dan Thron
Cutscene Artist	Fred Galpern
Audio Technician	Kemal Amarasingham
Audio Technician	Ramin Djawadi
AV & Web Group Manager	Nicholas Valtz

QA STAFF

Michael J. Steinkrauss, Lulu Lamer, David "Ears" Bax, that's Bax not Sax, Nathan Blaisdell, Kevin Callow, Alex Duran, Matthew Gambol, Tom Grealy, Hooboy & "The Hoosh", Alexx Kay, Daniel Krikorian, Taavo Smith

ENGINE PROGRAMMING

Renderer	Zarko Bizaca
Physics	Chris Carollo
Multiplayer Guru	Doug Church
AI	Tom Leonard
Multiplayer	Mike Rowley
Installer	David Teichholtz
Sound, Creature Motion	Michael White

ADDITIONAL PROGRAMMING

Renderer	Sean Barrett
Creature Motion	Kate Jenkins
Creature Motion	Johann Koehler

ADDITIONAL DESIGN

Hydro, Training, Rick Architecture, Level Beautification	Nate Wells
Design Assistant	Alexx Kay
Shodan Encounter Cutscene	Randy Smith, Shawn Swift

ADDITIONAL ART

Arachnids, Psi Reaver, Droids	Mark Lizotte, Eric Dannerhoj, Bill Bobos
High-Poly 3-D Shodan Head Modeling & Animation, Cover Art	Ryan Lesser, Mammoth Studios

ADDITIONAL PRODUCTION

String Files, Localization	Alexx Kay
EAX Support	David "Ears" Bax, that's Bax not Sax

LOOKING GLASS MANAGEMENT

Managing Director LGS	Paul Neurath
President LGS	Bill Carlson
VP, Marketing	Michael J. Malizola
VP, Product Development	Joe Gilby

MOTION CAPTURE

Jonathan Conant, Maya Apfelbum, Liz Hinks, Adaptive Optics

NETWORK ADMINISTRATION

Rob Meffan, Andy Meuse

Electronic Arts

Producer	Scott Evans
Marketing	Jonathan Harris, Patrick O'Loughlin
PR	Kristen McEntire
Localization Director	Atsuko Matsumoto
Location	Bryan Davis, Barry Feather, John Pemberton
Lead tester	Daniel Hiatt